THE ROMANCE OF SORCERY

Dieu se sert icy de ma bouche
Pour t'ánoncer la verité,
Si ma prediction te touche
Rends grace à sa Divinité.

J. Sauvé Scul.

NOSTRADAMUS
FROM AN ENGRAVING BY J. SAUVÉ

THE ROMANCE OF SORCERY

BY

SAX ROHMER

Introduction to the Causeway Edition
by Felix Morrow

WITH TWELVE ILLUSTRATIONS

CAUSEWAY BOOKS

NEW YORK 10016

CAUSEWAY: A bridge from here to there

Published by Causeway Books

95 Madison Avenue, New York, N.Y. 10016

Copyright © 1973 by Causeway Books

Library of Congress Catalog Card No.: 72-97372

ISBN: 0-88356-008-9

Printed in the United States of America

INTRODUCTION TO THE CAUSEWAY EDITION

The author of this book is best known to the wide world as the creator of Dr. Fu Manchu; the name immediately evokes the face of Warner Oland, who played this Chinese mystery figure in three unforgettable movies, followed by a fourth in which Boris Karloff became Fu Manchu. Perhaps even greater audiences the world over, many millions, read the thirteen Fu Manchu books and Sax Rohmer's other popular fiction in a dozen languages, or saw or heard adaptations on radio and television.

Sax Rohmer (1883–1959) wrote and published for fifty-five years, from 1904 to his death in 1959. At the height of his fame in the 1920s and 1930s he was one of the most widely read and highly paid writers in the world.

The present book is the only nonfiction book he ever wrote. He was thirty when it was published. He had already written his first Fu Manchu book and it was, indeed, the success of Fu Manchu in magazine publication and as a book that enabled Rohmer to write this long and serious work. In a biography of Sax Rohmer, his widow says of this time, after the first success of Fu Manchu: "Contrary to what might have been expected, Sax did not forthwith settle down to churning out a stream of Limehouse thrillers. With a little money in hand, he was able to devote the greater part of his time during 1913 to the composition of a long non-fiction work, *The Romance of Sorcery*. At the age of thirty, he was still sufficiently the dreamer to cherish visions of establishing himself as a serious student of the occult. Although perfectly aware that the book would make little financial profit, he tackled it with energy and enthusiasm." *

Not only did Sax Rohmer cherish visions of establishing himself as a student of the occult but, unknown to his wife, he was then already a member of the occult society The Hermetic Order of the Golden Dawn. Among his fellow members were William Butler Yeats, Arthur Machen, Arthur Edward Waite, and "Dion

* *Master of Villainy: A Biography of Sax Rohmer* by Kay Van Ash and Elizabeth Sax Rohmer. Bowling Green University Popular Press, 1972. Mr. Van Ash was Sax's young protégé and lived with them for many years. All quotations are from this biography.

v

Fortune" (Violet M. Firth). Another member (whom Rohmer disliked) was Aleister Crowley. Like many other members in the Golden Dawn, Rohmer was probably also a member of a Rosicrucian Society. Sax Rohmer's introduction to these societies came through his mentor in things occult, Dr. Watson Councell, the family physician of Rohmer's parents. Dr. Councell's book, *Apologia Alchymiae*, published in 1925, when Rohmer was 43, contains an introduction by Sax Rohmer, the only instance known when he wrote an introduction to another's work. It shows that Rohmer was still deeply interested in the occult. He also wrote two serious works of fiction of occult interest. *The Orchard of Tears* was published in 1918; *Wulfheim* was published by him under the pseudonym of Michael Furey in 1950 when Rohmer was 67 years old.

He originally wrote *Wulfheim* as a play about 25 years earlier, but failed to get it produced. The spirit in which he wrote it is revealingly described in the biography which his protegé wrote and co-signed with Rohmer's widow: "In what I can only regard as an attitude of defiance, he lived a hand-to-mouth existence on the proceeds of a few short stories and gave the rest of his time to a work that he could not sell at all, the second and, apart from *The Orchard of Tears,* the only other extant example of the non-commercial type of thing which he really wanted to write. This was a mystic play called *Wulfheim,* described as a masque with music, a mixture of theosophy and demonology."

The non-commercial type of thing which he really wanted to write. Why, then, did not Sax Rohmer write more of this type of thing, whether in fiction or nonfiction?

The reader of *The Romance of Sorcery* will, I believe, be as fascinated as I am by this question. For here is a book indubitably written by a very intelligent, even profound, student and practitioner of the occult. A student, moreover, who in a very sane and reflective way comes to the conclusion that the occult contains a great deal of truth which we can find only by the occult path. Sax Rohmer uses the term sorcery as a synonym for magic; he believes that the great magical tradition comes to us from ancient Egypt; and he believes that this magic, rightly understood and practiced, brings about mental and physical results which are very valuable for the human race. *Wulfheim,* written at age 67, says this in fiction as firmly as this book, written at age 30, says it in nonfiction. We know from his wife and his protegé that he not only remained true to these views, but that he practiced magic, using the rites and ceremonies in the *Egyptian Book of the Dead* and (no doubt) the magic he learned in the Golden Dawn. We can infer this from the occasions when his wife came upon Sax Rohmer unexpectedly and found him engaged in a magical rite. To complete the picture, one should mention the only article Rohmer ever wrote on occult magic, "Astral Voyages," in which he describes his experiments in astral projection, published in 1935 at age 52.

The Romance of Sorcery, soon after publication, brought the author an admiring letter from the great stage manager of illusion, Harry Houdini. A few years later they met and became close friends. Rohmer was able to share with Houdini their common interest in genuine occult phenomena. Houdini's exposures of fake mediums went hand-in-hand with his defense of bona fide mediums and occult experimenters—something which even some of Houdini's biographers have failed to understand. It was because they brought the whole subject of occultism into undeserved disrepute that Houdini exposed the trickery of pretenders. Long before he died, Houdini arranged with his wife a secret test of a message to reach her after death. And the medium Arthur Ford brought her that message the widow has told the world.

The sane experimentalism he shared with Houdini is the point of view from which Sax Rohmer wrote this book. It consists of an introductory chapter, "Sorcery and Sorcerers," indicating the Egyptian origins of magic and something of its history to our own time. Along the way he indicates his low opinion of such occultists as Eliphas Levi, his extreme skepticism of the magic of such as Francis Barrett, and that most of modern-day occultism is credulous nonsense. Then follows a series of chapters on notable occultists. He indicates great acceptance, even reverence, for the work of Apollonius of Tyana and Nostradamus in two long chapters. Dr. John Dee he finds deluded and imposed upon by the sinister Edward Kelly. Another long chapter judiciously concludes that Cagliostro was a fraud but sides with him against his papal executioners. A chapter on Madame Blavatsky finds that she failed to clear herself of charges of fraud, but is sympathetic to her theosophical beliefs to which Rohmer himself remained loyal throughout his life. A final long chapter, "Sorcery and the Law," tells the story of the medieval persecutions of witches, the "poor, tortured souls" so unjustly done to death. A short "Conclusion" finds Sax Rohmer placing himself on the side of the bona fide occultists and psychical researchers. "But," he concludes, "the difficulty of demonstrating the existence of occult phenomena to the general public can only be likened to that of demonstrating the perfume of a rose to a person who has never possessed the sense of smell, the beauty of an autumn sunset to a blind man, or the distinction in flavor between Astrakhan and American caviar to one of defective palate."

This whole book is infused with a quite extraordinary combination of good sense and occult faith. After reading it and enjoying it to the full, one can only regret that Sax Rohmer never wrote another in this field where genuinely good books are so few and far between.

I conclude with an attempt to answer the fascinating question, why he never wrote another. This is really also the question, why he did not devote his life to occult study, instead of writing thrillers. Both his wife and biographer have indicated that it was "the non-commercial type of thing which he really wanted to write." We know from his wife that he did "cherish visions of establishing himself as a serious student of the occult." Actually, he was already one, as this book demonstrates, and what she is really saying is that he longed to devote his life to occult study and practice.

Sax Rohmer's fear of poverty may have played a role. Until he created Fu Manchu he and his wife lived in dire poverty. But he could perhaps have paid his way with Fu Manchu and devoted the rest of his time to magic. True, when he became very successful, he developed a love of luxury. His biographers seem to think he turned altogether to popular fiction because he loved to live luxuriously—and one of them was his wife, who should know. But I would suggest another factor, to which she herself testifies but which, I think, she fails to understand.

INTRODUCTION TO THE CAUSEWAY EDITION

His wife was utterly terrified by his occult practices. For a time he persuaded her to use Tarot cards for divination, and the Ouija board, but she came to believe that these things were evil and would not have anything to do with them. She had "made an occasional use of the Tarot cards for some years, to the alarm and stern disapproval of Dr. Watson Councell, who urged her to throw them away. Eventually she did, but not until she had frightened herself so badly that she wishes she had taken his advice sooner. In five successive runs of the cards, she had seen the death of Sax exactly as it later occurred, the war in Vietnam, and her own end." Further, and this is even more significant, she insisted that Sax have nothing to do with his beloved magic:

"She recalls, with some vividness, a night when, waking to find herself alone, she had got up to look for her missing husband. This time she discovered him not in the company of Bohemian friends but alone in his study, with the *Egyptian Book of the Dead* open on the desk before him. He was holding aloft a peculiarly-shaped instrument and muttering some kind of conjuration . . . He did not tell her, but afterwards she concluded that he was probably trying to establish contact with the departed Houdini. 'Go away!' Sax said fiercely. 'You'll break the spell!' 'I will not go away!' Elizabeth said, with equal ferocity. 'If you carry on like this you'll go barmy!' Sax conceded that the spell was broken and ungraciously allowed himself to be conducted back to bed."

In his article on astral projection, Rohmer was noncommittal about the results, probably in order not to frighten his wife further. She, however, is quite forthright about saying that his astral experiments worked. "She swears that there was a night when she saw a shadowy 'second Sax' detach itself from the recumbent form of her husband, glide to the door of their bedroom, and turn to look back in her direction. But, she insists, that 'other form' was his evil counterpart. The face was that of a devil." No wonder, in the face of her fears of evil, that it was the first and last article of the kind that he wrote.

My hypothesis, then, is that his wife's fear of the occult and her complete opposition to occult practices by him were the determining factors which explain Sax Rohmer's silence after *The Romance of Sorcery*. I am quite sure that Kay Van Ash and Elizabeth Sax Rohmer's biography of him accurately describes his dependence on her; it is inconceivable that he would have persisted in his occult practices openly, and written about them, in the face of her fear and opposition. One final and illuminating fact. She never knew, until after his death, that he had been a member of The Hermetic Order of the Golden Dawn. By 1959, when he died, the secret rites and manuals of the Order had been published (in the 1930s) and a good deal else about it was known, including some of the members. Mr. Van Ash's explanation of Sax Rohmer's secrecy is that he remained loyal to his oath of secrecy. It is much more likely that he feared to tell her how long he had belonged.

In any event, readers who profit from *The Romance of Sorcery* will regret that Sax Rohmer wrote no other book in this field. With his silence the world lost a rarely level-headed interpreter of the occult.

Finally, this is the original, unabridged version of *The Romance of Sorcery*. It was published only once. The Preface is dated January 31, 1914. It was published in England that year and sheets sent to America for a binding by E. P. Dutton Publishers. Sax Rohmer's biographers say it was more widely read than Sax had anticipated, but that is very doubtful. There was only the one printing, the sheets divided between England and America, and first printings then were customarily small, probably only two thousand. Not until ten years later was there a cheap edition in England and America, and this was much abridged and without the illustrations. This, then, is the first reprint of the unabridged original.

September 1973   FELIX MORROW

PREFACE

ALTHOUGH would-be explorers of the occult continent may be numbered only by the employment of seven figures, it is notable as a curious fact that the world's master Magi have been neglected by popular biographers. Lives of all the great sorcerers there are, certainly, from Zarathustra to Éliphas Lévi, but without exception, so far as I am aware, these are designed for the use of the student: they are not for every man.

Fictionists have dipped into the magical pages, but lightly and warily. If we except some of the novels of Lord Lytton (who was an initiate, deeply versed) and the stories of Mr. Algernon Blackwood, to whom we are indebted for an account of a " Witches' Sabbath " little short of clairvoyant, I believe there is no piece of purely imaginative writing which can be regarded as the work of an Adept, or even of a serious student.

In the following pages, then, I have endeavoured to bring out the red blood of the subject, and have treated the various episodes with which I have had to deal in the same manner that I should treat the episodes of an ordinary romance. Whilst those curious to learn more of the arts of sorcery have not been neglected, above all I have placed, and have aimed at satisfying, the reader who opens this book in quest of entertainment.

The section " Sorcery and Sorcerers " will be found to contain some passages from Francis Barrett and from Dr. Wynn Westcott's valuable translation of one of Lévi's most extraordinary works. Neither of these authors will be familiar to the general reader, and I have borrowed freely in both directions. Their writings are illuminative, and should be considered, if only in brief, by any one who hopes to comprehend the aims of the sorcerers, as set forth in *The Romance of Sorcery*.

It may be asked of me why certain characters have been included here and others omitted. I can only say that I have sought for *variety*. To my decision to include a life of Nostradamus I was guided, in some degree, by the existence of a very general misapprehension regarding this great and wonderful man ; also by the fact that hitherto no complete life has appeared in the English language. Madame H. P. Blavatsky I have introduced, after much consideration, because certain phenomena associated with her activities come legitimately within the scope and limit of sorcery. I have dealt with these phenomena, but have not attempted, in so limited a space, even to outline her whole career.[1]

At the time that I was engaged upon the section " Apollonius of Tyana," an admirable edition of Philostratus's work, translated by Mr. F. C. Conybeare, M.A., was added to the Loeb Classical Library. This

---

[1] Since the above was written, a prominent theosophist, toward whose views I entertain profound respect, has taken me to task for discussing Madame in a work devoted to sorcery. My defence will be found in Webster's definition of the word.

lightened my labours, for the only other English version is that of E. Berwick, published in 1809. The freshness and freedom of Mr. Conybeare's rendering make quite delightful reading, compared with the severely staid manner of the former writer.

I have to acknowledge the generous assistance offered to me by M. Homolle of the Bibliothèque Nationale, and the untiring labours of M. Lejay Jean, of the same institution. Not only has M. Lejay aided me in my quest of material, but he has completed those inquiries regarding Cagliostro's house in the Rue Saint Claude and other matters which lack of time forced me to abandon.

A portion of the chapter "The Elementals" ("Sorcery and Sorcerers") is included by courtesy of the *Globe*, and at this place I must also acknowledge indebtedness to my friend Dr. R. Watson Councell for the freedom of his library. Of inestimable assistance, too, has been the exact knowledge of old French, and of old French history, which Mr. Fred W. Winter has placed at my disposal. The sections " Nostradamus " and " Sorcery and the Law," in particular, owe much to his scholarly attainments.

Finally, the adept guidance of Mr. Arthur N. Milne has been as that of a *pharos* in a night-storm, lacking which I could scarce have hoped to make safe harbourage.

S. R.

Herne Hill,
   January 31, 1914.

CONTENTS

LIST OF ILLUSTRATIONS

THE ROMANCE OF SORCERY

THE
ROMANCE OF SORCERY

SORCERY AND SORCERERS

I. THE VEIL

There was a Door to which I found no Key ;
There was the Veil through which I might not see :
 Some little talk awhile of ME and THEE
 There was—and then no more of THEE and ME.

T O-DAY is notable for a curious change in
Western thought, or, properly, in a phase of
Western thought, more appreciable by churchmen, theosophists, and other students of the Unseen
than by the laymen. I refer to a growing discontent
with, and a falling away from, revealed religion. It
is an age of groping ; and whereas one who stumbles
onward in the mist nearly always strays from the broad
highway into the bypaths that lead to the meres, some
may strike a fair and narrow road and emerge upon
the mountain top.

Of guides to these divers fairways there are many,
some of honesty unimpeachable if poor pilots, others
masters of their craft but slaves to greed. Apollonius
of Tyana was one of the former ; Cagliostro, possibly,
belonged to the latter class. No man who has pro-

claimed himself potent to raise the Veil has ever lacked disciples ; no man tendering such a claim ever shall, certainly not in this miracle-hungry century.

" What seek ye ? " demands the Adept.

Comes a chorus from poor purblind humanity :

" To bridge the gulf ! "

But over this gulf floats a mist, beyond the mist hangs a Veil. Has any man, braving the mist, ever thrown a bridge, however frail, across to the shadow bank ? Honest weighing of the evidence would certainly make it appear that so much has been accomplished. With what result ? With the result that the intrepid explorer has obtained a closer view of the Veil.

Now, all exploration of this kind unavoidably leads us into the realms of magic. These are extensive, certainly, and offer prospects more startlingly dissimilar, as we look to right or left, than any tract in nature, not excepting the famous Yellowstone Park. And modern occultism has not made more easy the way ; it has accomplished little beyond the coining of a number of new terms. Sorcery, I think, covers them all. Father Henry Day, S.J., speaking at Manchester, advanced a similar opinion, but classed all magic as Black, when he said :

" The Church condemns the new form of modern spiritism as she condemned the old superstitions. They are identical with devil-worship, with black magic, with the necromancy of the past. Whatever may be said of the pretensions of the spiritism of the day, the Church regards it as the continuation of Satan's revolt against God."

His words are characteristic of the unchanging attitude of the Church of Rome towards magical practices; and, in so far as they warn would-be dabblers to refrain from sorcery, they are of value. The dangers of magic are not chimerical, but very real.

Magical arts in the modern mind are curiously associated with the East—and particularly with Egypt. An inspection of the advertisements of the large body of professional seers will enable you to bear me out in this. Every nation has its superstitions; but, excepting the African medicine-man, and his counterpart among almost every primitive people, for the practising sorcerer proper we must go East. The palmists and crystal-gazers of Europe and America are no more than imitations of the Oriental original.

Whilst the word *Sorcery* has always seemed to me to be singularly elastic, it suggests to my mind an impression identical with that conveyed by *Magic*, with which I take it, in general, to be synonymous. Therefore, by sorcery I understand, and intend to convey, all those doctrines concerning the nature and power of angels and spirits; the methods of evoking shades of departed persons; the conjuration of elementary spirits and of demons; the production of any kind of supernormal phenomena; the making of talismans, potions, wands, etc.; divination and crystallomancy; and Cabalistic and ceremonial rites.

It may, perhaps, be said that no people has cultivated sorcery more assiduously than did the Chaldeans. The elaborate formulæ relating to demonology and possession which have been deciphered from the cuneiform, testify to the flourishing state of wizardry in Chaldea. But the elaborate and in many cases beautiful magic rituals formulated by the Egyptians for some reason possess a greater fascination for the modern student. Their system, indubitably, was more complete than any before or since.

Within the limits of this work it would be impossible even cursorily to scan the subject of sorcery in all its developments and in the guises lent to it by various nations. Therefore, I shall confine myself as closely as possible to those phases which we should bear in mind when we stand upon Calypso's island with Apollonius of Tyana and witness his translation from Rome ; when we disturb the ghostly studies of Nostradamus, seated upon his prophetic tripod ; when we intrude upon Count Cagliostro's Lodge of Isis, and, perceiving the beautiful Countess and thirty-six neophytes *in puris naturalibus*, retire in modest confusion.

I propose, now, to compare certain passages in *The Tales of the Magicians* (from Flinders Petrie's *Egyptian Tales*) with others in *The Thousand and One Nights*, in order to show that the traditions to this day regnant in the East have a genealogy which more often than not first started from the soil of Egypt.

In " Anpu and Bata " (*Egyptian Tales*) Bata is represented as placing his heart on the topmost flower of an acacia tree. By his heart is meant his *hati*—that is, more properly, his soul. This he did so that he could not be killed unless the tree were cut down. When the latter calamity occurred, the *hati* was found in a seed, which, being placed in a cup of water, expanded, and, his body reviving, he drank the water. He then changed into a sacred bull, which was sacrificed ; but two drops of its blood fell upon the ground, and these contained the *hati* or soul of Bata. They grew into two trees, which were cut down, but the *hati* passed into a shaving from one of them.

I shall invite you, next, to watch with me an en-

counter between rival sorcerers (actually, a sorceress
and an *'efreet*) from *The Thousand and One Nights*,
noting the curious analogies between the forms, animal
and vegetable, into which the *hati*, or soul, retreats
during the conflict. The episode will be found in
" The Story of the Second Royal Mendicant."

The daughter of a certain King, who was acquainted
with the secret arts, challenged " the 'Efreet Jarjarees,
a descendant of Iblees," to mortal encounter, and,
" taking a knife upon which were engraved some
Hebrew names, marked with it a circle in the midst of
the palace. Within this she wrote several names and
talismans, and then she pronounced invocations, and
uttered unintelligible words ; and soon the palace
around us " (I quote the Royal Mendicant) " became
immersed in gloom to such a degree that we thought
the whole world was overspread ; and lo, the 'Efreet
appeared before us in a most hideous shape, with
hands like winnowing-forks, and legs like masts, and
eyes like burning torches ; so that we were terrified
at him. The King's daughter exclaimed : ' No
welcome to thee ! '—at which the 'Efreet, assuming
the form of a lion . . . rushed upon the lady ; but she
instantly plucked a hair from her head and muttered
with her lips, whereupon the hair became converted
into a piercing sword, with which she struck the lion
and he was cleft in twain by the blow ; but his head
became changed into a scorpion. The lady immediately transformed herself into an enormous serpent,
and crept after the execrable wretch in the shape of a
scorpion, and a sharp contest ensued between them,
after which the scorpion became an eagle, and the
serpent, changing to a vulture, pursued the eagle for
a length of time. The latter then transformed himself

into a black cat, and the King's daughter became a
wolf, and they fought together long and fiercely, till
the cat, seeing himself overcome, changed himself
into a large, red pomegranate, which fell into a pool ;
but, the wolf pursuing it, it ascended into the air, and
then fell upon the pavement of the palace, and broke
in pieces, its grains becoming scattered, each apart
from the others, and all spread about the whole space of
ground enclosed by the palace. The wolf, upon this,
transformed itself into a cock, in order to pick up the
grains, and not leave one of them ; but, according to
the decree of fate, one grain remained hidden by the
side of the pool of the fountain. The cock began to
cry, and flapped its wings, and made a sign to us with
its beak ; but we understood not what it would say.
It then uttered at us such a cry that we thought the
whole palace had fallen down upon us ; and it ran
about the whole of the ground, until it saw the grain
that had lain hid by the side of the pool, when it
pounced upon it to pick it up ; but it fell into the
midst of the water, and became transformed into a
fish, and sank into the water ; upon which the cock
became a fish of a larger size and plunged in after the
other. . . ."

II. THE BIRTH OF SORCERY

A Hair perhaps divides the False and True ;
Yes ; and a single Alif were the clue—
   Could you but find it—to the Treasure-house,
And peradventure to THE MASTER, too—

The persistent tradition that the secret lore of the
Egyptian priests was written in certain " books "
finds some slight confirmation in " Ahura's Tale,"

from the second series of *Egyptian Tales*; for therein the *Book of Thoth* is thus described:

" He wrote it with his own hands and it will bring (raise) a man to the gods. To read two pages enables you to enchant the heaven, the earth, the abyss, the mountains and the sea; you shall know what the birds of the sky and the crawling things are saying; . . . And when the second page is read, if you are in the world of ghosts, you will grow again in the shape you were on earth. . . ."

The Brahmins, visited by Apollonius of Tyana, would seem to have possessed such a book, and the great sage himself claimed powers almost identical with those conferred by the *Book of Thoth*. But, concerning the latter, we read:

" This book is in the middle of the river at Koptos, in an iron box; in the iron box is a bronze box; in the bronze box is a sycamore box; in the sycamore box is an ivory and ebony box; in the ivory and ebony box is a silver box; in the silver box is a golden box, and in that is the book. It is twisted all round with snakes and scorpions and all the other crawling things . . . and there is a deathless snake by the box."

The *Harris Papyrus* has references to similar magical books (nor must we overlook *The Book of Dzyan*, which Madame Blavatsky claimed to possess), but none of these ancient manuscripts affords us much help in tracing the origin of sorcery. That the Egyptian priesthood conserved the art through many generations, that we are indebted to them for their preservation of the traditions, is almost indisputable. But whence was their knowledge derived? Research along ordinary lines has failed to enlighten us upon this point.

I shall venture, then, to cite here the views of a very advanced theosophical writer, but shall ask to be excused from any comment upon them :

We have to measure time by hundreds of thousands of years, he avers, if we endeavour to look back in imagination to the halcyon period of Egyptian civilization, and, by the use of figures on that scale, we are enabled to form an approximately correct conception of the origin of that wonderful structure, the Great Pyramid of Ghizeh, usually ascribed to a Pharaoh of the fourth dynasty, Cheops, or Khufu. Whilst he considers that many of the pyramids which decorate the banks of the Nile were really what Egyptologists suppose them to be—the tombs of kings, he believes that their form was adopted in imitation of that already exemplified by the early monument, dating back, even for the Egyptians of ten thousand years ago, to time immemorial.

The Great Pyramid, in this writer's opinion, is probably by far the oldest structure on earth. Its main purpose was to serve as a temple of initiation for those who were admitted to fellowship with the Atlantean Adepts, established in Egypt more than a hundred thousand years ago ! Its shape was designed to render it invulnerable to the geographical revolutions which were impending, and, in his own words, he " is given to understand " that since its erection it has actually been submerged beneath a northern inflow of the sea ; a consequence of an actual depression of the land now constituting Lower Egypt. But later undulations of the earth's crust in that region brought it to the surface again, uninjured and available in later times for the purposes to which it was originally assigned.

Great as the importance attaching to (really) Ancient

Egypt undoubtedly may be, he continues, we must not imagine that the centre of occultism established there was by any means the only region from which the Adepts directed their watchfulness over mankind. When we talk about the catastrophes that shattered, and to a large extent destroyed, the ancient Atlantean continent, we are apt to forget that a good deal of existing land in the western hemisphere has survived those mighty changes.

A great deal of Mexico and Peru has transmitted to our own time architectural remains that he contends to be distinctly bequests of Atlantean civilization : and there is a region in Central America which, from the maturity of that civilization till now, has been and still is a centre from which Adept influence radiates over the world.[1]

III. THE HOME OF THE *GINN*

> Myself when young did eagerly frequent
> Doctor and Saint, and heard great argument
> About it and about ; but evermore
> Came out by the same door wherein I went.

I have said that sorcery has come to us as a legacy from Ancient Egypt, and one of the most persistent traditions, instances of which appear from time to time in the press, has a foundation in the beautiful ritual known as *The Book of the Dead*. I refer to the uncanny properties ascribed to certain relics from the Nile land.

In the second series of Flinders Petrie's *Egyptian Tales* is a translation of a papyrus in the Ghizeh Museum, wherein we read :

" Now in the tomb was Na-Nefer-Ka-Ptah and with

[1] I understand that Yucatan is meant.

him was the *Ka* of his wife Ahura, for though she was
buried at Koptos, her *Ka* dwelt at Memphis with her
husband whom she loved."

The *Ka* is the Ego, and according to the Ancient
Egyptian belief it could, at the death of the body,
enter into any image or magical implement prepared
for its reception.   In the case cited above it dwelt in a
statue, and the compiler of Volume VIII of the *Col-
lectanea Hermetica* says :

" It seems exceedingly probable that as the mummy
was the material basis for the *Sahu* (Astral form) and
Khaibt (radiation), so the mummy-case with its
painted presentment of the living person was the
material basis for the preservation of the *Ka* of a low-
grade initiate or the *Khu* (the magical powers) of a
fully-equipped Adept."

Baron Textor de Ravisi says that " before the entire
resurrection of the body the justified *Ka* could, if it
chose, reanimate the body of the dead."   This is
almost identical with vampirism, where the corpse is
found fresh in the tomb. The same authority has
defined manifestations which are visible but intangible,
whereof the head is distinctly visible but the limbs
vaporous, to be composed of the Ego and the Soul.
Those manifestations which resemble the bodily form
of the deceased, but are intangible, are composed of
the Ego and the Astral body ; they are usually terrify-
ing. Manifestations of the Will and the Instinct,
re-united in the Spiritual body, are only visible to the
spiritual sense ; whilst manifestations procured through
a medium are due to the *radiations* of the Astral body
only, and possess none of the Ego, or individuality,
of the deceased.

Certainly, the Egyptians had a more closely defined

and altogether more comprehensible system than any since evolved ; in fact, it is indubitable that many later systems are based upon it, being no more than worthless elaborations of the original.

Egypt was the wonderland of the ancient world, but any deeper consideration of Ancient Egyptian magical lore unavoidably would lead us into a maze of technicalities wholly uninteresting to anyone but the student ; my present purpose will be better served if I pass on to a consideration of the sorcerer's more modern activity, for, by the all but unanimous testimony of the country's present inhabitants, the Nile land is still the theatre of singular supernatural happenings.

" In common with other countries of Islam," says Dr. Klunzinger (and this the *Koran* tells us), " Egypt is inhabited by a vast number of *ginn*. Like men they are born, mature, age, and die. They are male and female, black or white, some high of station, some lowly ; some are free and some slaves ; Moslem and Christian." In short, they are parallel with mankind, from whom they are distinguished by their lack of flesh and blood, and by reason of their attaining to a great age—namely, three hundred years, or more.

Each child has a companion *ginn*, born in the same hour. This " familiar," or *Karina*, is female in the case of a male child, and male in the case of a female. A child who dies in infancy is said to have been killed by the *Karina* ; and even in the official registers of deaths, until comparatively recently, the *Karina* was frequently entered as a recognized ailment.

Usually the *ginn* are said to be invisible ; but they can assume all kinds of intangible and vapoury forms, with the resemblances of men, animals, and monsters.

When a proper view is obtained of them they may at once be distinguished by their perpendicular eye.

The art of calling up these dread beings, in order to exorcise them, or to make them do one's bidding by invoking them by name, is cultivated throughout the Moslem world by great numbers of men, and by some women. By the instrumentality of the *ginn*, the "servants of the secret," or by the knowledge of one of the "secret names of God," those acquainted with occult lore can perform miracles. That the greater number of these Moslem sorcerers are poor men—often mendicants—may, therefore, appear remarkable; but it is claimed that self-denial is essential in a compact with a *ginn*. Some sorcerers of Moslem Egypt are said to be formally married to a *ginnee*, or female *ginn*, and to perform their wonders by means of their supernatural spouse.

A mysterious Moslem gentleman suspected of being wedded to a *ginnee* appeared in Egypt in the early part of the nineteenth century, styling himself Säid Abd-el-Rahmán el Adàros, and claiming to have come from India. He sailed up the Nile with a vessel and extensive retinue, and proclaimed that he designed to travel in the Sudan. Eye-witnesses swore to having seen him take pieces of money from beneath his carpet whenever he so willed, and that he could with a breath change silver coins into gold ones. Suffice it that the mysterious gentleman was denounced to the Government as a sorcerer and escorted from the country!

An old Moslem authority says : " Let a Christian beware of calling up a Moslem *ginn*. The *ginn* will avenge himself for this affront and immediately put his summoner to death."

In the modern magic books of the East we read how

to gain the affections of another ; to awake at will ;
to unfasten chains ; to recapture an escaped slave ; to
keep a wife from faithlessness ; to cause the belly of
a thief to swell up ; to make a man or an ox pursue
him ; to discover buried treasure ; to call up *ginn* ;
to find pieces of gold under one's pillow. I will instance
a charm for calling up *ginn* : the *naïveté* of the concluding sentence is quaint.

Fast for seven days, and let body and clothes be
clean. Read first the chapter of the *Koran*, " The
Angel," to the word *hazîr*, fourteen times after the
sunset prayer ; then pray with four genuflections,
uttering the *fatha* seven times at each, and when on
the seventh night you have read that chapter fourteen
times, ask of God whatsoever you wish. The *ginn*,
who are the servants of this chapter, will now appear
" and will give you information *respecting the treasure
and how you may obtain possession of it.*"

A certain individual, who asserted that he had
undergone such a course of self-mortification and
spirit-seeking, informed the author of *Upper Egypt*
that he had seen all kinds of horrible forms in his
magic circle, but that he saw them also when his eyes
were shut. At last, becoming quite terrified, he fled
from the place.

The following is said to be a love-charm :

" On a Wednesday after the Vesper prayer, and
when your shadow measures twenty paces, write the
following formula (*châtim*) with rose-water and sesame
water on paper or parchment. Roll this up and throw
it on the ground. Then write the formula on the palm
of the left hand and fumigate with mastic, benzoin, and
coriander. Say over the chapters *Amran* and *Ichlâs*
while your hand is held above the smoke, and then

pick up the talisman from the ground. Touch your
body with it, and that of the person on whom you
have designs. Hang it to . . . your right side, and
you will see something wonderful. God's protection
is with thee. But use the talisman only for what is
lawful ! ''

The formula consists of certain words written so as
to form a hollow square, with words also written across
the corners. Enclosed within the square on each
side are the words *Bil hák ansilnah u bil hák nésil*, that
is, " In right (not unallowed) we have made him (the
spirit) descend, and in right he descendeth." The
words *Gabraîl, Mikaîl, Israfîl, Israîl*, the names of
the four archangels, are written so as to form the sides
of the square ; across the corners are *Abu békr, Omr,
Otman, Ali*, the four chief companions of the Prophet.
Outside the square on each side is *Biduh*, the name
of a *ginn*.

The magic mirror enjoys great popularity. A boy
(not more than twelve years of age), a virgin, or a
black female slave is directed to look into a cup filled
with water or into a pool of ink ; the *skryer* is
furthermore fumigated with incense, whilst certain
sentences are murmured by the magician. After a
time, when the boy (for a boy is usually employed)
is asked what he sees, he reports that he sees persons
moving in the mirror. The magician orders the boy
to lay certain commands on the spirit. The commands are obeyed at once. The magician asks the
spectators to name any person whom they would wish
to appear in the mirror, no matter whether the person
be living or dead. The boy commands the spirit to
bring the individual desired. In a few seconds he is
present, and the boy proceeds to describe him.

ה־כ

Vehuiah · Jeliel · Sitael · Elemiah · Mahasiah · Lelahel · Achaiah · Cahethel · Haziel · Aladiah · Lauviah · Hahaiah · Ieiazel · Mebahel · Hariel · Hakamiah · Lovah · Caliel

Lauviah · Pahaliah · Nelchael · Ieiael · Melahel · Hahuiah · Nithhaiah · Haaiah · Ierathel · Seehiah · Reiiel · Omael · Lecabel · Vasariah · Iehuiah · Lehahiah · Chavakiah · Menadel

Aniel · Haamiah · Rehael · Ihiazel · Hahahel · Michael · Veualiah · Ielahiah · Sealiah · Ariel · Asaliah · Mihael · Vehuel · Daniel · Hahasiah · Imamiah · Nanael · Nithael

Mebahiah · Poiel · Nemamiah · Ieialel · Harahel · Mitzrael · Umabel · Iahhel · Annauel · Mehekiel · Damabiah · Manakel · Eiael · Habuiah · Rochel · Iabamiah · Haiaiel · Mumiah

THE CABALA

FROM *THE MAGUS*

" Which description, however, according to our own observation," says one writer, " is always quite wide of the mark." But E. W. Lane's experiments in this art (called *darb-el-mendel*) with the Sheikh Abd-El-Kadir El-Maghrabee, as recounted in *The Modern Egyptians*, may be consulted as a check to this opinion.

An account of a curious case of magic in Cairo, during the last century, may be given here, to show how great a degree of faith the Egyptians in general place in the arts of enchantment.

Moustafa Ed-Digwee, chief secretary in the Cadi's Court, in Cairo, was dismissed from his office, and succeeded by another person of the name of Moustafa, who had been a money-changer. The former sent a petition to the Pasha, begging to be reinstated ; but before he received an answer he was attacked by a severe illness, which he believed to be the effect of enchantment : he persuaded himself that Moustafa the money-changer had employed a magician to write a spell which should cause him to die ; and therefore sent a second time to the Pasha charging the new secretary with this crime.

The accused was brought before the Pasha, and confessed that he had had resort to malign arts, naming the magician whom he had employed. The latter was arrested, and, being unable to deny the charge brought against him, was thrown into prison, where he was sentenced to remain until it should be seen whether or not Ed-Digwee would die.

He was confined in a small cell, at the door of which two soldiers were placed in turn to watch over the prisoner. Lane, in dealing with this incident, says :

" Now for the marvellous part of the story.

" At night, after one of the guards had fallen asleep,

the other heard a strange, murmuring noise, and, looking through a crack of the door of the cell, saw the magician sitting in the middle of the floor, muttering some words which he (the guard) could not understand. Presently the candle which was before him became extinguished ; and, at the same instant, four other candles appeared, one in each corner of the cell.

" The magician then rose, and, standing on one side of the cell, knocked his head three times against the wall ; and each time that he did so, the wall opened and a man appeared to come forth from it. After the magician had conversed for some minutes with the three personages whom he had thus produced, they disappeared ; as did, also, the four candles ; and the candle that was in the midst of the cell became lighted again, as at first : the magician then resumed his position on the floor, and all was quiet. Thus the spell that was to have killed Ed-Digwee was dissolved.

" Early next morning, the invalid felt himself so much better that he called for a basin and ewer, performed the ablution, and said his prayers ; and from that time he rapidly recovered. He was restored to his former office ; and the magician was banished from Egypt."

The same author tells us also that not long after this incident another enchanter was expelled from the country, for writing a charm which caused a Moslem girl to be affected with an irresistible love for a Copt Christian.

IV. THE SIBYLS

The Revelations of Devout and Learn'd
Who rose before us, and as Prophets burn'd,
Are all but Stories, which, awoke from sleep,
They told their comrades, and to sleep return'd.

We shall see, presently, that not only Apollonius of
Tyana but also Dee, Nostradamus, and Cagliostro were
notable, chiefly, as prophets. If divination be but
elementary magic, it is more highly esteemed by the
layman than by the student, and the Sibylline lights
flare dimly through the darkness of to-day, as flared
such smoky torches in the blacker gloom of Babylon,
Memphis, Delphi, Rome.

In an examination of such a subject, the mind of the
inquirer too readily may be prejudiced by the fact that
the science or art of divination has been cast into
disrepute by the impostors who practise it at the
present day : yet, apart from its modern revival, it
is worthy of consideration alike by historian and arch-
æologist, if only because so many able men of bygone
centuries have placed the greatest faith in the oracular
responses.

Therefore, whoever would seek for pearls in the
ocean of obscurity which overtides the history of
oracular manifestation must arm against the influences
of modern environment and modern thought ; must
recede from this age of sceptics, through the middle
ages of fanatic Christianity, pass by the birth of the
New Creed, by the death of the gods, and take pause
before the Capitol of Rome at what time Cæsar makes
his last visit to the Senate House.

It must be remembered that Rome, during the

centuries of her ascendancy, gave to the world some
of the keenest intellects, some of the most highly-
trained observers whose laurelled images adorn man's
gallery of genius.   If we discredit the opinions of such
as these because of the pagan credulity of the age they
ornamented, we err ; for were they not more advan-
tageously circumstanced to weigh in the balance the
omen of the soothsayer, whose eyes attested to the
justice of his warning ; to accept or reject the pronouncements of the Sibyls, who themselves had converse with these mystic sisters ; who, as Æneas at
Cumæ, heard the words spoken by Herophile from the
cavern ; who, some among them, lived to see the
Oracle fulfilled ?

Since in the wheel of the centuries Rome is the hub,
and, in any retrospective criticism, scarce may we see
beyond its shadow, our inquiry concerning the ancient
Oracles fairly may be said to centre upon the seven
hills.   The Sibyls claim priority, of course ; and therefore at this point a brief survey of the Sibylline traditions prevalent in Ancient Rome may not be out of
place.

According to Marcus Varro, if we are to credit
Lactantius, the Sibyls were ten in number. "... First
there was the Persian of whom Nicanor made mention,
who wrote the history of Alexander of Macedon ; and
the second was the Libyan, whom Euripides mentions
in the prologue of the Lamis ; the third was the Del-
phian, of whom Chrysippus speaks in that book which
he wrote on divination ; the fourth was the Cimmerian
in Italy, whom Nævius in his books of the Punic War
and Piso in his annals name."

Proceeding, we learn that the fifth was the Ery-
thræan, whom Apollodorus, of Erythræa, affirmed to

have been his own countrywoman, and that she prophesied to the Greeks who were moving against Ilium,
both that Troy would meet with destruction and that
Homer would write falsehoods ; that the sixth was the
Samian, of whom Eratosthenes wrote that he had
found records in the ancient annals of the Samians.
The seventh was the far-famed Cumæan, variously
named Herophile, Deiphobe, Demophile, Phenomine,
Demo, and Amalthea. She it was who brought the
celebrated " nine books " to King Tarquinius Priscus.

The eighth Sibyl was the Hellespontine, born in the
Trojan country, in the village of Marpessus, near
Gergitha. Heraclides of Pontus wrote that she lived
in the time of Solon and Cyrus. The ninth was the
Phrygian, who prophesied at Ancyra. And the tenth
was the Tiburtine, named Albunea, who was worshipped at Tibur as a goddess, hard by the banks of
the river Anio, in which stream her image was said
to have been found, holding a book in hand. Her
oracular responses the Senate transferred to the
Capitol. To Lactantius we also are indebted for this
item of information : " Of all these Sibyls, the songs
are both made public and held in use except those of
the Cumæan, whose books are kept secret by the
Romans ; neither do they hold it lawful for them to
be inspected by any but the fifteen men." These
fifteen men were, of course, the Quindecemviri, or
college of priests, to whom the care of the Sibylline
books was entrusted at Rome.

From the fact of the concealment of the Cumæan
Oracles it has been contended, contrary from the
opinion of Pliny, who says that the Sibylline books
were destroyed by fire in the year 83 B.C., that none
were lost in the burning of the Capitol but the Cumæan,

since none but the Cumæan were concealed there.
But, in addition to these, there were kept in the Capitol
some Oracles prescribed by the Pythia at Delphi ; so
that some doubt must always prevail respecting the
fate of the Delphic as well as of the Cumæan Oracles.

In short, even at the time when the Oracles were
most highly venerated, at the time when the Cumæan
Sibylline books might be consulted only by a decree of
the Senate, the history of their authorship was veiled
in much mystery.

On more than one occasion the probity of the
Quindecemviri openly was questioned by the populace ;
it being charged against them that they misused their
privilege, pandering to the Senate and delivering to
the people reports regarding the Sibylline pronouncements, falsified, and wholly fictitious.

As to the time when the several Sibyls lived, again
we find contrary opinions, conflicting evidences, and
irreconcilable accounts. If Osopæus be worthy of
credence, then, according to him, the Sibyl at Delphi
was a Phrygian, " more ancient than Orpheus." One
Sibyl lived in the time of the Jewish Judges ; the
Cumæan, in the time of Amasias ; the Samian, in
the time of Josiah. There was a Sibyl in Samos in the
time of Darian Astyages, and the Sibylla Cumana prophesied in the Fiftieth Olympiad, or the Fifty-fourth.
" The Delphica is the oldest Sibyl," we read, " and
lived before the Trojan War. Homer borrowed many
of her verses." But against this we have the opinion
of Gallæus, who thought that the Sibyls plagiarized
Homer !

Out from this mass of perplexing evidence who would
proceed to a just and impartial judgment of the Oracles
which played so important a part in the history of

Greece and, consequently, in that of Rome (for all that
was notable of Greece was absorbed into the life of
Rome ; and, let it not be forgotten, the lotos with the
henbane) must brush aside the irrelevant, the prejudiced, the morbid and emotional, and leave upon
his table the one essential fragment—the fragment
that remains, concrete and convincing, when the dust
of disputatious criticism has gone the way of all dust.
The one substantial datum which may be established
is this : the Sibyls, whether justly or as a result of a
species of auto-hypnosis, believed themselves to be
inspired and were believed to be inspired by generations
of Greek and Roman philosophers and thinkers. So
much for their pretensions.

As to their later acceptance by contemporary
authorities, a moment's consideration of the facts
available—and these are multitudinous—will reveal
how they were accepted without question until that
same state of affairs became regnant in Rome which
rules among ourselves to-day.

The false Oracles of the temple of Isis, unveiled,
intact in all their trickery, by the spade of the ex-
cavator at Pompeii, afford but one instance among
many. The Romans saw impostors practising false
oracular mummery about them ; and as to-day none
but the superstitious are disposed to hearken to the
Sibyls of Bond Street, so, in that distant yesterday, it
came about that none but the gullible and the morbid
remained susceptible to the pseudo-wisdom of such
false prophets as those of Pompeii. The true was
mutilated by the false until the true was lost. Once
lost it was all but forgotten, and at last its very existence was denied. It is thus that many arts and
sciences, possibly worthy of a better fate, have been

attacked, have been shattered, by the charlatan or
the impostor, who has seen in them a means of de-
frauding his fellow-men, and who has not scrupled to
exercise his ingenuity at the expense of the afflicted.
With gross injustice, or in ignorance, Lytton classed
Apollonius of Tyana among these.

The wonders attributed to the Sibyl who lived in
the cave at Cumæ are an instance of how the possibly
true may be so overlaid by the false and apocryphal
that, to one looking back in quest of verity, the true
has become but dimly perceptible, if perceptible at all.

Of this Cumæan Sibyl it was related that Apollo
had become enamoured of her, and had offered to grant
her whatever she might ask of him. She asked that
she should be permitted to live for as many years as
she held grains of sand in her hand. The god at once
granted her request, but then she refused to reciprocate
his love. Therefore he pronounced that her long life
should be to her a curse rather than a blessing, for that
she should be without freshness and beauty. She was
reputed to be seven hundred years old when Æneas
came to Italy, but doomed to live nearly as many more
ere the number of her years would equal the sands she
had held ; and her ultimate destiny was to wither
away and become only a voice.

It is upon stepping into such a quagmire of the pre-
posterous as this that we stumble and all but lose
sight of the faint light which must guide us to the solid
shore beyond. For one wonders, whilst wading through
this morass of pagan fable, if light and darkness, seemingly substantial and palpably impalpable alike, are
not the mere creations of such a one as Virgil, at
best ; the monstrous figments of some pagan impostor's mendacious mind, at worst.

However, the Delphic Oracle is preserved to us in Herodotus (vi. 86). Glaucus, son of Epicydes, is said to have received from the Milesians a large sum of money, and to have given a pledge to restore it when properly demanded. When, however, the demand was made, Glaucus professed to be ignorant of any such obligation. Whilst the matter was pending, he went to Delphi and consulted the Pythian Oracle, receiving the following response :

> Glaucus of Epicydes, greater gain
> Immediate is it by oath to overcome,
> And take the money as by force ; swear then,
> Since death awaits the man that keeps his oath.
> But Orcus has a nameless son, nor hands
> Nor feet are his, but swift he moves along,
> Till, having seized a whole race, he destroys,
> And all the house. But the race of man
> Who keeps his oath is better afterward.

In common with the great majority of such Oracles, this response is characterized by a predominant element of uncertainty and enigmatical obscurity, leavened with a pinch of sound advice.

Not even the new thought that exercised a revolutionary intellectual influence in the dawn of Christianity could quench the light of the Oracles. Few among the early Christian writers would seem to have doubted the authenticity of the Sibyls ; and no further reference is necessary here to the power which these mystic books exercised over the whole of pagan Greece and Rome.

V. ORIENTAL ORACLES

Why, all the Saints and Sages who discuss'd
Of the Two Worlds so wisely—they are thrust
  Like foolish Prophets forth ; their Words to Scorn
Are scattered, and their Mouths are stopt with Dust.

Although, in Roman times, the Egyptian Oracles became so debased, it should not be forgotten that during the height of Egypt's grandeur the policy of the kingdom was largely, if not wholly, dictated by the pronouncements of the mouthpiece of the gods, or first prophet. Egyptian history contains the names of numberless such prophets. The prophets were the high priests, and though the Pharaoh ruled Egypt the high priest ruled Pharaoh. Whether or not the prophecies of the priests of Amen were inspired, they, *sans doute*, were dictated by a shrewd regard for the welfare of the community and informed with a forceful statesmanship that must command the student's admiration.

In the reign of Shepses-Ka-f, we read of one Ptah-Shepses, who was the " prophet of the god Sekar " and (from which his influence may be adjudged) " chief of the priesthood of Memphis." The Sphinx, too, was regarded as prophetic, and an inscription upon it tells us that ". . . a great enchantment rests upon this place from the beginning of time, as far as the districts of the lords of Babylon, the sacred road of the gods to the western horizon of On-Heliopolis, because the form of the Sphinx is a likeness of Sheper-ra, the very great god who abides at this place, the greatest of all spirits, the most venerable being who rests upon it."

Tehuti-mes IV ascribed his elevation to the throne to the active protection and aid of the oracular Horem-

Khu ; and the inscription upon the memorial stone before the breast of the Sphinx tells us how, " when hunting lions in the valley of the gazelles," he rested in the shadow of this potent one's image. " It seemed to him as though this great god spoke to him with his own mouth."

Here, it is difficult to decide whether the Sphinx should be regarded as oracular, whether the true Oracle was Tehuti-mes, or whether the alleged communication of the god was no more than a cloak to hide the prince's intrigue to secure the throne. Be this as it may, he caused it to be proclaimed that the god had said to him, ". . . Thou shalt wear the white crown and the red crown. . . . The world shall be thine in its length and in its breadth . . . the sand of the district in which I have my existence has covered me up. Promise me that thou wilt do what I wish. . . ." When Tehuti-mes IV came to the throne, certainly he kept the promise which he had made, thought he had made, or averred that he had made, to the oracular deity ; he cleared away the accumulated sand and freed from its confinement the gigantic body of the Sphinx.

Throughout the eastern nations, this yearning to know the unknowable—which, indeed, is inherent in modern western man to this day—exhibited itself constantly. It was this trait of Oriental character that made the institution of prophets, seers, and Oracles an essential part of the scheme of things. In Assyrian history, it is related that Esarhaddon, being hard pressed by a group of nations to the north-east of Assyria, led by a certain Kashtariti, and among whose followers the Gimirites, the Medes and Manneans were the most prominent, asked for an Oracle from Shamash regarding the outcome of the situation. The priest, acting as mediator, thus addressed the god :

" O Shamash ! great Lord ! As I ask thee do thou in mercy answer me. From this day, the third day of this month of Iyan, to the eleventh day of the month of Ab of this year, a period of one hundred days and one hundred nights, is the prescribed term for the priestly activity. Will within this period Kashtariti, together with his soldiery, will the army of the Gimirites, the army of the Medes, will the army of the Manneans, or will any enemy whatsoever succeed in carrying out their plan, whether by strategy or by main force, whether by the force of weapons of war and fight or by the axe, whether by breach made with machines of war and battering rams or by hunger, whether by the power residing in the name of a god or goddess, whether in a friendly way, or by friendly grace, or by any strategic device, will these aforementioned, as many as are required to take a city, actually capture the city of Kishsassu, penetrate into the interior of that same city of Kishsassu, will their hands lay hold of that same city of Kishsassu, so that it falls into their power ? Thy great divine power knows it. The capture of that same city of Kishsassu, through any enemy whatsoever, within the specified period, is it definitely ordained by thy great and divine will, O Shamash ? Will it actually come to pass ? "

The exact phraseology and exhaustive character of this invocation would reflect little discredit upon an up-to-date solicitor !

Methods of delivering Oracles are so numerous and diverse that little or no relationship can be established between any several examples.

Pausanius tells us that the Oracle of Hermes at

Pharæ was "the casual utterances of men." One who wished to consult the Oracle came in the evening to the statue of Hermes in the market-place, that stood beside a hearth altar to which bronze lamps were attached. Having kindled the lamps and put a piece of money on the altar, he whispered into the ear of the statue whatsoever he desired to know, and departed, closing his ears with his hands. Whatever human speech he first heard on removing them, he accepted as an Oracle.

The famed Pythoness of Delphi appears to have chewed leaves of the sacred laurel and then to have drunk water from the prophetic stream called Kassotis, which flowed underground. But the height of the afflatus was attained when she seated herself upon the tripod ; and here she was supposed to be inspired by a mystic vapour that arose from a fissure in the ground. The Pythoness was ordinarily no seeker after notoriety, no courtesan, and no representative of a highly placed family : but a virtuous woman of the lower class. The Persian Oracles (other than the Sibyl mentioned by Nicanor) had distinctive characteristics ; and in the science of divination, or in affecting an acquaintance with the science, the Aztec priests undoubtedly excelled ; "and," according to Prescott, "while they seemed to hold the keys of the future in their own hands, they impressed the ignorant people with the sentiments of superstitious awe, beyond that which has probably existed in any other country—even in Ancient Egypt."

The further the inquirer proceeds, the more evident does it become that Oracles, in some shape or form, be they the word of Hebrew prophet, the song of the Sibyl, the dream of one sleeping in the shadow of a god, the inspired speech of the Pythoness, have done much to shape the world !

I do not design to analyse the oracular records in quest of divine inspiration ; I but hope to show, so clearly that there can remain no doubts, the fact that Oracles, howsoever inspired—whether the mere repetitions of essential political dogmas, the echoed promptings of a concealed Chorus, or something un-suborned by man—have time and time again weighed down the doubtful balance ; have made and unmade kings ; have set up and cast down thrones ; have wrought and have ruined kingdoms ; have been, if not the guiding hand, the instrument whereby much of the Old World was fashioned, and whereby much of the New was made possible.

Shortly after the defeat of Mohammed by the Coreish (the Meccans) at Ohod, a scene occurred which illu-mines the manner in which the Oracles of Mohammed were given to the Faithful.

Among the slain was Sàd, son of Rabî, a leader of the Bani Khazraj. He left a widow and two daughters ; but his brother, in accordance with the practice of the times, took possession of the entire inheritance. The widow—not unnaturally—was grieved at this ; and, being a discreet and prudent woman, determined to obtain redress, if redress were obtainable. Accord-ingly she invited the Prophet to a feast, with some twenty of his intimates. A retired spot among the palm trees of the widow's garden was well sprinkled with water, and the repast spread.

Mohammed arrived, and with his companions took his seat upon the carpets prepared. Sympathetically he spoke to the widow of her bereavement, with such pathos that all the women wept, and the eyes of the

Prophet himself filled with tears. The supper disposed of, a feast of fresh dates followed ; whereupon the widow arose, and addressed her guest as follows :

" Sàd, as thou well knowest, was slain at Ohod. His brother hath seized the inheritance. There is nothing left for the two daughters ; and how shall they be married without a portion ? "

Mohammed, much moved by the simple tale, replied:

" The Lord shall decide regarding the inheritance ; for no command hath yet been revealed to me in this matter. Come again unto me when I shall have returned home." With this he departed.

Later, as with his companions he rested at the door of his own house, symptoms of inspiration came upon him—he was oppressed, and we are told that the drops of sweat fell like pearls from his forehead. Then he commanded that the widow of Sàd and his brother should be summoned ; and when they were brought before him, he pronounced thus :

" Restore unto the daughter of Sàd two-thirds of that which he hath left behind him and one-eighth part for his widow : the remainder is for thee."

The widow, rejoicing, then uttered the Takbir, " Great is the Lord ! "

This incident has been cited at length as illustrating quite peculiarly the manner wherein Oracles have formed the basis upon which rest the structures of some of the laws, and laws yet operative, of mankind ; for this ordinance, thus oracularly proclaimed, was the origin of an important provision in the Mohammedan law of inheritance.

A yearning to peep between the bars of the fast-locked gate of futurity is innate with all mankind, and, though the Sibyl may be the most sorry impostor, by no

assertion of our higher education may we abrogate
the power she has usurped.   That Oracles hold, to-day,
the keys of the Senate House and of the holy places, may
not truly be said ; but that they have held those keys
in the past may not fairly be denied.   Upon the predictions of Oracles the ancient wars were waged, the
ancient kings were crowned, the ancient states were
builded.

Whatever the *source* of those oracular utterances,
whatever the faith of those who interpreted them, that
they were the finger-posts along the old roads, pointing
the way to conquest or the way to disaster, cannot be
gainsaid.

> *Cæsar :* The ides of March are come.
> *Soothsayer :* Ay, Cæsar ; *but not gone.*

The tragedy of *Julius Cæsar* turns upon that axis,
as the ancient world turned upon the axis of the Oracle.

VI.   EXTRAORDINARY MODES OF DIVINATION

> The Worldly Hope men set their Hearts upon
> Turns Ashes—or it prospers ; and anon,
>   Like snow upon the Desert's dusty face,
> Lighting a little hour or two—is gone.

I have dealt at some length with what I may term
" official" Oracles for the reason that the subject bears
so directly upon the life of Nostradamus, as will presently appear ; for Michel de Notre Dame became, in
a sense, the official prophet of France.   Before we
dismiss altogether the subject of divination, we might
profitably glance at some of the more extraordinary
windows of futurity opened by peering mankind ; for
the doings of the seer have enriched the annals of
occultism with some singular pages.   Thus, Julian the

Apostate, in his necromantic practices and nocturnal sacrifices, is said to have immolated many children in order to consult their intestines (*anthropomancy*).

When he was at Carra, in Mesopotamia, he is said to have retired to the Temple of the Moon with some companions, and, his mystic operations concluded, to have left the temple locked and sealed, and with a guard over the door. He never returned to Carra, being slain in the war ; and when, in the reign of Jovian, the place was opened, a woman was found hanging by her hair, her hands outstretched, her body cut open and the liver removed.

Divination by means of table-turning was known to the Egyptian priests, apparently from the earliest times. It has come to us by way of Rome, for to the Romans the practice passed.

The instrument known as *planchette* is no more than a variation of the gyrating table ; and tripod-turning enjoyed a considerable vogue in Rome, when the Romans, I presume, had tired of the original Egyptian form of the practice (the gyrating of a kind of sieve).

Tertullian speaks of those who, "putting their faith in angels or demons, made goats and even tripods prophesy to them."

This table-turning of Old Rome, however, was invested with all the pomp of religious ceremonial ; being indeed a wholly demoniacal business. In the report of the confession of certain conspirators who, under Valens, had consulted a prophetic tripod (*dactylomancy*) as a preliminary measure to that of assassinating the Emperor, we find the conspirators saying :

" We have constructed this accursed little tripod, most sublime judges, in the semblance of the Delphic tripod, and we have fashioned it, with solemn incantations, from the branches of a consecrated laurel. In accordance with ancient custom, we have surrounded it with divers ornaments, and consecrated it by means of imprecations, charms, and mystic verses ; and this being done, we *moved* it."

The report further tells us how the conspirators purified the apartment in which the mystic rites were to be performed. Around the edge of the metal basin in which the tripod was to be turned, were engraved, at equal distances one from another, the twenty-four letters of the alphabet.

In the form of the ensuing ceremony, and in the part played by these twenty-four letters, we perceive a certain similarity between this tripod and the *planchette*. For the officiating priest (robed in white linen and with shaven skull, and bearing a sprig of vervain in his hand) took note of the letters which were struck by the rings suspended from the table, as it turned about.

Upon this occasion the rings struck *Th* and *E* in reply to the conspirators' query as to who was to succeed Valens. This was taken as a confirmation of the popular belief that Theodorus should be the future Emperor. I now come to the really notable part of this episode in the history of sorcery.

Valens, at this time, found himself equally curious for reliable information upon this matter of the succession, and had recourse to the magical art of *alectromancy*.

A cock (he should have been white and deprived of his claws) was placed within a circle marked about with the letters of the alphabet, covered with grain, from which the bird was allowed to peck at discretion. In this way, the cock laid bare the letters *Th*, *E*, *O*, and *D.* The Emperor seems to have entertained no doubt that *Theodorus* was the name indicated, since he promptly had Theodorus put to death. The existence of *Theodosius* had been overlooked, alike by the conspirators and by Valens, and Theodosius succeeded to the Empire.

At this place I may touch upon the methods of those priests called *oneiropoletæ* (" vendors of dreams "). These priests slept within the precincts of the temple with the supplicants who sought the revelation of the gods, and communicated to them the divine instructions received in their dreams. A hypnotic sleep was induced, too, by means of certain passes with the hands or by making the supplicant stare fixedly in a mirror floating upon the surface of a fountain. St. Augustine tells of a priest of his own Church and time who was an adept in this art.

Animal magnetism, in one form or another, plays an important part in many sorceries. In Cochin-China there exist those who, it is said, are able, solely by the effort of their will, to propel heavy barges ! I will not cite the authority responsible for this statement, but pass on to the account of an eye-witness of some of the phenomena at command of the Lamas of Tibet ; for the arts of Tibet are indissolubly bound up with the fame of Madame Blavatsky.

One of the feats related is as follows :

In order to discover a criminal, the Lama seats himself upon the ground before a small, square table, on which he lays his hand, whilst he chants from a certain book. After a time, he rises, lifting his hand ; whereupon the table is likewise seen to rise, following his hand—until it has risen to the level of the Lama's eyes.

It next commences a rotary motion; and its speed becomes so great that he appears hard put to it to follow, even by running. Finally, having pursued various directions, the table falls. Its fall is said to indicate the point of the compass toward which search should be made for the culprit.

The traveller whose account has furnished me with the foregoing, avers that he was four times a witness of this surprising feat. Search failed, however, to bring the culprit (in this case a thief) to light; until, when the quest had been abandoned, a man resident in the indicated direction killed himself. The stolen property, we are told, was discovered to be concealed in his hut !

In conclusion I may mention an account of *Bokte* sorcery for which we are indebted to the French traveller, M. Huc. According to the latter, a *Bokte* of the Lama convent of Rache-Churin, to a wild vocal accompaniment by brother Lamas, ripped himself entirely open with a sacred scimitar, and, during his sufferings, submitted to interrogation anent the future —his answers being regarded as oracular.

The devout curiosity of the pilgrims (who flock to these bloody ceremonies) being satisfied, M. Huc tells us that the *Bokte* passes his hand rapidly over his stomach, and it " becomes as whole as it was before," without the slightest trace remaining of the diabolical operation—with the exception of an extreme lassitude ![1]

[1] An Indian doctor with whom I am acquainted has himself witnessed an identical experiment.

VII. "THE ENIGMA OF THE SPHINX"

Would you that spangle of Existence spend
About THE SECRET—quick about it, Friend !
 A Hair perhaps divides the False and True—
And upon what, prithee, may life depend ?

Sorcery, or that form of sorcery which may be termed ceremonial, owes its survival, in a great measure, to Alphonse Louis Constant or "Éliphas Lévi." I consider that Éliphas Lévi may justly be called the last of the sorcerers. Yet, outside the study of the student of occultism, Lévi is unknown. How many readers of *A Strange Story, Zanoni,* and those others of Lytton's works dealing with the supernatural, are aware that the author was one of the privileged few whom the great master of magic accepted as disciples, was a pupil of Éliphas Lévi ? Lord Lytton as a sorcerer is an unfamiliar figure ; nevertheless, as a sorcerer, and an Adept, he is regarded by those qualified to judge.

Much of Lévi's work has been translated into English—notably, by Mr. A. E. Waite—but it possesses scant interest for the general reader, being prolix and incomprehensible. That part of his writings which is available in English may be said to be representative, and what I have seen of his untranslated work does not impress me with its lucidity.

Possibly an explanation of Lévi's mystical and misleading phraseology is to be found in his *Magical Ritual* (translated from MSS. and edited by W. Wynn Westcott, M.B.). In the chapter, "The Tower—La Maison de Dieu," we read :

"Do you know why the Fiery Sword of Samael is stretched over the Garden of Delight, which was the cradle of our race ?

" Do you know why the Deluge was ordered to efface
from the earth every vestige of the race of the giants ?

" Do you know why the Temple of Solomon was
destroyed ?

" These events have been necessary because the
Great Arcanum of the Knowledge of Good and of Evil
has been revealed.

" Angels have fallen because they have attempted
to divulge this Great Secret.   It is the secret of Life,
and when its first word is betrayed that word becomes
fatal.   If the Devil himself were to utter that word,
he would die."

This word, we are told, will destroy each one who
speaks it and every one who hears it spoken.   If it
were spoken aloud in the hearing of the people of a
town, that town would be given over to anathema.
If that word were to be whispered beneath the dome
of a temple, then within three days the temple doors
would fly open, a Voice would utter a cry, the divine
occupant would depart, and the building would fall in
ruins.   No refuge could be found for one who revealed
it : if he mounted to the topmost part of a tower, the
lightning flash would strike him ; if he tried to hide
himself in the caverns of the earth, a torrent would
whirl him away ; if he sought refuge in the house of a
friend, he would be betrayed ; if in the arms of the
wife of his bosom, she would desert him in affright.

In his passion of despair he would renounce his
science and knowledge, and, condemning himself to
the same blindness as did Œdipus, would shriek out—
" I have profaned the bed of my mother ! "

" Happy is the man who solves the Enigma of the
Sphinx, but wretched is he who retails the answer to
another."

He who has solved the secret and guards its secrecy is described as the " King of Earth " ; he disdains mere riches, is inaccessible to any suffering or fear from destiny ; he could wait with a smile the crash of worlds. This secret is, moreover, profaned and falsified by its mere revelation, and never yet has a just or a true idea come from its betrayal. " Those who possess it have found it. Those who pronounce it for others to hear have lost it—already."

Those who would understand the mysteries and perform miracles are warned by Éliphas Lévi to weigh well their knowledge and power ere entering upon the attempt ; for if they be in any way deficient, he says, they stand upon the brink of an abyss.

" But if you have secured the Lamp and Wand of Initiation, if you are cognizant of the secrets of the Nine, if you never speak to God without the Light which proceeds from Him, if you have received the mystical baptism of the Four Elements, if you have prayed upon the Seven Mountains, if you know the mode of motion of the Double Sphinxed Chariot, if you have grasped the dogma of why Osiris was a black god, if you are free, if you are a King, if you are in truth a priest in the Temple of Solomon—act without fear, and speak, for your words will be all-powerful in the spiritual kingdom. . . ."

Furthermore, however, it is necessary to know the names and powers of the twelve precious jewels which are included in the crown of gold of the sun, and the names of the chief powers of the moon. Also, one must be familiar with the keys of the Fifty Gates, the secret of the Thirty-two Paths, and the characters of the Seven Spirits.

Incense plays a very important part in ritualistic

sorcery, as it played an important part in Egyptian
sorcery. Thus : for conjurations on Sunday the
incense should be cinnamon, frankincense, saffron,
and red sandal-wood. For Monday : camphor, white
sandal-wood, amber, and cucumber seeds. For Thursday : ambergris, cardamom, " grains of paradise,"
balm, mace, and saffron ; and so on.

It may be of interest to mention here the constituents
of *Kyphi*, the celebrated incense of Ancient Egypt.
A recipe for its preparation is contained in the Ebers
papyrus, and Ebers says that three different varieties
were made up by L. Voigt, a Berlin chemist. That
from the formula of Dioscorides was the best. It consisted of resin, wine, *Rad. Galangæ*,[1] juniper berries,
root of aromatic rush, asphaltum, mastic, myrrh,
Burgundy grapes, and honey.

Lévi says of the Seal of Solomon :

" It consists in the interlaced triangles ; the erect
triangle is of flame colour, the inverse triangle is
coloured blue. In the centre space there may be drawn
a Tau cross and three Hebrew Yods, or a *crux ansata*
(*ankh*), or the Triple Tau of the Arch-masons. He who
with Intelligence and Will is armed with this emblem
has need of no other thing ; he should be all-potent,
for this is the perfect sign of the Absolute."

Éliphas Lévi also instructs us upon the formation
and consecration of the Magic Wand. He who would
possess it must select the wood of an almond or nut
tree which has just flowered for the first time ; the
bough should be cut off at one blow by the " magical
sickle." It must be bored evenly from end to end
without causing any crack or injury, and a magnet-
ized steel needle of the same length as the bough must

[1] Galangal root.

be introduced. One end must be closed by a clear, transparent glass bead, and the other end by a similar bead of resin : the ends should be covered then with sachets of silk. Two rings must next be fitted near the middle of the wand, one of copper and one of zinc, and two lengths of fine copper chain rolled around the wand. Upon the wand should then be written the names of the Twelve Spirits of the Zodiacal Cycle, with their sigils added, as below :

Aries	. . .	Sarahiel
Taurus	. . .	Araziel
Gemini	. . .	Saraiel
Cancer	. . .	Phakiel
Leo .	. . .	Seratiel
Virgo	. . .	Schaltiel
Libra	. . .	Chadakiel
Scorpio	. . .	Sartziel
Sagittarius	. .	Saritiel
Capricornus	. .	Semaqiel
Aquarius .	. .	Tzakmaqiel
Pisces	. . .	Vacabiel

Finally, upon the copper ring must be engraved in Hebrew letters, from right to left, the words " The Holy Jerusalem," H QDShH JRUShLIM ; and upon the zinc ring in Hebrew letters, from right to left, the words " The King Solomon," H MLK ShLMH, Heh Melek Shelomoh.

When the wand is complete, it must be consecrated by the invocations of the Spirits of the Four Elements and the Seven Planets, by ceremonies lasting over the seven days of a week, using the special incense and prayers for each day.

The consecrated wand, in common with all magical

instruments, should be kept wrapped in silk, and never allowed in contact with any colour but black. The ideal receptacle for it is a cedar or ebony box.

With this wand, duly made and fully consecrated, "the Magus can cure unknown diseases, he may enchant a person or cause him to fall asleep at will, can wield the forces of the elements and cause the Oracles to speak."

VIII. THE SOUL OF THE WORLD

Ah Love ! could you and I with Him conspire
To grasp this sorry Scheme of things entire,
   Would not we shatter it to bits—and then
Remould it nearer to the Heart's Desire !

I shall now draw your attention to the philosophy of the last of the Magi, as expounded in that chapter of *The Magical Ritual* called " L'Amoureux " :

He enjoins us to bear in mind that equilibrium results only from the opposition of forces, the active having no existence without the passive ; that light without darkness is formless ; and " Yea " can win no triumph save over " Nay." Love, also, gains added strength from hate, and hell is the hotbed of such plants as shall bear root in heaven.

He tells us, too, that the great Fluidic Agent which is called the " Soul of the World," and which is represented with the horned head of the Cow of Isis to express animal fecundity, is a *blind* force.

The power which the Magus wields is composed of two opposing forces, which unite in love and disjoin in discord ; love associating contraries, whilst hate makes of similars rivals and enemies. Hatred succeeds to love when by saturation the void has become filled, " unless the full cannot become empty " ; but the usual result is an " equilibrated saturation, due to mutual repulsions."

Sexual love the Magus regards as a physical manifestation ; repugnance and pain may be forgotten by those who are under its sway. This is a form of inebriation arising from the attraction of two contrary fluids ; and at the conjunction of the positive and negative poles there results an ecstasy and orgasm during which the loved one seems the brilliant phantom of a vision.

Our consideration is solicited for the bodily and mental disorders which result from solitude and its accompanying fluidic congestions, due to want of equilibrium : such as nervous maladies, hysteria, hypochondriasis, megrim, vapours, and insane delusions. It becomes possible, in the light of the new wisdom, to understand the ailments of maidens, and of women of an uncertain age, of widows and of celibates.

Inspired by this natural law of equilibrium, " you may often predict the future course of a life, and may cure many such ailments, often by distracting the attention when unduly fixed, and so may the Magus become as great a physician as Paracelsus, or as renowned a diviner as was Cornelius Agrippa. You will come to understand the diseases of the soul ; the fact that learned and chaste persons often hunger after the pleasures of vice will be noticed, and so will it be observed that men and women steeped in vices turn at times to the consolations of virtue ; and thus you may predict the occurrence of strange conversions and of unexpected sins, and great astonishment will be shown at your facility in discerning the most carefully concealed secrets of the heart and home.

" Girls and women may be by such means of divination shown in dreams the forms of lover and husband ; such confidantes are potent auxiliaries in magic arts ; never abuse their position, never neglect their interests, for they are good gifts to the Magus. In order to possess an assured sway over the heads and hearts of women, it is essential to obtain the favour of both Gabriel, the Angel of the Moon, and of Anäel, the Angel of Venus."

Certain female evil demons must be overcome and cast down in order that perfect equilibrium be established. Foremost of these are :

Nahémah, princess of the Succubi.

Lilith, queen of the Stryges, tempting to debauchery, and destroyer of maternal desire.

" Nahémah presides also over illicit and sterile caresses.

" Lilith rejoices in strangling in their cradles children whose origin has been soiled by the touch of Nahémah."

The truly wise master of the Cabala, we are told, understands the concealed meaning of these names, and of such demoniac evil powers, which are also called the material envelopes or cortices or shells of the Tree of Life, soiled and blackened by the outer darkness ; they are as branches which are dead, having been torn off the tree, whence issue light, life, and love.

Finally, these, according to Lévi, are some of the privileges of a Magus :

Aleph.—He sees God and is able to commune with the seven Genii around the throne.

Vau.—He understands the reasons for the Present, the Past, and the Future.

Zain.—He holds the secret of what is meant by the resurrection from the dead.

A few of his powers are these :

Cheth.—The power of making the Philosopher's Stone.

Teth.—The possession of the Universal Medicine.

Samech.—To know in a moment the hidden thoughts of any man or woman.

Peh.—To foresee any future events which do not depend upon the will of a superior being.

Resh.—Never to feel love or hatred unless it is designed.

Shin.—To possess the secret of constant wealth, and never to fall into destitution or misery.

These privileges are the final degree of Human Perfectibility ; these are open to attainment by the elect, by those who can dare, by those who would never abuse them and who know when to be silent.

IX. THE ELEMENTALS

> Then said the second—" Ne'er a peevish boy
> Would break the Bowl from which he drank in joy ;
>   And he that with his hand the Vessel made
> Will surely not in after-wrath destroy."

It will be seen that this form of sorcery has to do largely with the doctrine of Elemental Spirits. The existence of such intelligences has been credited from the earliest times, and the *ginn* and *'efreet* of Arabian lore are Elementals under another name.

There are early Assyrian incantations addressed to Elementals, and the 108th chapter of the Ancient Egyptian *Book of the Dead* is called " The Chapter of Knowing the Spirits of the West."

According to the Abbé de Villars, the air is full of an innumerable multitude of creatures of human form, somewhat fierce of aspect, but in reality tractable, great lovers of the sciences, excessively subtle, eager to serve the sage, but hostile to the fool. Their wives and daughters are beauties of a masculine type, and may be likened to the Amazons. The seas and rivers are thus inhabited as well as the air, and the beings who dwell therein were denominated Nymphs or Undines by the Adepts of the past. Few males are born to them, but the women are numerous, and they are very beautiful, so that the daughters of men cannot compare with them. The earth, too, is populated to a point within a short distance of its centre with Gnomes, who are people of a low stature, the guardians of buried treasure, of mines, and of gems. They are ingenious, amicable toward mankind, and may be commanded with ease. " They supply the Children of the Sages with the money which they need, and desire no other wages for their labours but the glory of the service."

The Gnomides, their wives, are diminutive, but exceptionally pretty, and very quaint in their attire. Regarding the Salamanders, or igneous inhabitants of the fiery region, they serve the philosophers, but do not court their company, and their wives and daughters are even more elusive. The wives of the Salamanders, however, are more beautiful than any of the other Elementals, for their element is purer, and " you will be even more charmed with the beauty of their minds than with their physical perfections.

" Yet you cannot but pity these helpless creatures when I tell you that their souls are mortal, and that they have no hopes of enjoying that Eternal Being whom they know and religiously adore. Composed of the purest parts of the elements which they inhabit, and having no opposing qualities, they subsist, it is true, for many ages ; yet what is time in comparison with eternity ? They must eventually return to the abyss of oblivion. So much does this knowledge afflict them that they are frequently inconsolable. But God, whose mercy is infinite, revealed to our fathers, the philosophers, a remedy for this evil. They learned that in the same manner that man, by the alliance which he hath contracted with God, hath been made a partaker in divinity, so may the Sylphs, Gnomes, Undines, and Salamanders, by an alliance with man, be made partakers of immortality and of the bliss to which we aspire, when one of them is so happy as to be married to a sage, while Elementaries of the masculine kind can attain to the same glorious end by effecting a union with the daughters of the human race."

This belief is responsible, of course, for the many fairy wives of fable. In the legends and folk-stories of nearly all countries, Asiatic and European, we find the enchanted-spouse motif occurring again and again, and some very curious parallels exist between such fables of the East and of the West ; so that the idea of the fairy wife would appear to be common to all peoples, or traceable to some parent legend of remote antiquity.

In the medieval French romance of *Mélusine*, the maiden of that name weds Raymond, on the condition that he shall never seek to see her upon a certain day in every week. To this he solemnly pledges himself. Eight sons are born of the union, and seven of these become great warriors. All goes well until the unhappy Raymond is persuaded, by the specious arguments of his brother, to break his solemn vow.

On the day of Mélusine's usual withdrawal from his

society, he goes in search of her, and finds her in a bath,
the lower part of her body having been transformed
into that of a serpent ! When, later, in the course of a
quarrel, Raymond unjustly reproaches Mélusine as " a
false serpent," she, though against her will, takes flight
through the open window in the likeness of a dragon.

This sufficiently remarkable fable becomes more
remarkable still when considered side by side with
" The Story of Hasan of El-Basrah " in *The Thousand
and One Nights*. Hasan becomes enamoured of a
damsel who " surpassed in her loveliness the beauties
of the world, and the lustre of her face outshone the
bright full moon ; she surpassed the branches in the
beauty of her bending motions, and confounded
the mind with apprehension of incurring calumny. . . .
She had a mouth like the seal of Suleyman, and hair
blacker than the night of estrangement is to the
afflicted, distracted lover, and a forehead like the new
moon of the Festival of Ramadan, and eyes resembling
the eyes of the gazelles, and an aquiline nose brightly
shining, and cheeks like anemones, and lips like coral,
and teeth like pearls strung on necklaces of native gold,
and a neck like molten silver, above a figure like a
willow-branch."

This damsel was the daughter of one of the Kings of
the *ginn*, and when, by means not over-scrupulous, he
had secured her for his wife, Hasan, like Raymond,
passed many years in happiness with her. Then, in
her husband's absence, the daughter of the *ginn* is
given access to a certain magical " dress of feathers,"
contrary to the solemn injunctions of Hasan.

In the Arabian story this incident takes the place of
Raymond's intrusion upon the bath of Mélusine. For
the fairy wife " took the dress and opened it, and took

her child in her bosom . . . and became a bird. . . ."
Having left a message that Hasan, if he desired to meet
her again, should come to her " in the islands of Wak-
Wak " (said to lie east of Borneo), " she flew away with
her children and sought her country."

Perhaps one of the oldest myths of this class is the
Hindu legend of Urvasi and Pururavas ; but there is
another very ancient Hindu legend, wherein Bheki,
the frog, is a beautiful maiden who consents to wed a
King on the extraordinary condition that he shall never
show her a drop of water.   Being faint, on one occasion,
she is said to have asked for water, and he thoughtlessly
giving her some, she immediately disappeared.

Paracelsus seems to have been responsible for the
creation of the term " Undines " (the water Elementals).
In Fouqué's romance upon the subject, Undine takes
the knight of her choice down into a submarine palace,
where she marries him, making him promise that he
will never speak angrily to her when on, or near to, any
water.   Needless to say, he breaks his promise.

In addition to these stories, there are numberless
other fairy-wife fables in the literature of East and
West, as that of King Ruzvanshah, a Persian story,
and the Turkish fable of the King of Yemen, both of
whom espoused daughters of the *ginn*.   The conditions
of the union are very nearly identical in every case.

One of the most uncanny creatures of the human
invention, the werewolf, may be included among fairy
spouses ; and a belief in the existence of these was
current in ancient and medieval times, and prevails
to this day among many savage races, and even in out-
of-the-way parts of France, Russia, and Bulgaria.

In a quotation by Halliwell from a Bodleian MS. we
read that :

" Ther ben somme that eten . . . men, and eteth noon other . . . fro that tyme that thei be a-charmed with mannys . . . for rather thei wolde be deed . . . men shulde be war of hem."

Wlislocki, writing so recently as 1891, tells us of a gipsy fiddler's wife at Tórész, in the north of Hungary, about ten years earlier, who kept the family in mutton and enabled her husband to establish a profitable business as an innkeeper by her nocturnal expeditions in wolf's shape. The village priest cured the woman, we are informed, by sprinkling her and the house with holy water, and the peasants murdered the husband. At the time that Wlislocki wrote there were then living in the village, according to his account, two of the men who participated in the deed.[1]

Similar fables of semi-fairy unions, except that the husband is the supernatural partner, are the Græco-Roman myth of Cupid and Psyche and the Sicilian tale of the girl who wedded a green bird, which, on bathing in a pan of milk, became a handsome youth. But the favourite motif, which runs through the mythology of the East and West, while it cannot fairly be traced to any one source, is that of the fairy wife.

X. THE " CELESTIAL INTELLIGENCER "

With them the seed of wisdom did I sow,
And with mine own hand wrought to make it grow ;
And this was all the Harvest that I reap'd—
" I came like Water, and like Wind I go."

One of the most remarkable works ever contributed to the literature of the occult is that called *The Magus*. I append the full title at the end of this chapter (p. 51).

[1] So recently as the winter of 1913, a report reached me, from a British Tropical Colony, of a were-wolf. The circumstances were attested by several witnesses.

Ophis.

The Spirit
Antichrist.

F. Barrett Del.   Pub. by Lackington & Allen.   R. Griffith Sculp.

EVIL SPIRITS

FROM *THE MAGUS*

In the section of this huge and elaborate work entitled " Natural Magic," the author says, " There are some *collyriums* which make us see the images of spirits in the air or elsewhere ; which I can make of the gall of a man and the eyes of a black cat, and some other things. The same is made, likewise, of the blood of a lapwing, bat and a goat ; and if a smooth, shining piece of steel be smeared over with the juice of mugwort, and be made to fume, it causes invocated spirits to appear."

Furthermore he tells us that in the colic, if a live duck be applied to the belly, it takes away the pain, and the duck dies. If one take the heart out of any animal, and, whilst it is warm, bind it to a patient suffering from a quartan fever, it drives it away. " So if any one shall swallow the heart of a lapwing, swallow, weasel, or a mole, while it is yet living and warm with natural heat, it improves his intellect, and helps him to remember, understand, and foretell things to come. Hence this general rule—that whatever things are taken for magical uses from animals, whether they are stone, members, hair, excrements, nails, or anything else, they must be taken from those animals while they are yet alive, and if it is possible, that they may live afterwards.

" If you take the tongue of a frog, you put the frog into water again : and Democritus writes, that if any one shall take out the tongue of a water-frog, no other part of the animal sticking to it, and lay it upon the place where the heart of a woman beats, she is compelled, against her will, to answer whatsoever you shall ask of her. Also, take the eyes of a frog, which must be extracted before sunrise, and bound to the sick party, and the frog to be let go again blind into the water, the party shall be cured of a tertian ague ; also, the same will, being bound with the flesh of a nightingale in the skin of a hart, keep a person always wakeful without sleeping.

" So the right eye of a serpent, being applied to the soreness of the eyes, cures the same, if the serpent be let go alive. So, likewise, the tooth of a mole, being taken out alive and afterwards let go, cures the tooth-ache ; and dogs will never bark at those who have the tail of a weasel that has escaped. Democritus says, that if the tongue of the chameleon be taken alive, it conduces to good success in trials, and likewise to women in labour ; but it must be hung up on some part of the outside of the house ; otherwise, if brought into the house, it might be most dangerous.

" There are very many properties that remain after death ; and these are things in which the idea of the matter is less swallowed up in them ; even after death, that which is immortal in them will work some wonderful things : as in the skins we have mentioned of several wild beasts, which will corrode and eat one another after death ; also, the drum made of the rocket-fish drives away all creeping things at what distance soever the sound is heard ; and strings of an instrument made of the guts of a wolf, and being strained upon a harp or a lute, with strings made of sheep-guts, will make no harmony."

THE

MAGUS

OR

CELESTIAL INTELLIGENCER

BEING

A Complete System of

OCCULT PHILOSOPHY

IN THREE BOOKS :

Containing the Ancient and Modern Practice of the Cabalistic Art, Natural and Celestial Magic, &c ; showing the wonderful Effects that may be performed by a knowledge of the CELESTIAL INFLUENCES, *the occult properties of metals, herbs and stones,*

and the

APPLICATION OF ACTIVE TO PASSIVE PRINCIPLES.

Exhibiting

THE SCIENCES OF NATURAL MAGIC ;

Alchymy, or Hermetic Philosophy ;

also

The NATURE, CREATION, AND FALL OF MAN ;

His natural and supernatural Gifts ; the magical Power inherent in the Soul, &c. ; with a great variety of rare Experiments in Natural Magic :

THE CONSTELLATORY PRACTICE, or TALISMANIC MAGIC ;

The Nature of the Elements, Stars, Planets, Signs, &c. ;
The Construction and Composition of all Sorts of Magic Seals, Images, Rings, Glasses, &c. :
The Virtue and Efficacy of Numbers, Characters, and Figures, of good and evil spirits.

MAGNETISM,

And Cabalistical or Ceremonial Magic ;

In which the secret Mystries of the Cabala are explained ; the operation of good and evil spirits ; all kinds of Cabalistic Figures, Tables, Seals, and Names, with their Use, &c. The Times, Bond, Offices, and Conjuration of Spirits, to which is added

Biographia Antiqua, or the Lives of the most eminent Philosophers, Magi, &c.

The Whole Illustrated with a great Variety of

CURIOUS ENGRAVINGS, MAGICAL AND CABALISTICAL FIGURES, &c.

By

FRANCIS BARRETT, F.R.C.

Professor of Chemistry, Natural and Occult Philosophy, the Cabala, &c., &c.

LONDON

Printed for Lackington, Allen and Co., Temple of the Muses, Finsbury Square.
1801.

XI. THE SHADOW ARMY

We are no other than a moving row
Of Magic Shadow-shapes that come and go
Round with the sun-illumined lantern held
In Midnight by the Master of the Show.

Book II, Part III of this huge and elaborately illustrated work (original copies of which are rare) deals
with the "Particular Composition of the Magical
Circle."

The following instructions, we learn, are the principle
and sum-total of all that has gone before, only, says
The Magus :

"We have brought it rather into a closer train of
experiment and practice than any of the rest ; for
here you may behold the distinct functions of the
spirits ; likewise the whole perfection of magical
ceremonies is here described, syllable by syllable."

But as the greatest power is attributed to the circles
("for they are certain fortresses "), I shall now give
some particulars respecting the composition and figure
of a circle.

The forms of circles are not always one and the
same, but are changed according to the order of spirits
that are to be called—their places, times, days, and
hours ; for in making a circle it should be considered
in what time of the year, what day, and what hour ;
what spirits you would call, and to what star or region
they belong, and what functions they have : therefore, to begin, let there be made three circles of the
latitude of nine feet, distant one from another about
a hand's breadth.

First, write in the middle circle the name of the hour
wherein you essay the magical task ; in the second

place, write the name of the angel of the hour ; in the third place, the seal of the angel of the hour ; fourthly, the name of the angel that rules the day, and the names of his ministers ; in the fifth place, the name of the present time ; sixthly, the names of the spirits ruling in that part of time, and their *presidents* ; seventhly, the name of the head of the sign ruling in the time ; eighthly, the name of the earth, according to the time of conjuration ; ninthly, and in order to complete the middle circle, write the name of the sun and moon, according to the said rule of the time : " for as the times are changed, so are the names."

In the outer circle let there be drawn, in the four angles, " the names of the great presidential spirits of the air that day wherein you do this work, viz. the name of the king and his three ministers. Without the circle, in four angles, let *pentagons* be made. In the inner circle write four divine names, with four crosses interposed : in the middle of the circle, viz. towards the east, let be written Alpha ; towards the west, Omega ; and let a cross divide the middle of the circle."

When the circle is thus finished, according to rule, one must proceed to consecrate and bless it, in the following manner :

" *In the name of the holy, blessed, and glorious Trinity, proceed we to our work in these mysteries to accomplish that which we desire ; we therefore, in the names afore- said, consecrate this piece of ground for our defence, so that no spirit whatsoever shall be able to break these boundaries, neither be able to cause injury nor detriment to any of us here assembled ; but that they may be com- pelled to stand before the circle, and answer truly our demands, so far as it pleaseth Him who liveth for ever and ever; and who says, I am Alpha and Omega, the Beginning and the End, which is, and which was, and which is to come, the Almighty; I am the First and the Last, who am living and was dead; and behold I live for ever and ever; and I have the keys of death and hell. Bless, O Lord! this creature of earth wherein we stand; confirm, O God! thy strength in us, so that neither the adversary nor any evil thing may cause us to fall, etc., etc. Amen."*

It must also be borne in mind that the angels rule the hours in a successive order, according to the course of the heavens and the planets to which they are subject; so that the same spirit which governs the day rules also the first hour of the day; the second governs the second hour, and so on throughout; " and when the seven planets and hours have made their revolution it returns again to the first which rules the day." Therefore we shall now consider the names of the hours.

	Names of Hours of the Day.		Names of Hours of the Night.
1	Yain	1	Beron
2	Janor	2	Barol
3	Nafnia	3	Thami
4	Salla	4	Athar
5	Sadedali	5	Methon
6	Thamur	6	Rana
7	Ourer	7	Netos
8	Thamic	8	Tafrac
9	Neron	9	Saffur
10	Jayon	10	Agle
11	Abai	11	Calerva
12	Natalon	12	Salam

The following particulars should also be studied:

Benediction of Perfumes

" The God of Abraham, God of Isaac, God of Jacob, bless here the creatures of these kinds, that they may fill up the power and virtue of their odours ; so that neither the enemy nor any false imagination may be able to enter into them ; etc. Then sprinkle the same with holy water."

The Exorcism of Fire into which the Perfumes are to be put

" I exorcise thee, O thou creature of fire, by the only true God Jehovah, Adonai, Tetragrammaton, that forthwith thou cast away every phantasm from thee, that it shall do no hurt to any one. We beseech thee, O Lord, to bless this creature of fire, and sanctify it so that it may be blessed to set forth the praise and glory of thy holy name, and that no hurt may be permitted to come to the exorcizer or spectators ; etc. *Amen.*"

Of the Habit of the Exorcist

" It should be made of fine white linen and clean, and to come round the body loose, but close before and behind."

Of the Pentacle of Solomon (for the figure see Plate)

" It is always necessary to have this pentacle in readiness to bind with, in case the spirits should refuse to be obedient, as they can have no power over the exorcist while provided with and fortified by the pentacle, the virtue of the holy names therein written presiding with wonderful influence over the spirits.

" It should be made in the day and hour of Mercury upon parchment made of kidskin, or virgin, or pure, clean, white paper ; and the figures and letters wrote in pure gold ; and it ought to be consecrated and sprinkled (as before often spoken) with holy water."

When the vesture is put on, it will be convenient to say the following oration :

An Oration when the Habit or Vesture is put on

" Anoor, Amacor, Amides, Theodonias, Anitor ; by the merits of the angels, O Lord, I will put on the garment of salvation, that this which I desire I may bring to effect, through thee, the most holy Adonai, whose kingdom endureth for ever and ever. *Amen.*"

XII. THE MASSING OF THE SHADES

Shapes of all Sorts and Sizes, great and small,
That stood along the floor and by the wall ;
    And some loquacious vessels were ; and some
Listened, perhaps, but never talk'd at all.

I have omitted many of the elaborate particulars which follow, firstly, in order that I may not weary you, and, secondly, because it forms no part of my intention to tempt the curious to dabble in a dangerous pursuit ; but the lengthy ceremonial being duly performed, we are assured that there will appear infinite visions, apparitions, phantasms, etc., beating of drums, and the sound of all kinds of musical instruments ; " which is done by the spirits, that with the terror they might force some of the companions out of the circle, because they can effect nothing against the exorcist himself : after this you shall see an infinite company of archers, with a great multitude of horrible beasts, which will arrange themselves as if they would devour the companions ; nevertheless fear nothing."

Thereupon, the exorcist, holding the pentacle in

his hand, must say, " Avoid hence these iniquities, by virtue of the banner of God." At this, the spirits will be compelled to obey the exorcist, and the company shall see them no more.

Then let the exorcist, stretching out his hand with the pentacle, say :

" Behold the pentacle of *Solomon*, which I have brought into your presence ; behold the person of the exorcist in the middle of the exorcism, who is armed by God, without fear, and well provided, who potently invocateth and calleth you by exorcising ; come, therefore, with speed, by the virtue of these names Aye Saraye, Aye Saraye ; defer not to come, by the eternal names of the living and true God, Eloy, Archima, Rabur, and by the pentacle of Solomon here present which powerfully reigns over you, and by the virtue of the celestial spirits, your lords ; and by the person of the exorcist, in the middle of the exorcism ; being conjured, make haste and come, and yield obedience to your master, who is called Octinomos."

This invocation being performed, immediately there will be hissings in the four parts of the world, whereupon the exorcist must say :

" Why stay you ? Wherefore do you delay ? What do you ? Prepare yourselves to be obedient to your master in the name of the Lord, Bathat or Vachat rushing upon Abrac, Abeor coming upon Aberer."

Then they will immediately come in their proper forms ; and :

" When you see them before the circle, show them the pentacle covered with fine linen ; uncover it, and say, ' Behold your confusion if you refuse to be obedient ' ; and suddenly they will appear in a peaceable form, and will say, ' Ask what you will, for we are prepared to fulfil all your commands, for the Lord hath subjected us hereunto.' " [1]

For the guidance of the amateur sorcerer it may be mentioned that the spirits of the air of Monday are subject to the west wind, which is the wind of the moon ; their nature is to give silver and to convey things from place to place ; to make horses swift, and to disclose the secrets of persons, both present and future.

Their Familiar Forms are as follows :

They appear generally of a great and full stature, soft and phlegmatic, of colour like a black, obscure cloud, having a swollen countenance, with eyes red and full of water, a bald head, and teeth like a wild boar ; their motion is like an exceeding great motion of the sea. For their sign there will appear an exceeding great rain, and their particular shapes are :

A King, like an archer, riding upon a doe.

A little boy.

A woman hunter with a bow and arrows.

A cow ; a little dog ; a goose.

A green or silver coloured garment.

An arrow ; a creature with many feet.

The spirits of the air of Friday are subject to the west wind ; their nature is to give silver, to incite men, and incline them to luxury, to cause marriages, to allure men to love women, to cause or take away infirmities, and to do all things which have motion.

Their Familiar Shapes

They appear with a fair body, of middle stature, with an amiable and pleasant countenance, of colour

---

[1] There is a very fine account of a conjuration in Lytton's *A Strange Story*.

white or green, their upper parts golden ; the motion
of them is like a clear star.   For their sign will appear
naked virgins round the circle, which will strive to
allure the invocator to dalliance with them ; but :

Their Particular Shapes are

A King, with sceptre, riding on a camel.
A naked girl ; a she-goat.
A camel ; a dove.
A white or green garment.
Flowers ; the herb Savine.

But there are repulsive Elemental forms, as well, in
addition to those mentioned by Barrett, having, for
instance, the appearances of huge insects, with heads
of birds or of human beings.   A gruesome theory,
employed finely in fiction by Sheridan le Fanu, has been
advanced, according to which the creatures seen by
sufferers from delirium tremens, by opium-smokers and
by other drug-slaves, are simply forms taken by the
lowest class of Elementals which the action of the
poison has in some way rendered visible.[1]

I will transcribe here, in dismissing Francis Barrett,
an interesting " advertisement " from *The Magus* :

Advertisement

*The Author of this work respectfully informs those who
are curious in the studies of Art and Nature, especially
of Natural and Occult Philosophy, Chemistry, Astrology,
etc., etc., that, having been indefatigable in his researches
into those sublime sciences, of which he has treated at*

---

[1] I had originally intended to include a *complete* ceremony of conjuration in the foregoing chapters, but it has been pointed out to me
that this might be undesirable in a book of the present description.

large in this book, that he gives private instructions and lectures upon any of the above mentioned sciences; in the course of which he will discover many curious and rare experiments. Those who become students will be initiated into the choicest operations of Natural Philosophy, Natural Magic, the Cabala, Chemistry, the Talismanic Art, Hermetic Philosophy, Astrology, Physiognomy, etc., etc. Likewise they will acquire the knowledge of the Rites, Mysteries, Ceremonies, *and* Principles *of the ancient Philosophers, Magi, Cabalists, Adepts, etc. The purpose of this School (which will consist of no greater number than Twelve Students) being to investigate the hidden treasures of Nature; to bring the mind to a contemplation of the* Eternal Wisdom; *to promote the discovery of whatever may conduce to the perfection of Man; the alleviating the miseries and calamities of this life, both in respect of ourselves and others; the study of morality and religion here, in order to secure to ourselves felicity hereafter; and finally the promulgation of whatever may conduce to the general happiness and welfare of mankind. Those who feel themselves thoroughly disposed to enter upon such a course of studies, as is above recited, with the same principles of philanthropy with which the Author invites the lovers of philosophy and wisdom to incorporate themselves in so select, permanent, and desirable a society, may speak with the Author upon the subject, at any time between the hours of Eleven and Two o'clock, at* 99, Norton Street, Mary-le-Bonne. *Letters (post paid) upon any subject treated of in this Book will be duly answered, with the necessary information.*

XIII. THE LIGHT

Wake ! for the Sun, who scatter'd into flight
The Stars before him from the Field of Night,
 Drives Night along with them from Heav'n and strikes
The Sultán's turret with a Shaft of Light.

I have left you thus long to the guidance of Francis
Barrett in order that the complex nature of the Cabalistic art, as expounded by its professors, might become
more readily appreciable. To my seeming, there is
something pathetic in its very complexity. These
groping spirits, after all, were worshippers—the Un-
knowing calling to the Unknown, and their strange
hymns have echoed hollowly down the avenue of the
ages—hollowly and mockingly.

Through the gateway opened by the Cabalists we
may enter a stupendous whispering-gallery ; there we
may hearken to echoes bidding us hither and thither.
Francis Barrett believed himself a guide to the Light ;
Éliphas Lévi proclaimed that the Secret of the Sphinx
was his, yet renounced his writings at the end, and
died in the faith of Rome.

It is for each to judge for himself whether the seekers
sought a true light or pursued a will-o'-the-wisp. But
the endless task, begun by some primitive man of a
younger world, proceeds, feverishly, to-day. There
are sorcerers in London, in Paris, in New York, and
in every other important centre. I do not mean mere
students of the literature of the subject, but practical
sorcerers. However, upon this point I shall say no
more.

We are promised a great Adept in the near future—
a Buddha who shall pour the light of the East into the
darkness of the West. The West is ripe for his coming,
but one may speculate upon his greeting.

APOLLONIUS OF TYANA

I. AT THE TEMPLE OF ÆSCULAPIUS

THERE is so much of the marvellous in the life of the man of Tyana, that if I am to begin by doubting the possession by Apollonius of supernatural powers, I can see no end to my doubts other than that of doubting if he ever existed at all! I prefer to take him as I find him—as a white figure in a black age, a philosopher unsullied by the mires through which his footsteps led him, a seer and a master of obscure wisdom. That some of his adventures remind one of the Arabian wonder stories, and some of them of the claims of modern theosophy, concerns me not at all. I am prepared, equally, to give patient hearing to Egyptian magician, English theosophist, or alchemistical philosopher.

We shall find ourselves moving in spacious times, in an age of marble villas and white raiment; and if on occasion I shall ask you to step aside with me into some shady portico to consider matters, I shall do so in no sceptic spirit. Upon this understanding, then, we commence the task.

It was in the darkness which immediately preceded the dawn of Christianity that Apollonius was born. He is said to have seen the light in a meadow, in the Greek city of Tyana, his mother having been inspired by a dream to walk out into a certain meadow and

pluck the flowers. Her maids who were with her
wandered away in quest of the blooms, and she fell
asleep upon the grass.

She was awakened by the crying of swans and by
the loud flapping of their wings, and, rising in alarm,
bore her child. Philostratus naïvely writes:

" People of the country say that just at the moment
of the birth a thunderbolt seemed about to fall to earth
and then rose up into the air and disappeared ; and
the gods thereby indicated, I think, the great distinction to which the sage was to attain, and hinted in
advance how he should transcend all things upon
earth and approach the gods."

His early studies were under a Phœnician teacher at
Tarsus, but Apollonius found the atmosphere of that
city little to his liking. He accordingly removed,
with his father's consent, to Ægæ, taking up his
residence in the temple of Æsculapius, where he applied
himself with tremendous ardour to the Pythagorean
doctrines.

He early outsoared his new preceptor, one Euxenus,
but, recognizing that he owed him something, persuaded the elder Apollonius to present Euxenus with
a country villa, where there were shady groves and
cooling fountains calculated to appeal to one kindly
disposed toward Epicurus.

" Now," said Apollonius, " you live there your own
life, but I will live that of Pythagoras."

He forthwith renounced flesh diet and wine, par-
taking only of dried fruit and vegetables ; for he said
that flesh was unclean, but that all the fruits of the
earth were clean. Whilst he thus conceded that wine
was clean, he declared that it darkened the ether of the
soul. He next abandoned shoes, and clad himself in

linen, declining to wear any animal product. Also, he ceased to cut his hair.

From this time onward his reputation steadily increased, together, it would appear, with his command of ready speech. He is said to have effected a number of remarkable cures.

On one occasion he found a stream of blood upon the altar (that of Egyptian bulls which had been sacrificed), together with a pair of Indian gold vases, set with jewels.

" What is all this ? " Apollonius asked of the priest ; " for some one is making a very handsome gift to the gods."

He was answered that a rich Cilician was supplicating the god to restore to him one of his eyes. Apollonius, however, was convinced that the supplicant had lost the eye as the penalty of some horrible and cruel deed.

" The priest accordingly made inquiries about the Cilician and learned that his wife had by a former marriage borne a daughter, and he had fallen in love with the maiden and had seduced her, and was living with her in open sin. The mother had surprised the two, and had put out both her eyes and one of his by stabbing them with her brooch-pin."

One Maximus of Ægæ is responsible for recording a number of the incidents which marked the sojourn of Apollonius at the temple, including that of his encounter with the debauched and infamous governor of Cilicia. When Apollonius was twenty years of age his father died, and Apollonius gave the bulk of the property to his elder brother : the remainder he divided among the other relatives. His words on that occasion, granting that they have come down to us as uttered, were typical of the polished form observable in his most careless remarks ; but we must remember that they reach us through the refining sieve of Philostratus.

"Anaxagoras of Clazomenæ," he is reported as saying, "kept his philosophy for cattle rather than for men when he abandoned his fields to flocks and goats ; and Crates of Thebes, when he threw his money into the sea, benefited neither man nor beast."

He thus early showed his real contempt for wealth : and he also proclaimed his intention to remain celibate.   In laying such restraint upon himself while yet a youth, he is declared to have surpassed Sophocles, "who only said that in reaching old age he had escaped from a mad and cruel master."

II. BABYLON AND THE MAGI

"Loquacity," said Apollonius, "has many pitfalls, but silence none."

Such were the views of the man who, by nature loquacious and by virtue of his training a fluent speaker, from the time that he quitted Ægæ preserved an unbroken silence for five years ! His renunciation of flesh, wine, and woman seems but dim in the background of this, his giant renunciation of speech, that speech which, in Apollonius, was an attribute truly godlike.

This curious ordeal, of course, was the one prescribed by Pythagoras for his disciples.   As Iamblichus says :

"He instructed those who came to him to observe a quinquennial silence, in order that he might by experiment learn how they were affected as to continence of speech, the subjugation of the tongue being the most difficult of all victories, as those have unfolded to us who instituted the Mysteries."

During this period he travelled about Pamphylia and Cilicia ; and, on one occasion, entering the market-place of Aspendus, he found that certain rich men had made a corner in corn.

Clinging to the statue of the Emperor Tiberius was the unhappy governor, but even that dread sanctuary could not save him from the wrath of the populace ; for they were preparing a fire, in order to burn him alive !

Apollonius made his stately way through the enraged mob, and with a gesture asked of the governor what wrong he had done. The latter explained that he had done none, being as greatly wronged as the people, but that they would not grant him a hearing. What followed serves to illustrate, in a remarkable manner, the magnetic force of personality already possessed by Apollonius.

He turned to the throng, raising his hands for silence ; and that enraged populace, so wrought upon by the imminent prospect of starvation as thus to have attacked the governor, to have courted the deathly wrath of Tiberius, were still—hushed in wonderment.

The governor named those responsible for the situation, and Apollonius silently directed that they be summoned. When they arrived, we are told, he had much ado to refrain from speech against them, so deeply was he affected by the sight of the hungry men, women, and children. He refrained, however, writing out his indictment, which the governor read aloud :

" Apollonius to the corn-dealers of Aspendus. The

earth is the mother of us all, for she is just ; but you, because you are unjust, have pretended that she is your mother alone ; and if you do not repent I will not permit you to remain upon her."

So profound was the terror inspired by this singular man of silence that the dealers immediately unlocked their granaries and filled the market-place with corn.

Of the further adventures of Apollonius during his term of silence, records are lacking ; his chroniclers seem to have realized that his words were the golden treasury of his wisdom and that his silence was but a novitiate. At the conclusion of this period he visited the beautiful temple of the Apollo of Daphne at Antioch, with its guardian groves of giant cypress trees, cool springs, and white porticoes. And at Antioch, we are told, he performed, at sunrise, certain secret rites, the nature of which he communicated only to those who, like himself, had passed a period of years in silence.

It was in Antioch, too, that he formed the scheme of extensive travel which was to lead him to Babylon and the Magi, to Egypt and the Naked Sages, to the Mountain of the Brahmins, and to Rome and Tigellinus. When, finally, he set out he had with him only two attendants, both of whom had belonged to his father's house.

Reaching ancient Nineveh, he was joined by the man whose tireless pen was to preserve the lightest sayings of Apollonius for posterity, the man who was destined to become the modest friend and faithful companion of his wanderings—Damis, a native of the city. Advancing his claims to join Apollonius, Damis said :

" I know the languages of the various barbarous races, and there are several—for example, the Armenian tongue, and that of the Medes and Persians, and that of the natives of Kadus—and I am familiar with all of them."

" And I," replied Apollonius, ". . . understand all languages . . . and all the secrets of human silence."

Thus it happened that a satrap in command of a frontier garrison on the Babylonian border saw approaching his post a man of majestic mien, accompanied by a party of travellers. Full of the importance of his office, however, he confronted the imposing leader and submitted him to a violently conducted examination. But the calm and singular replies of the mysterious stranger at last had effect, and the satrap lost all hold upon his elusive courage.

" By the gods," he said, with awe, " who are you ? "

" . . . I am Apollonius of Tyana."

That name already had been noised abroad in Babylon ; for the satrap, addressing him as " divine Apollonius," endeavoured now to press gifts upon the famous visitor. But Apollonius proceeded on his way, predicting, from the portent of a slain lioness with eight whelps which they came upon, that he would stay in Babylon for one year and eight months ; which was actually the period of his visit. Of Babylon we are told that its fortifications extended 480 stadia and formed a complete circle, and its wall was 150 feet high and nearly one hundred in thickness. The city was split by the Euphrates into equal halves, and beneath the river stretched a secret passage linking the palaces upon either bank. The beauteous Semiramis was said to have had this tunnel constructed, temporarily diverting the stream into lakes for the purpose.

The palaces they found to be roofed with bronze,

but the chambers of the women were adorned with silver, with solid gold ornaments and statuettes and with golden tapestries, as also were some of the other apartments. They visited a chamber having a domed roof studded with sapphires, amid which were golden figures of the gods. It was here that the King delivered judgment ; and golden wrynecks were " hung from the ceiling, four in number, to remind him of Adrastea, the goddess of justice, and to remind him not to exalt himself above humanity." These figures were said to have been arranged by the Magi.

Entering by the great gate, Apollonius was invited to kiss a golden image of the King—a ceremony imposed upon all save Roman officials.

" Who," inquired Apollonius, looking at the image, " is that ? "

He was told that it was the King.

" This King whom you worship," he replied, " would acquire a great boon if I merely commended him as of honourable and good reputation ! "

He passed into Babylon.

That such assurance was not unjustified is shown by the fact that he was honourably received. For the vestibule of the temple in which the monarch awaited him was of great length, and from afar the King saw that majestic figure approaching.

" This," he cried, " is Apollonius, whom my brother said he saw in Antioch. He depicted just such a man as now comes to us ! "

Thus had the fame of the man of Tyana preceded him, heralding his coming and preparing the way. His stay in Babylon was notable for several reasons. For instance, he proved to his own satisfaction and to that of all beholders that an eunuch may fall in love, but

I do not propose to deal with the incident.   Above all,
he visited the Magi.

Unfortunately Damis was not acquainted with what
took place during the several interviews, for Apollonius
forbade him to accompany him in his visits : so that all
we know of the Magi from Apollonius is contained in
the following :

" What," asked Damis once, " of the Magi ? "

" They are wise men," replied Apollonius ; " but
not in all respects."

It is fortunate that the faithful Damis was not
similarly excluded from the Hill of the Brahmin Sages,
to which (one year and eight months having elapsed
since Apollonius entered the city of Babylon), I shall
now hasten, not even pausing at the glorious Court of
the Indian King Phraotes, probably near Peshawar,
which he visited on the way.

III. THE MAGIC OF THE BRAHMINS

Entering the land of the far-famed Brahmins with
Apollonius, we find ourselves whirled away into a maelstrom of weird happenings.   Amid the phantasmagoria
created for our wonderment by the man of Tyana's
chronicles it is quite possible to discern, however, some
familiar forms.   The supernatural feats of the Lamas,
to which I have drawn your attention earlier, evidently
have a genealogy which touches at some point the
Brahmin sorceries ; if, indeed, the occult wisdom of
those sages were not the common fund upon which,
later, yogin, mahatma, and conjuring fakir alike have
drawn.

It is no part of my intention to weary you with an

inquiry into the real identity of these Brahmins, although it would be interesting to disperse the mist which, figuratively and actually, enveloped them. By Brahmins, to-day, we do not understand magicians, but that these who entertained Apollonius were wonder-workers, dreaded and respected, is very evident.

For four days, we are told, Apollonius and his party journeyed across a fertile country, then to find themselves close to the stronghold of the Sages. Their guide, at this point, exhibited signs of excessive fear, declining to proceed further. In fact, he threw himself from his camel in a state of pitiable panic. A short distance ahead rose the Hill of the Brahmins, and, as the party halted, a youth was seen running towards them. He was of extremely dusky complexion, but between his eyebrows there gleamed a crescent-shaped mark. As a badge he bore a golden anchor.

" Hail, Apollonius ! " he cried.

His words struck all the party with great wonderment, but Apollonius turned to Damis, saying, " We have reached men who are unfeignedly wise, for they seem to have the gift of prescience."

This messenger directed that the company should halt at that spot, and that Apollonius alone should follow him ; such was the command of the Masters. Alone, then, Apollonius advanced to the stronghold of sorcery.

The hill upon which the Brahmins dwelt was of about the same height as the Athenian Acropolis, and its summit was enveloped in a kind of mist, which wholly obscured the walls from view. Apollonius asserts that, ascending upon the southern side, he came upon a well above the mouth of which there shimmered a deep blue light, which at noon ascended aloft, coloured like a rainbow. Hard by was a fiery crater, which sent up a *lead-coloured* flame, though it emitted neither smoke nor smell. The well was called the Well of Testing and the fire the Fire of Pardon. Here, moreover, were two jars of black stone, respectively the Jar of the Rains and the Jar of the Winds.

The summit of this hill was locally regarded as the navel of the earth, and upon it fire was worshipped with mystic rites, the fire being derived from the sun, to which luminary a hymn was sung there each day at noon. This fire-worship may perhaps afford a clue to the doctrine of the Brahmins.

Entering without fear, as became a student of the higher mysteries, Apollonius was received by the Sages, who were seated upon seats of black copper, but the chief Brahmin, Iarchas, occupied a seat higher than the rest, chased with golden figures. He exhibited a perfect acquaintance with the history of Apollonius and with every particular of his journey thither.

I should like to deal at length with this reception, but to do so would be to depart from my present purpose. Following some philosophic conversation, then, the Brahmins proceeded to a temple, where, in the course of their worship (and it should be noted that Apollonius participated in this) they struck their rods upon the ground and were levitated some distance into space !

One is tempted to suppose that these rods must have been akin to the wand described by Éliphas Lévi ; for Lévi says of the wand that, when it is " duly made and fully consecrated, the Magus can cure unknown diseases ; he may enchant a person, or cause him to fall asleep at will, *can wield the forces of the elements*, and cause the Oracles to speak." Apollonius was in-

formed that Iarchas was a reincarnation of the mighty
monarch Ganges, and told that he himself had in
a former incarnation been an Egyptian sea-captain.
Here again we catch a glimpse of familiar doctrines.
But I hasten to recount the episodes which attended
the arrival of a certain King who came to take counsel
with the Sages.

The King entered, ablaze with gold and jewels, and
Apollonius, modestly, was about to retire, but was
prevented by Iarchas, the chief Brahmin. The King,
who was accompanied by his brother and by his son,
seems to have treated his hosts with a deference which,
in an Indian monarch, can only have proceeded from
dread, and shortly, in a formal speech, Iarchas " *bade*
the King take food."

Four tripods immediately moved forward of their
own volition ! Upon them were cup-bearers of black
brass, which resembled the figures of beautiful youths.
And the earth magically strewed soft grass beneath
them. Dried fruit, bread, and vegetables were served
and set before the royal guest and Apollonius by these
mysterious automata ; and we learn that two of the
tripods flowed with wine, whilst the others furnished,
respectively, hot and cold water. We are reminded
of Homer :

> That day no common task his labour claim'd :
> Full twenty tripods for his hall he fram'd,
> That, plac'd on living wheels of massy gold
> (Wondrous to tell), instinct with spirit, roll'd
> From place to place, around the blest abodes
> Self-mov'd, obedient to the beck of gods.

Vessels and goblets formed of enormous jewels were
passed to the guests by the bronze cup-bearers ; and
these contained a mixture of wine and water.

The happenings at the abode of the Brahmins have afforded Apollonius's critics (and the critics of his biographer, Philostratus) with matter for ridicule. By some who have sought, amid the seemingly fabulous, for the real episodes of his life, these adventures of Apollonius have been deliberately ignored. But I as deliberately select them, since I wish to present him as a magician and as one who consorted with magicians.

Aaron's rod had powers strangely similar to those possessed by the rods of the Brahmins, and Éliphas Lévi evidently was of opinion that his wand was capable of performing feats more wonderful even than that of levitation. The bronze cup-bearers must be a stumbling-block for the sceptical, but theosophy teaches an absolute control of mind over matter. Thus, a theosophist will perceive little of the remarkable in these bronze waiters. You and I may doubt if jewels ever existed large enough to have been used as goblets ; but the authors of *The Arabian Nights* had no such doubts. In short, an examination of occult phenomena, conducted from the common level, usually can yield no other result than increased incredulity ; but those who stand upon the ladder of the Secret Wisdom tell us that they can see much further ; that a great and wondrous landscape unfolds, map-like, to their view. Some, who have ascended many rungs, believing that, the topmost attained, the human veil would wholly be lifted from their eyes, have learned that that ladder is endless.

Therefore, without essaying to mount, let us endeavour to review the marvels recorded of Apollonius in the spirit, not of scoffers, but of those who, whilst failing themselves to perceive any light, are sufficiently generous to admit that their vision and not the light may be in fault.

A conversation which followed this magical banquet is worthy of record. Apollonius asked the Brahmins of what they supposed the Cosmos to be composed.

" Of the elements."

" Are there then four ? " he asked.

" Not four," said Iarchas, " but five."

" And how can there be a fifth," demanded Apollonius, " beside water and air and earth and fire ? "

" There is the ether," replied the Brahmin, " which we must regard as the element of which the gods are made ; for just as all mortal creatures inhale the air, so do immortal and divine natures inhale the ether."

Apollonius asked which was the first of the elements.

" All are simultaneous," Iarchas answered, " for a living creature is not born by degrees."

" Am I," said Apollonius, " to regard the universe as a living creature ? "

" Yes," replied the other " . . . for it engenders all living things."

" Should I then term the universe female ?—or male ? "

" Of both genders," said the other, " for by commerce with itself it fulfils the rôle both of mother and father in bringing forth living creatures ; and it is possessed by a love for itself more intense than any separate being has for its fellow, a passion which knits it together into harmony. . . ."

Then we have a glimpse of the alchemistical philosophy (if not of the true philosopher's stone) in the following words of Iarchas :

" Respecting the stone which attracts and binds to itself other stones, you must not be sceptical ; for you may see the stone yourself if you will, and admire its properties. The largest specimen is of the size of a finger-nail, and it is conceived in a hollow of the earth at a depth of four fathoms ; but it is endowed with such force that the earth swells and breaks open in many places where the stone is. . . ."

It was impossible to secure it, Apollonius was told, except by the most subtle artifices of science ; for it vanished if unskilfully sought. "We alone," said the Brahmin, "can secure, partly by performance of certain rites, and partly by certain forms of words, the *pentarbe*. . . ."

Touching this interesting point—the elusive nature of the *pentarbe*—the original text of Philostratus is susceptible of more than one construction ; but a French translator renders it thus : "Il n'est permis à personne de la chercher, car elle s'évanouit si l'on ne la prend pas par artifice."

"In the night-time," Iarchas related, "it glows like fire, for it is red and emits rays ; and if you look at it, it smites your eyes with a thousand glints and gleams. And this light within it is a spirit of mysterious power, for it absorbs to itself everything in its neighbourhood."

This account has quite a unique interest ; for the philosopher's stone possessed by the Adept Trautmansdorf was stated, by those alleged to have seen it, to have been about as large as a bean, of a garnet-red colour, and to have emitted light in the dark.

Iarchas, then, exhibited to Apollonius the *pentarbe* and all that it was capable of performing. He also gave to the man of Tyana seven mystic rings, named after the seven stars ; and it is said that Apollonius wore each of them in turn on the day of the week which bore its name.

During his sojourn among these thaumaturgists, he himself performed wonderful cures of the halt, the blind, and the possessed ; but what he learnt of the Brahmins' lore we can only assume from his subsequent life and works.

And on departing from the Hill of the Sages we are told that he kept the Ganges on his right hand, but the Hyphasis on his left, going down toward the sea a journey of ten days from the sacred ridge.   And as he and his followers descended they saw a great many ostriches, and many wild bulls, and numbers of asses and lions and pards and tigers, and " another kind of apes than those which inhabit the pepper trees, for these were black and bushy-haired, and were dog-like in features and as big as small men."

In this way they came to the sea, where passenger ships rode.   And we read that the sea called Erythra, or " red," was really of a deep blue colour, but that it was so named from a King Erythas, who gave his own name to it.

Having reached this point, Apollonius sent back with the guide the camels to Iarchas, together with the following letter :

" Apollonius to Iarchas and the other Sages greeting.

" I came to you by land, and you presented me with the sea ; but by sharing with me the wisdom which is yours, you have opened for me the road to the heavens. All this I shall tell to the Hellenes ; and I shall communicate my words to you as if you were present, unless I have in vain drunk of the draught of Tantalus. Farewell, ye goodly philosophers."

IV. THE FAIR WOMAN OF CORINTH

Apollonius returned once more to his beloved Greece, where his subsequent divinations, including that of the plague at Ephesus, calling up of spirits, and miraculous cures, are too numerous to be dealt with here. I proceed to the day of the Epidaurian festival at Athens, whereat he received a serious affront at the hands of the hierophant, who denied him admission to the rites, saying that he would never initiate a wizard and charlatan, nor unveil the Eleusinian mystery to a man who dabbled in impure rites. Thereupon Apollonius retorted with dignity :

" You have not yet mentioned the chief of my offences, which is that knowing, as I do, more about the initiatory rite than you do yourself, I have nevertheless come to you for initiation, as if you were wiser than I am."

These words the bystanders applauded with true Hellenic appreciation, saying that he had answered with characteristic vigour ; whereupon the hierophant, perceiving that his exclusion of Apollonius was unpopular with the crowd and likely to react upon himself, adopted a tone of conciliation :

" Be thou initiated," he said, " for thou seemest to be some wise man that has come here."

" I will be initiated," Apollonius replied, " at another time, and " (glancing at the hierophant who succeeded the one he addressed, and who was destined to preside over the temple four years later) " it is he who will initiate me."

This augury was fulfilled.

One of the most remarkable incidents of Apollonius's remarkable career took place at about this time.

There was in Corinth a man named Demetrius, a student of philosophy who had embraced in his system all the masculine vigour of the Cynics. We shall see more of Demetrius later. Of him Favorinus, in several of his own works, made the most generous mention; and the attitude of Demetrius toward Apollonius was one of reverence and admiration; for he regularly sought his company and was anxious to become his disciple, being so impressed with his doctrines as to convert to the cult of Apollonius the more advanced of his own pupils. Among the latter was one Menippus, a Lycian twenty-five years of age, a man of good judgment, " and of a physique so beautifully proportioned that in mien he resembled a fine and gentlemanly athlete."

The handsome Menippus, returning one day to Cenchræ, and walking alone along the road, engaged, I assume, in reflections befitting a Cynic philosopher, met with an amorous adventure. A woman approached him whose beauty was such as to drive all thoughts of Cynicus from his mind, and whose glance pierced his philosopher's cloak and found a youthful heart beneath.

She was daintily and richly attired, and, the licence of the period allowing of such overtures, she clasped his hand, declaring that she had long been in love with him! Furthermore she confided to him that she was a Phœnician and lived in a suburb of Corinth, where she desired him to call upon her.

" When you reach the place this evening," she whispered to him, " you will hear my voice as I sing to you, and you shall have such wine as you never before drank. There will be no rival to disturb you; and we two beautiful beings will live together."

To this proposal Menippus consented :

" For although he was in general a strenuous philosopher, he was nevertheless susceptible to the tender passion ; and he visited her in the evening, and for the future constantly sought her company by way of relaxation."

Then came a day when Apollonius surveyed Menippus as a sculptor might do, sketching a mental outline of the youth and examining him. From the eye of Apollonius no weakness could be hidden, no foible concealed, no secret veiled.

" You are a fine youth," he said, " and hunted by fine women ; but in this case you are cherishing a serpent, and a serpent cherishes you."

The respect in which the great sage was held no doubt secured his immunity from the kind of retort natural in such case. Menippus, however, demanded his reasons for so extraordinary a statement.

" This woman," Apollonius warned him, " is of a kind you cannot marry. Do you think that she loves you ? "

Menippus replied that he had every reason to think so. His manner presumably revealed to his questioner the depths of his infatuation, for :

" Would you then marry her ? " asked Apollonius.

The youth, whose philosophy evidently had failed him in his direst need, replied that to do so would be delightful. His desire to conceal the truth is shown ; for when the omniscient sage, perceiving that the affair was serious, asked when the wedding was to be, the enamoured Menippus answered :

" Perhaps to-morrow ; for it brooks no delay."

That the ceremony actually took place on the morrow we are not told, but on the occasion of the

"THE MAN OF TYANA"--BUST OF APPOLLONIUS IN THE CAPITOLINE, ROME

wedding banquet Apollonius presented himself before the whole of the guests, his presence, probably, being not entirely welcome to Menippus.

" Where," inquired the inflexible man of Tyana, " is the dainty lady at whose instance ye are come ? "

She entered at that moment ; but her loveliness had no power to soften the heart of Apollonius.

" Here she is," replied Menippus, and rose, blushing, from his seat.

" And to which of you belong the silver and gold and all the rest of the decorations of the banqueting hall ? "

" To the lady," replied the youth, " for this is all I have of my own."   And he pointed to the philosopher's cloak which he wore.

Apparently ignoring the lovers, Apollonius turned to the guests, a man detached from earthly things, whose sandals were set upon the ladder of the gods.

" You know of the gardens of Tantalus, how they exist and yet do not exist ? "

Can we not hear his stern voice ; see the company grouped about him, all eyes upon the bearded face ; see Menippus standing protectively by his beautiful mistress ?

" As such," continued Apollonius, " you must regard this world of ours, for it is no reality, but the semblance of a reality.   And that you may realize the truth of what I say, this is one of the vampires, that is to say of those beings whom the many regard as lamias. These beings fall in love, and they are devoted to the delights of Aphrodite, but especially to the flesh of human beings, and they decoy with such delights those whom they mean to devour at their feasts."

Now, it will be evident at once that we may place

at least two constructions upon this speech ; we may accept it literally, as did Damis, and after him Philostratus, or we may regard it somewhat in the light of a parable. The clue, I think, to the light in which Apollonius designed that it be viewed we may find in the words " whom *the many* regard as lamias."

This point of view, however, I shall not discuss further ; but when we remember that the vampire, the most gruesome ghoul in the gallery of human superstitions, to this day thralls the imagination in Greece, as well as in Russia, Servia, Hungary, and parts of Germany, it is no wonder that Damis, a true man of his age, adopted a different view, and has so recorded the incident as to bear it out.

No doubt the words of Apollonius struck consternation to the hearts of his audience.

" Cease your ill-omened talk," cried the object of his denunciations, " and be gone ! "

But when we read that the golden goblets and the rich appointments of the villa were proved " as light as air " and melted from sight, whilst all the retinue of servants vanished before the rebukes of Apollonius, whereupon " the phantom pretended to weep, and prayed him not to torture her, nor to compel her to confess what she really was," again we hesitate, scarce knowing how to construe. I will conclude the episode in the words of Philostratus :

" But Apollonius insisted and would brook no denial, and then she admitted that she was a vampire, and was feasting Menippus with pleasures and devouring his body, for it was her habit to feed upon young and beautiful bodies, because their blood is pure and strong."

Curiously enough, this incident is dealt with by

Sinistrari of Ameno, a seventeenth-century writer, who speaks of :

" The case of Menippus Lycius, who, after frequent intimacies with a woman, was by her entreated to marry her ; but a *certain philosopher*, who partook of the wedding entertainment, having guessed what that woman was, told Menippus that he had to deal with a *Compusa*, that is a Succuba Demon ; whereupon the bride vanished, bewailing. . . ."

V. TIGELLINUS

Passing over his subsequent travels, throughout which he addressed himself to executing reforms, notably in the various temples, and, in addition, gave utterance to a number of remarkable predictions, let us see what befell the man of Tyana in Rome.

The Rome to which Apollonius now directed his steps was the Rome of deeds more than humanly bloody, the Rome of magnificent vice, the Imperial city whose wit was directed to the eulogy of incestuous courtesans, whose genius employed itself with devising new subtleties of debauchery ; a garden of horror wherein living torches flamed by night, proclaiming redly the capital of the world—the Rome of the immortal madman, Nero.

Its walls not yet in sight, Apollonius met with one Philolaus of Cittium, near to the Grove of Aricia. This philosopher was a fugitive from the capital, and he spoke of the deeds of Nero in a hushed voice, glancing about him in fear lest his words be overheard. He warned Apollonius that he would in all probability be arrested by the officers set over the gates, and earnestly counselled him to retrace his steps, pointing out that, whatever he might choose to incur of risk to his own person, he was not entitled to subject his band of followers to the dangers of Rome.

" Do you at least save these, your companions," he implored.

Upon which Apollonius, turning to Damis, said :

" Of all the blessings which have been vouchsafed to me by the gods, often without my praying for them at all, this present one is the greatest ; for chance has thrown in my way a touchstone to test these young men, of a kind to prove most thoroughly which of them are philosophers, and which of them prefer some other line of conduct than that of philosophy."

And in fact the poor-spirited members of the company were now detected readily enough ; for, under the influence of Philolaus's words, some of them declared themselves ill, others unprovided for the journey, others homesick, others visited by warning dreams ; and in the end the thirty-four philosophers surrounding Apollonius, whose philosophy crumbled not at the mere name of Nero, were reduced to eight !

This, then, was the tried band which approached the gates of Rome, and, despite the doubts and fears of Philolaus, entered unchallenged.

Apollonius, we are informed, took up his residence in a temple, crowds flocking to see and hear the sage of Tyana. And at about this time, from Corinth came Demetrius, attaching himself to Apollonius and at the same time publicly expressing suicidal opinions against the Emperor.

In consequence, Apollonius and his fellows were looked at askance, and it was generally believed that he had encouraged Demetrius to proceed thus, which belief was strengthened on the occasion of Nero's completion of the great baths in Rome.

Now, the better to understand Demetrius's subsequent action, it is necessary to remember that bathing was a veritable vice with certain Romans, and some of them would bathe six or seven times a day, and remain in the tepidarium for hours together, in a condition of semi-conscious lassitude.

From the tepidarium one could enter either the sudatorium (vapour bath) or the calidarium (water bath). In the former, the bather reposed in an atmosphere of spicy fragrance, whilst slaves massaged and scraped his body. Thence he passed to the water, sweet with fresh perfumes, and, retiring by another door, enjoyed a cooling shower. Returning to the tepidarium, he was anointed, if of the wealthier class, by his slaves, with rare ointments and oils of the costliest description, whilst soft music played in an adjoining chamber !

The Imperial Thermæ of Nero were veritably a small town, comprising not only all the chambers for bathing, but huge apartments devoted to gymnastic games, extensive libraries, lovely gardens, lecture halls, spacious theatres and schools, restaurants, tennis-courts, and porticoes. Many Roman citizens loafed away the greater part of their lives in the Imperial Thermæ, entering directly the doors opened in the morning, and remaining there until they closed at night.

Nero, with the Senate and the whole of his Court, coming to open the great baths, Demetrius, from within the thermæ, delivered himself of a pungent philippic against bathers ; declaring that, far from the habit being a cleanly one, these bathers enfeebled and polluted themselves! He then proceeded to show that such institutions were a useless expense.

We are prepared, of course, to learn that he was instantly slain, since none other than Nero was the object of his attack; but it was actually because none other than Nero was its object that he escaped. For " he was only saved from immediate death as the penalty of such language by the fact that Nero was in unusually good voice when he sang on that day, and he sang in a tavern which adjoined the gymnasium, naked except for a girdle round his waist, like any low tapster."

Such were the mountebank caprices upon which depended life and death in the Rome of the mad Emperor.

Demetrius, however, did not wholly escape the peril which he had openly courted by his language; for Tigellinus banished him from Rome, on the ground that he had ruined the bath by the words he had used; " and he began to dog the steps of Apollonius— secretly. . . ."

Suspicion of the man of Tyana was intensified by words which he uttered in connexion with a prodigy. For at about that time there was an eclipse of the sun and a clap of thunder was heard, " a thing which very rarely occurs at the time of an eclipse." Thereupon Apollonius glanced up to heaven and said:

" There shall be some great event and there shall not be."

At the time, those who heard these singular words were at a loss to comprehend their meaning; but three days later every one understood what was meant; " for while Nero sat at meat, a thunderbolt fell on the table, and clove asunder the cup which was in his hands and was close to his lips."

Evidently, it was argued, the fact that he had so
narrowly escaped being struck was intended by the
words that a great event should happen and yet should
not happen. Tigellinus, when he heard the story, began
to dread the mysterious Apollonius "as one who
was wise in supernatural matters; and though he
felt that he had better not prefer any open charges
against him, lest he should incur at his hands some
mysterious disaster, nevertheless he used all the eyes
with which the government sees, to watch him,
whether he was talking or holding his tongue, or
sitting down or walking about, and to mark what he
ate, and in whose houses, and whether he offered
sacrifice or not."

His opportunity arose when Nero had an attack of
what was apparently influenza. The temples were
filled with crowds who supplicated the gods to restore
the Emperor's voice; and Apollonius denounced this
folly, speaking of those who took "pleasure in the
mimes of buffoons."

Spies reported these words to Tigellinus; Apollonius
was immediately arrested, upon a charge of impiety
against the divine Nero, and one of those base creatures
who, in that and subsequent reigns, fattened upon
blood-money, was retained as his accuser.

We now come to a very curious incident, which
shows Apollonius an apt pupil of the Brahmin Masters,
and illustrates, I think, how hypnotism played a part
in the very earliest sorceries.

The creature who was paid to compass his destruction had his tirade written upon a scroll, and this, we
read, he brandished like a sword against Apollonius,
crying that it should ruin and slay him. The two,
accused and accuser, came before Tigellinus, and we

can imagine that scene as vividly as though art had limned it for posterity ; the craven prostrated to the ground, crawling in the dust, I conceive, to the feet of the formidable judge, and Apollonius, white-robed, composed, a man conscious of inner power, advancing stately, as one who numbered kings among his friends and gods among his counsellors. Also, we can see the judge, but vaguely, since imagination must fail to depict him as he was. Let us step aside for a moment, and glance at him, the accumulated evils of his age incarnate in one man.

Sofonius Tigellinus, Prætorian Prefect, had been so created by Nero, in the words of Tacitus, "purely from partiality to the inveterate lewdness and infamy of the man." He was grand master of debauchery and vice. Doubtless to him, and not to Nero, were due the Christian persecutions and the burning of Rome ; for his was the evil power behind the throne. His infamy is assured of immortality by one achievement alone : the banquet on the lake of Agrippa—which was in the gardens adjoining his house.

"For this purpose," says Tacitus, "he built a raft which supported the banquet, which was moved by other vessels, drawing it after them : the vessels were striped with gold and ivory, and rowed by bands of pathics, who were ranged according to their age and accomplishments in the science of debauchery. He had procured fowl and venison from remote regions, with sea-fish even from the ocean : upon the margin of the lake were erected bagnios, filled with ladies of distinction : over against them naked courtesans were exposed to view : now, there were beheld obscene gestures and motions ; and as soon as darkness came on, all the neighbouring groves and circumjacent

dwellings resounded with music, and glared with
lights. . . ."

This, then, the giver of the banquet on the lake of
Agrippa, was the man before whom Apollonius of
Tyana stood, accused of a crime than which no greater
was recognised in Rome. This was the man who
took from the informer's hand the scroll of indictment,
unrolled it, and prepared to read—which point of my
narrative brings me to the really extraordinary part
of the interview.

For, to the eyes of Tigellinus, the scroll appeared
quite blank ; not a single word, not a letter, was traced
upon it !

Needless to say, Sofonius Tigellinus was a prey to
ceaseless fear—fear of the supernatural, of that under-
world to which he had consigned so many unhappy
souls. He came to the conclusion, we are told, that he
had to do with a visitant from Hades—which renders
it the more remarkable that he should have decided
to interview him in private. Yet such was his decision, prompted, we must assume, by an anxiety to
placate.

Apollonius, at that interview, explained his motive
in practising wisdom, declaring that the sole use he
made of it was to gain a knowledge of the gods and an
understanding of human affairs, for that the difficulty
of knowing another man exceeded that of knowing
oneself.

" And how about the demons," said Tigellinus, " and
the apparitions of spectres ? How, O Apollonius, do
you exorcise them ? "

" In the same way," he answered, " as I should
murderers and impious men."

The reference to Tigellinus himself was broad enough,

for all the world knew that he was Nero's master and
guide in every excess of cruelty and wanton violence.
But Tigellinus seems to have overlooked it.

"And," he continued, "could you prophesy if I
asked you to?"

"How," said Apollonius, "can I, being no prophet?"

"And yet they say that it is you who predicted that
some great event would come to pass and yet not come
to pass."

"Quite true," said Apollonius, "is what you heard,
but you must not ascribe it to any prophetic gift, but
rather to the wisdom which God reveals to sages."

"And why do you not fear Nero?"

"Because the same God who allows him to seem
formidable has also granted to me the absence of fear."

"Then what do you think of Nero?"

And Apollonius answered:

"More highly than you do; for you think it dignified
for him to sing, but I think it dignified for him to be
silent."

Tigellinus was astonished at the calm effrontery of
his prisoner.

"You may go," he said, "but you must give sureties
for your person."

To which Apollonius answered:

"And who can give surety for a body that no one
can bind?"

This answer, we learn, struck Tigellinus as inspired
and above the wit of man; and since he was not anxious
to offend a god, he said:

"You may go wherever you choose, for you are too
powerful to be controlled by me."

So ended this notable encounter between the power of
Rome and the powers of mystical philosophy.

During the remainder of his sojourn in the capital,
Apollonius is recorded to have performed many supernatural feats, not the least remarkable being the
following :

A girl on the point of marriage seemingly died,
and her bier was followed by him who was to have
been her husband, in all the affliction usual in like cases
of interrupted wedlock. As she chanced to be of
consular family, all Rome condoled with him.

Apollonius met this mournful procession.

" Set down the bier," said the man of Tyana to the
attendants. " I will dry up the tears you are shedding
for the maid."

Almost all the spectators thought that he was about
to pronounce a funeral oration ; but what he actually
did "was to touch the maid, and, after uttering a few
words over her in a low tone of voice, he wakened
her from that death with which she seemed to be
overcome."

The grateful family presented Apollonius with
150,000 drachmas, which he in return begged them to
settle upon the bride as a marriage portion.

When Nero took his departure for Greece, after
issuing a proclamation that no one should teach philosophy in public, the wonderful man of Tyana " turned
his steps to the western regions of the earth."

VI. THE CHARGE OF SORCERY

We shall be compelled to pass over much of the
travels and exploits of Apollonius, in Egypt and elsewhere, if we are to give any consideration to the crown-
ing adventure of his life ; the accusation of sorcery

and conspiracy with Nerva against Domitian. Concerning the sage's friendly dealings with Vespasian and Titus I shall not pause to deal, otherwise than by mentioning how he is recorded to have predicted to the latter the manner of his death. That Titus was favourablydisposed toward him is shown by his having said to Apollonius, on one occasion: "Although I have captured Jerusalem, you have captured me."

His sojourn among the Naked Sages of the Nile affords few incidents of note. Of these Sages, Philostratus wrote: "They wear next to no clothes, in the same way as people do at Athens in the heat of summer," an interesting aside upon Athenian sartorial customs. The Sages met in a small grove, but their shrines were built, not within the grove, but apparently in various spots in the immediate neighbourhood. The Nile seems to have been the chief object of their worship; the dome of heaven their only roof. But they had built a kind of caravanserai for the reception of strangers, and it was "a portico of no great size, being about equal in length to those of Elis, beneath which the athletes await the sound of the midday trumpet."

Nilus, the youngest of the Naked Sages, joined Apollonius, who journeyed on through Phœnicia and Cilicia to Ionia and Achaia, and thence to Italy. Space forbids us to dally with the lovesick young man who was enamoured of a nude statue of Aphrodite in the isle of Cindus, or to pause in Tarsus, whilst Apollonius heals the youth bitten by a mad dog. We must hasten to Ephesus.

There Apollonius learned that Domitian had put to death three of the vestal virgins who had broken their vows, and, later, after the murder of Sabinus, was proposing to marry the widow of his victim (she was Domitian's own niece). Apollonius thereupon commenced to demonstrate in public against the Emperor.

Aware, in his wisdom, that Nerva would ere long ascend the throne, he declared on one occasion that not even tyrants can force the hand of destiny, and, directing the attention of his audience to the brazen statue of Domitian which had been erected close by that of Meles, he said :

" Thou fool, how wrong are thy views of Destiny and Fate ! For even if thou shouldst slay the man who is fated to be despot after thyself, he shall come to life again."

Report of this reaching Rome, Domitian wrote to the governor of Asia, ordering that Apollonius be arrested and brought before him. The man of Tyana forestalled the order, however, and voluntarily set out for Rome.

In the gardens of the villa where, of old, Cicero had discoursed, he talked with Demetrius, who met him at Dicæarchia. The latter showed great alarm for his safety, saying that his having foreseen the order of arrest, and only ten days after its issue appearing in Rome, without having heard, by natural means, that he was to be subjected to a trial, would be ascribed to the hardihood of sorcery.

" If you have not forgotten the affairs of Nero's reign," said Demetrius, " you will remember my own case, and that I showed no craven fear of death. But then one gained some respite : for although Nero's harp was ill attuned to the dignity that befits an Emperor, yet in other respects its music harmonized his mood not unpleasantly with our own, for he was often induced thereby to grant a truce to his victims and stay his murderous hand. At any rate he did not slay me, although I attracted his sword to myself as much by your discourses as by my own, which were delivered against the bath ; and the reason why he did not slay me was that just then his voice improved, and he achieved, as he thought, a very brilliant performance.

"But where now is the royal songster, and where the harp to which we can make our peace-offerings ? The outlook to-day is unredeemed by music, and full of rancour, and this tyrant is as little likely to be charmed by himself as by others. It is true that Pindar says, in praise of the lyre, that it charms the savage breast of Ares, and stays his hand from war ; but Domitian, although he has established a musical contest in Rome, and publicly offers a crown to the victor, nevertheless slew several of those who piped and sang in his last musical contest ! "

Neither the arguments of Demetrius, however, nor the added advice of Damis, could turn Apollonius from his purpose.

" I will boldly wrestle with the tyrant," he declared, " hailing him with the words of Homer : Mars is as much my friend as thine."

Accordingly he set sail, in three days reached the mouth of the Tiber. and was drawn once more into the maelstrom of Rome. Of the counts of the indictment against him he learned that they were numerous and varied.

" Your style of dress is assailed in them," he was told, " and your way of living in general, and your having been worshipped, and the fact that in Ephesus you delivered an Oracle regarding the famine ; also that you have uttered certain sentiments detrimental

to the Emperor, some of them openly, some of them
obscurely and privately, and some of them on the
pretence that you learned them from the gods. But
the charge which most appeals to the credulity of
Domitian, although I cannot credit it, knowing that
you are opposed even to shedding the blood of sacri-
ficial victims, is this : they say that you visited Nerva
in the country, and that you cut up an Arcadian boy
for him when he was consulting the auspices against
the Emperor ; and that by such rites as these you
awakened his ambitions ; and that all this was done
by night when the moon was already on the wane.
This is the accusation compared with which we need
not consider any other. . . ."

Apollonius was arrested and thrown into prison.
During the time that he was incarcerated, a spy of
Domitian's was introduced amongst the prisoners, but
the sage of Tyana, with his usual tact and command
of apt speech, frustrated the man's designs.

Came the morning of his summons to the Palace,
and he was conducted thither by four guards, Damis
following in his train.

" Now the eyes of all were turned upon Apollonius,
for not only were they attracted by his dress and
bearing, but there was a godlike look in his eyes, which
struck them with astonishment ; and moreover, the
fact that he was come to Rome to risk his life for his
friends won the goodwill even of those who, hitherto,
had been evilly disposed toward him."

Before the Palace of the Cæsars, beholding the
throng of sycophants, courtiers and courted, he made
a notable remark.

" It seems to me, O Damis," he said, " that this
place resembles a bath ; for I see people outside

hastening in, and those within hastening out ; and some of them resemble people who have been thoroughly well washed, and others those who have not been washed at all."

Coming into the Emperor's presence, Apollonius found Domitian to be wearing a wreath of green leaves. He had been sacrificing to Athene in the Hall of Adonis ; and the apartment was full of flowers.

The Emperor turned around, and met the grave glance of the philosopher. A man whom fear of that end which ultimately visited him had made mad, Domitian found a threat in every eye—even in that of his wife—and rightly ; a menace in every shadow— and with justice. As the majestic power which seems to have proceeded from Apollonius once had awed Tigellinus, so now it touched the timid, cruel heart of Domitian, filling it, not with admiration, not with compassion, but with dread.

Apollonius, a rhetor of Hellenic subtlety, guided the ensuing conversation into those channels which he, and not Domitian, wished it to pursue, concluding with a defence of Nerva which inflamed the Emperor to fury.

" The accusation," cried Domitian, " shall unmask everything ; for I know, as well as if I had been present and taken part . . . all the oaths which you took, and the objects " (especially, he was thinking of his own death) " for which you took them, and when you did it, and what was your preliminary sacrifice."

From the time of this interview onward to the trial, he subjected Apollonius to every insult, cutting off his hair and his beard and confining him among the lowest and vilest felons. Regarding these measures, the following *rencontre* may be quoted :

"I had forgotten," said Apollonius, "that it was treasonable to wear long hair," and, speaking of his fetters : "If you think me a wizard, how will you fetter me ? And if you fetter me, how can you maintain that I am a wizard ? "

Replied the Emperor :

" I will not release you until you have turned into water, or a wild animal, or into a tree."

" I will not turn into any of these," said Apollonius, " even if I could, for I will never betray men who, in violation of all justice, stand in peril ; and what I am, that will I remain."

" And who," asked the Emperor, " is going to plead your cause ? "

" Time," replied Apollonius, " the spirit of the gods, and the wisdom which inspires me."

In this prison he remained for some days, and it was here one morning, a little before midday, that Damis said to him :

" O man of Tyana " (he took a particular pleasure, we read, in being so called), " what is to become of us ? "

" What has become of us already," answered Apollonius, " and nothing more."

" And who," said Damis, " is so invulnerable as that ? Will you ever be liberated ? "

" So far as it rests with the verdict of the court," said Apollonius, " I shall be liberated this day ; but so far as depends on my own will, now and here."

With this he mysteriously removed his leg from the fetters, saying to Damis :

" Here is proof positive to you of my freedom, so be of good cheer ! "

Damis has recorded that it was then for the first time that he fully understood the nature of Apollonius,

" to wit that it was divine and superhuman, for without any sacrifice—and how in prison could he have offered any ?—and without a single prayer, without even a word, he quietly laughed at the fetters, and then inserted his leg in them afresh, behaving like a prisoner once more."

True to his prediction, he was that day released from his fetters and sent elsewhere to await trial, and on the day following he called Damis and said :

" My defence has to be made on the day appointed, so do you betake yourself to Dicæarchia—*it is better to go by land*—and when you have greeted Demetrius, turn aside to the sea-shore where the island of Calypso lies ; for there you shall see me."

" Alive ? " asked the faithful Damis.

" As I myself believe," Apollonius replied with a smile, " alive ; but as you will believe, risen from the dead."

Accordingly, Damis tells us that he went away with sorrow in his heart ; for although he did not wholly despair of the Master's life, yet he feared exceedingly. And on the third day he arrived at Dicæarchia—and heard the news of the great storm which had raged throughout those three days ; for a gale had burst over the sea, sinking some of the ships that were making for Dicæarchia, and driving out of their course those which were heading for Sicily and the Straits of Messina. Then, and not till then, did he comprehend why it was that Apollonius had bidden him go by land.

VII. THE TRIAL—AND AFTER

It is sunrise, and the doors of the court are thrown wide to admit the throng which flocks to hear the great Apollonius plead the cause of mystic philosophy.

" And those about the Emperor say that he had taken no food that day, because he was so absorbed in examining the documents of the case. For they say that he was holding in his hands a roll of writing of some sort, sometimes reading it with anger and sometimes more calmly. And we must needs figure him as one who was angry with the law for having invented such things as courts of justice."

Apollonius, awaiting his summons to appear before the Emperor, was approached by an official of the tribunal.

" Man of Tyana, you must enter the court with nothing on you."

" Are we then to take a bath," inquired Apollonius, " or to plead ? "

" The rule," explained the other, " does not apply to dress, but the Emperor forbids you to bring in either amulet, or book, or papers of any kind."

" And not even a cane, for the back of the fool who gave him such advice as this ? "

Whereupon the informer who was to accuse him— one of those contemptible creatures who fattened upon the fears of Domitian—cried out :

" O my Emperor, this wizard threatens to beat me, for it was I who gave you this advice ! "

" Then," retorted Apollonius, " it is you who are a wizard rather than myself ; for you say that you have persuaded the Emperor of my being that which so far I have failed to persuade him that I am not."

But let us hasten to the trial.

The court, though prepared for the accommodation of a large audience, scarce could contain the multitude that flocked thither ; for not only was the famous man of Tyana to confront the Emperor, but all the illustrious of Rome were present. What a hush must have fallen—what a silence come upon citizen and patrician alike—when the accused made his stately entry !

Apollonius, at this time, was already an old man ; he had been deprived of his patriarchal beard and of his long white locks ; but we may be sure that with them had gone none of his dignity, that his eyes had lost none of their fire, of that fire which told of secret power.

He ignored the Emperor's presence completely, not even glancing in his direction.

" Turn your eyes upon the god of all mankind ! "

It was the voice of the parasite—the informer.

Apollonius raised his eyes to the ceiling !

Thus he was standing, I assume, a man scorning to compromise with his conscience, when the Emperor opened his examination:

" What induces you, Apollonius," he said, " to dress yourself differently from everybody else, and to wear this singular garb ? "

" The earth which feeds me," said Apollonius, " also clothes me, and I do not like to trouble the poor animals."

" Why is it that men call you a god ? "

" Because," was the answer, " every man that is thought to be good is honoured by the title of god."

" And what," demanded the Emperor, " suggested

your prediction to the Ephesians that they would suffer from a plague ? "

" I used," said Apollonius, " a lighter diet than others, and so was first to be sensible of the danger."

Thus far, you will perceive, the rhetor had scored over the Emperor. The latter now spoke as follows :

" Tell me, you left your house on a certain day, and you travelled into the country, and sacrificed a boy— I would like to know for whom ? "

To which Apollonius replied :

" Good words, I beseech you ; for if I did leave my house, I was in the country ; and if this were so, then I offered the sacrifice ; and if I offered it, then I ate of it ! But "—and I doubt not his glance sought the villainous informer—" let these assertions be proved by trustworthy witnesses ! "

We are told that his words were greeted with applause. That applause must have been so general and so significant of popular opinion—particularly, no doubt, the popular opinion of informers—as to determine the timid Domitian to conciliate the plauditors.

" I acquit you of the charges," he said, concluding the trial abruptly ; " but you must remain here until we have had a private interview."

Full well Apollonius knew how much this meant and how little, for :

" I thank you indeed, my sovereign," he replied, " but I would fain tell you that by reason of these miscreants your cities are in ruin, and the islands full of exiles, and the mainland of lamentations, and your armies of cowardice, and the Senate of suspicion. Grant me, then, opportunity to speak ; or send some one to take my body. My soul you cannot take.

Nay, you cannot even take my body. Not even thy deadly spear can slay me, since I tell thee I am not mortal ! ''

And with these Homeric words *he vanished from the court !*

So, at any rate, it is recorded ; and I count it no part of my duties to inquire whether the disappearance were due to natural or to supernatural causes. When we shall have witnessed the scene which followed, at Dicæarchia, no doubt our judgment will be aided to a wise decision.

For Damis had arrived on the previous day and had discussed with Demetrius the preliminaries of the trial, the account of which had filled the latter with the keenest apprehension. On the day following, their talk had been of nothing else, and as they wandered sadly along the edge of the sea immortalized by the woes of the lovely, deserted Calypso, they were almost in despair of the Master's return.

Discouraged, then, and sick at heart, they sat down in the Chamber of the Nymphs, by the fountain of white marble.

There the grief of poor Damis broke out afresh :

'' O ye gods ! '' he cried, '' shall we ever behold again our good and noble companion ? ''

A voice answered :

'' Ye shall behold him ; nay, ye have already beheld him ! ''

How they leapt to their feet, whirling about in a kind of joyous fear ; how pale they grew, those two philosophers, to find the man of Tyana standing there by the fountain !

'' Art thou alive ? '' whispered Demetrius.

Apollonius stretched out his hand.

" Take hold of me," he said, " and if I evade you, then I am indeed a phantom come to you from the realm of Persephone, such as the gods of the under-world reveal to those who are dejected with much mourning. But if not, then you shall persuade Damis also that I am both alive and that I have not abandoned my body."

Demetrius ventured to touch the great Master, thus wondrously translated from Rome to the Isle of Calypso. They were, in fact, no longer able to disbelieve, " but rose up and threw themselves upon his neck and kissed him."

VIII. ASSASSINATION OF DOMITIAN

A rumour, we are told, now ran through the Hellenic world that the thaumaturgist was alive, and had arrived at Olympia.

At first the rumour seemed unreliable ; for besides being humanly unable to entertain any hope for him, since they had heard that he was cast into prison, there also circulated such rumours as that he had been burnt alive, dragged about with grapnels fixed in his neck, and had been cast into a deep pit, or into a well. But when the rumour of his arrival was confirmed, thousands flocked to see him from the whole of Greece, exceeding the throngs which attended the Olympic festivals ; and all were filled with the wildest enthusiasm and agog with curiosity and expectation.

" People came from Elis and Sparta, and from Corinth away at the limits of the Isthmus ; and the Athenians, too, although they are outside the Pelo-ponnese ; nor were they behind the cities which are at the gates of Pisa, for it was especially the most celebrated of the Athenians that hurried to the temple, together with the young men who flocked to Athens from all over the earth. Moreover, there were people from Megara staying in Olympia, as well as many from Bœotia and from Argus, and all the leading people of Phocis and Thessaly."

And now it was September 18, in A.D. 96, a date with which the fame of Apollonius will ever be associated. Urged to the deed (as we may fairly assume) by the Empress Domitia, a freedman obtained a private audience with Domitian, and, seizing a suitable opportunity, plunged a dagger into his body.

The Emperor was a man yet full of physical vigour, and, though bleeding freely from the wound, he threw the assassin, gouged out his eyes, and crushed his skull with the base of a gold cup used in religious ceremonies. The cries of assailed and assailant, and the sounds of conflict, brought the guard upon the scene.

Ensued that which is by no means unparalleled in Roman history (wherein, later, we read of the Prætorian Guard putting up the Imperial purple to auction). Finding the Emperor swooning, the guard dispatched him ! Domitian's sun was set ; the star of Nerva risen.

So much for what befell in Rome ; I shall ask you to be translated to Ephesus.

At about noon, Apollonius was delivering an address in the groves of the Colonnade, just at the moment when Domitian met his death in Rome ; and suddenly he dropped his voice, as if something terrified him, and then, though with hesitancy, continued his exposition ; finally, he lapsed into silence.

His next words were perhaps the most dramatic of his life ; for with an awful glance at the ground, and stepping forward three or four paces, he cried :

" Smite the tyrant, smite him ! "

All Ephesus—for all Ephesus, be assured, was there—was struck dumb with amazement; but he, pausing like one who peers through the gloom and at last sees his object clearly, said :

" Take heart, for the tyrant has been slain this day ; by Athene, even now at the moment that I uttered my words ! "

We know that his inner sight had not misled him, and ere long all Ephesus knew, when the messengers from Rome came racing with the tidings.

This, the sage's most famous exhibition of supernatural power, concludes the memoirs of Damis, to which we owe our knowledge of Apollonius. The man of Tyana died at a great age, probably nearly if not quite a hundred years ; and respecting the place of his death much controversy has been. Ephesus, Lindus, and Crete would seem to have equal claims.

I shall add no opinion to those which already have been expressed, I shall quote no word from the works of those, ancient and modern—Dion, Vopiscus, Lampridius, Hierocles, Eusebius, Lactantius, St. Justin, Jerome, Sidonius, Lucian, Apuleius, Caracalla, Blount, Voltaire, Baur, Froude, Pettersch, d'Aussy—who have sought to deify and who have sought to besmirch Apollonius of Tyana. His whole life was a great mystery ; his end one befitting the man who said :

" Live unobserved, and, if that cannot be, slip unobserved from life."

MICHEL DE NOTRE DAME, CALLED NOSTRA-DAMUS

I. MEDICINE IN THE SIXTEENTH CENTURY

THE period of unrest amongst the Latin States which marked the opening of the sixteenth century is notable for the number of men whose names are a byword in the history of Europe. Louis XII of France carried on an unsuccessful campaign against the armies of Ferdinand and Isabella, meeting with defeat at the hands of the great captain, Gonsalvo de Cordova, who had played no small part in the subjugation of the Moors of Granada ; and Bayard, the knight " sans peur et sans reproche," was carving a name to be immortal in the annals of chivalry. Cæsar Borgia pursued his wild career of intrigue and crime, now seeking the aid of this State, now of that, in his insatiable ambition to become paramount amongst the rulers of his time. Machiavelli was compiling his book *Il Principe*, taking his stand on the Borgian ogre ; whilst Christopher Columbus prepared the way for the great rivalry in the New World, which was to culminate before the end of the century in the victory of Sir Francis Drake over the might of Spain.

Into this maze of momentous happenings, on Thursday, December 14, 1503—a year which saw the death of Rodrigo Borgia, Pope Alexander VI—was born at

St. Rémy, a small town in Provence, Michel de Notre Dame, or, as he was more generally known, Michel Nostradamus.

Of Jewish origin, his family had been but recently converted to Christianity, and was included in the celebrated tax of 1512. Michel, who was fully acquainted with the ancient Jewish religion, and who knew also to which tribe he belonged, manifested considerable pride in declaring " the tribe of Issachar is renowned for the gift of prophecy ; and we read in the first book of *Chronicles*, 32nd verse, 12th chapter, that the men of this tribe are learned and experienced, and capable of discerning and remarking the times— *de filiis quoque Issachar viri eruditi, qui noverunt, singula tempora.*"

His father, Jacques de Notre Dame, was a notary, and his grandfather, Pierre de Notre Dame, a celebrated physician to the Duc de Calabre, son of René the Good, King of Navarre and Count of Provence ; whilst the maternal grandfather of Nostradamus had also been a physician and counsellor of the same King, René. Upon this subject Jean Astruc, in dealing with the genealogy of Nostradamus, says : " His origin on his mother's side was not obscure, for through her he was descended from Jean de St. Rémy, counsellor and physician to King René."

Certain historians have thought that Michel was of noble origin, although Pitton denies this in his *Sentiments sur les histoires de Provence*. From authentic sources, however, we are enabled to state with certainty that his family was honest and learned, patronized by the great and loved of the people. The author of the *Commentaires*, after having proved that the forbears of Nostradamus were men of learning, says : " The mouths of the envious who, ignoring the truth, have slandered his origin, are closed."

Nostradamus very early gave evidence of his remarkable genius. When little more than a child he was sent by his father to study at Avignon, and it is said of him that he assimilated the teachings of his professors with such facility that these marvelled. Possessed of a wonderful memory, he added to this precious faculty a sound judgment, penetration, tact, vivacity, gaiety, and finesse in conversation. Whilst yet young, he instructed his fellow-students, and frequently explained to them numerous terrestrial and celestial phenomena, exhibiting thus early a profound interest in the science of astronomy.

At this period astronomy formed part of the science of philosophy, and Nostradamus proved better qualified to instruct his schoolfellows upon the movements of the planets, and the annual revolution of the earth around the sun, than were the learned professors of the college of Avignon; and his own tutor frequently charged him to teach in his stead. His father, however, unwilling that his son should devote himself to astronomy, desired him to undertake the study of medicine, and accordingly, for this purpose, sent him to Montpellier, where his prodigious faculty for assimilating knowledge rapidly brought him to the front.

Let us glance at the outer man. Nostradamus was well made, but of no more than medium height. His face was oval, his forehead high, broad, and bulging, and his eyes were grey and brilliant; his nose was aquiline, his cheeks were fresh and rosy, and his hair was of a deep chestnut hue. He wore his beard long, and was noticeable for his expression of abstraction.

I do not propose to dwell upon the career of Nostradamus as a student, but to deal with his life as physician, philosopher, and prophet, and I come to the first great event in his history when, at the age of twenty-two years, even before he had had conferred upon him the degree of doctor, he gained for himself a reputation which surpassed that of the most learned physicians of his time.

In 1525 a pestilence broke out and ravaged Montpellier and the surrounding country, and Nostradamus, aware that certain districts were without doctors, quitted Montpellier and set out upon a tour of the villages attacked by the contagion. Departing from the methods employed by the Faculty of Montpellier, he made up new remedies ; and whilst those of his colleagues proved of no avail against the dread disease, and frequently hastened death, his own effected marvellous cures. His devotion to the stricken people was only equalled by the wonderful skill that he displayed in dealing with the cases to which he attended ; and, although many refrained from entrusting themselves to the care of so young a physician, the excellence of his remedy soon became known, even as far as Toulouse and Bordeaux, and he had ultimately many more patients than he found it possible to cope with.

Astonished at his phenomenal success, the other doctors invited him to name the composition of the drug with which he had succeeded in arresting the progress of the pestilence. But he merely replied that he held a certain powder, the recipe for which was in the possession only of his own family. That this was nothing less than the great *Elixir*, more than one student of alchemy has believed.

The old and learned professors of the Faculty of Montpellier, having heard of the successes attained by their young pupil during his journey, recalled him after the pestilence had been stayed, to confer upon him the degree of Doctor. In 1529, after having effected a great number of marvellous cures, and having established a reputation, he returned to Montpellier, loaded with honours, but, for all that, poor.

Nostradamus, having, as we have seen, employed remedies which were unauthorized by the Faculty, was interrogated with defiance ; but it is said that he was received as Doctor amid the applause and admiration of the learned assembly. History has preserved to us the name of the person who most frequently interrogated Nostradamus. This was the celebrated Antoine Romier, one of the most noted physicians of the sixteenth century.

Before the French Revolution there was still to be seen, on the registers of the Faculty of Montpellier, the signature of Nostradamus, and beneath, the following date, written in his hand : XXIII Octobre MDXXIX.

Some time later, his name had become so popular that the students actually demanded that he should be appointed as their professor. Their wishes were acceded to, and, if we are to believe Astruc, and Bouche's *Histoire de Provence*, the young doctor Nostradamus was named Professor to the Faculty of Montpellier.

II. THE BLACK PIG AND THE WHITE PIG

Ere long, however, Nostradamus, who loved travel, tired of Montpellier. He left this city, his chair, his pupils, his friends, and re-visited the country of Provence, the scene of his former successes. Everywhere he was received with acclamation and affection ; every town was *en fête* to welcome him.

At the gates gathered those whom he had restored to health, and before their preserver marched young boys and girls who strewed his path with flowers.

The notable people of the district extended to him invitations to visit them and to remain for several months in their families. In fact, according to the chronicles of the time, never had king, prince, or mighty noble a more genuinely affectionate welcome from the Midi than that accorded the young Professor of the Faculty of Montpellier.

One of the greatest savants of the century, Jules César Scaliger, having heard—as all France had heard —of the immense reputation of Nostradamus, communicated with him in order that he might judge for himself if the commotion had any real foundation.

Although it has been said that Scaliger was the son of an obscure sign-painter, he was in reality a descendant of the famous Della Scala family of Verona, one member of which had been the patron of Dante. A physician of no small repute, he was also one of the most renowned classical scholars that Europe has produced.

The young professor, then, immediately availed himself of the invitation extended and proceeded to the town of Agen. During his sojourn there, Scaliger frequently plied his colleague with questions concerning the manner in which the latter had practised his profession during the recent plague, and the replies he received, says a contemporary chronicler, were of so learned a nature that the classic was constrained to confess that this was no ordinary man. A friendship sprang up between these two—a bond so strong that Nostradamus was persuaded to set himself up in Agen.

This town, honoured in the presence amongst its citizens of two such remarkable intellects, offered them considerable presents to induce them to remain permanently within its walls. These they declined, however, saying that they could not belong solely to the town of Agen, since they did not belong even to themselves ; and that if the authorities had presents to give, they should, rather than occupy themselves with them, think of the unfortunate, of the infirm, of the sick, and of the aged. This response appealed to the people so keenly that on the morrow they went to meet Scaliger and Nostradamus, who were out walking, and carried them in triumph through the town.

A man of the age of Nostradamus, handsome and enjoying so great a reputation, naturally excited the attentions of family men who possessed marriageable daughters, and several people of considerable standing presented themselves with a view to arranging an alliance. They were, however, refused by the young savant, and many of the disappointed had convinced themselves that he would never marry, when at last he espoused a young girl of high station, " very beautiful and of an amiable disposition," by whom, says his great friend Chavigny, he had two children—boy and girl. But his wife and children died young, and Nostradamus, stricken with grief, resolved upon leaving Agen, where he had lived for four years, in order to travel far from the scene of his triple bereavement and to make new acquaintances.

He now journeyed in turn through La Guienne, Languedoc, Italy, and France; and although he did not stay long enough in these places to learn much of the country through which he passed, he took care to acquaint himself with men of his profession and to profit thereby. We notice this spirit and taste in the observations which he makes in his two books, upon the divers methods of practising medicine which he remarked during his wanderings, and the conclusions at which he arrived concerning the merits of the many doctors with whom he came into contact. But to these I shall refer later.

One of the earliest signs of his ability in divination was demonstrated whilst he was travelling through Lorraine. In this country he made the acquaintance of the Seigneur de Florinville, who requested Nostradamus to visit his château to treat his wife, who was stricken by some infirmity.

Whilst walking one day with his host in the courtyard, the two fell to discussing omens. During their conversation two sucking-pigs—one white, the other black—strayed into the yard and approached them. The Seigneur took this opportunity to ask of Nostradamus what would be the destiny of these two pigs.

" You," replied Nostradamus, " will eat the black one, but the other will be devoured by a wolf."

The answer was in accordance with the wishes of de Florinville; for, although in public he treated his guest as an intimate friend, he seems secretly to have regarded him as an impostor. Certain that it was now in his power to expose Nostradamus, he gave instructions to his chef to kill the white pig and to serve it for supper.

In obedience to his master's command, the cook killed the white pig, dressed it, and placed it upon the spit ready for roasting at the proper time. Shortly afterwards, however, he was called away from the kitchen upon some errand, and, during his absence, a tame wolf-cub, the property of the Seigneur, entered, and, discovering the carcass of the white pig, immediately set to eating it. The animal had eaten about half of this delicacy when the chef returned and surprised the wolf at his meal.

Fearing that he would be reprimanded for his carelessness, the cook immediately seized the black pig, killed it, and prepared it for supper in place of the white one.

Supper was served, and all the guests took their places at the board. The Seigneur de Florinville, who of course knew nothing of what had taken place in the kitchen, felt assured that he would now achieve his ill-mannered triumph over Nostradamus, and, addressing the latter with a confident air, he remarked that they were about to eat the white pig, inasmuch as the wolf had not done so.

Nostradamus replied that he was in error, and expressed his conviction that the meat now placed before them was the flesh of the black pig. Thereupon de Florinville sent for the chef and asked him before all whether that which was upon the table was the white pig or the black.

The poor servant was covered with confusion—he had known nothing of his master's evil scheme—and stammered out that he had cooked the black pig, as the white one had been devoured by the wolf-cub during his absence from the kitchen.

De Florinville's state of mind may be better imagined than described, and certainly his discomfiture was well merited. Reports of this absurd incident were very soon noised abroad, and, as such things are usually made much of, were considerably exaggerated. But the episode served, nevertheless, to show the ability of Nostradamus as a diviner.

III. THE PLAGUE

The wanderings of Nostradamus lasted for about ten years, during which period comparatively little is known of his doings, and we again hear of him in the year 1543, when he returned to Provence rich in experience.

It is certain that during his absence from the country of his birth he had observed very closely everything connected with the practice of medicine amongst the peoples with whom he came into contact. In the preface to his *Opuscule* he tells us that " the administration of pharmacy in Marseilles was very bad," but that he had the good fortune to meet with a learned personage, by name Louis René ; and he also names a few excellent chemists, to whom he refers with due measure of praise.

As neither envy nor jealousy formed part of the character of Nostradamus, he knew how to render justice where justice was due ; and if he criticized certain doctors of Avignon, he at least was loud in his praises of those who practised at Montpellier ; and

in each instance he named the object of his attack or
of his approval. His criticisms, if severe, were just,
and gained for him a large number of admirers and
friends.

On his return to Provence, the town of Marseilles
sent to him a deputation of savants with a request
that he would now take up his residence and live
permanently within her walls; but the numerous
friends he had made at Salon, a little town situated
between Aix, Avignon, and Arles, succeeded in per-
suading him to reside there. It was in Salon that he
made the acquaintance of Anne Pons Jumel, or Ponsart
Jumelle, a young lady, wealthy and of good family,
whom he married in 1544; and by this second wife he
had six children.

We know only of four, however—three boys and one
girl. The eldest took the name of Michel, and studied
his father's profession, but without much success.
The second was César, who has written a history of
Provence. The third son became a Capuchin friar;
but of the daughter we know nothing.

Concerning the son Michel, a certain writer says that,
impelled by a marked propensity towards astrology,
he took advantage of the occasion when the little town
of Pouzin, in Vivarais, was besieged by the royal
troops, in 1575, to predict that it would perish by fire,
and, in order that for once in his life he might give
utterance to a true prediction, he himself set fire to
several houses on the surrender of the town. He was
caught in the act, and taken before d'Espinay Saint-
Luc on the fall of Pouzin. Saint-Luc sarcastically
inquired of him if he had foreseen any accident that
might happen to *himself*.

" No," was the reply.

" Then your science fails you ! " said Saint-Luc—
and killed him forthwith.

I cannot vouch for the truth of this story.

When the civil war broke out between the Catholics
and Huguenots of Provence, Charles IX sent the Comte
de Crussol with orders to the Comte de Tendes, governor
of the province, that the latter should exert all his
influence in order to pacify the opposing factions, or
bring the rebels to a sense of their duty. The Sieur
de Flassans, one of the Huguenot leaders, was no
sooner warned of the approach of the King's messengers,
than he marched on the town of Barjols at the head of
five or six thousand men and sixty cavaliers ; and was
also accompanied by a great number of partisans.
The Comte de Crussol, who commanded the royal
troops, sent a herald to de Flassans commanding him
to lay down his arms, to which the latter replied that
he would do nothing of the kind, but would await de
Crussol.

Realizing the temper of the Huguenots, de Crussol
had no alternative but to accept the challenge thrown
out by de Flassans. Accordingly he set out towards
Barjols, and, in passing through Salon, decided to visit
Nostradamus and ask of him what would be the outcome of his enterprise.

The seer received the inquiring soldier, and in reply
to his question told him that " he would leave the
trees laden with new fruit " (*qu'il y laisserait les arbres
chargés de nouveaux fruits*).

In the result of the expedition will be seen the grim
truth of this prediction. The King's troops inflicted
a severe defeat upon the Huguenots, and, forcing the
town, captured a great number of prisoners, most of
whom were hanged as rebels and heretics. So numerous

were the executions that it is said there were few
trees in the neighbourhood which were without their
ghastly testimony to the hatred between Catholic
and Huguenot. This, in itself, was an omen—a fore-
shadowing of that bloody harvest in the orchards of
the King which later was to redden the annals of France.

Almost every day Nostradamus predicted events
which seldom failed to occur at the time he had fore-
told, and, in consequence, his prophecies became the
subject of fierce debate amongst the learned of the
period.   Naturally enough, he made for himself
enemies as well as friends. The former asserted that
his gift of prophecy was the outcome of a compact
with the devil, whilst the latter replied hotly that he
was divinely inspired ; and here we may give a verse
from Ronsard, then regarded as the prince of French
poets, in which he addresses this reproach to France :

> *Tu te mocques aussi dès Prophètes que Dieu*
> *Choisit en tes enfans, et les fait au milieu*
> *De ton sein aparoistre, afin de te prédire*
> *Ton malheur à venir, mais tu n'en fais que rire.*

I venture to render it as follows :

> Nor heedest thou Prophets ; for when God hath blest
> Some one of thy kindred, some child of thy breast,
> With grace to forewarn thee of menaces near,
> Thy greeting is laughter, thine answer a jeer.

Meanwhile, despite the slander of his enemies, the
renown of Nostradamus was such that he attracted
to his house learned prelates of the Church, illustrious
soldiers, and eminent men of every profession, who
considered themselves honoured in having been entertained by the physician and seer of Salon. Even

dukes, princes, kings, and queens paid him the honour of visiting the town to consult him.

Never had Salon seen so rich and so numerous a company, or so continuous a flow of highly placed personages as these, who came to pay homage to the great man, to listen to his lectures, or to receive treatment at his hands. It was a veritable pleasure, we are told, to hear Nostradamus, and they counted themselves fortunate who entered into conversation with him. He differed in many respects from other physicians of the period, but notably in one—he cured.

The name of Nostradamus, then, had long been pronounced with the most profound respect when an event occurred which added a new lustre to his reputation. In 1546 a horrible scourge broke out in the town of Aix and physicians were summoned to arrest the progress of the disease. So swift was its operation, so deadly, that many of them were themselves stricken down by the pestilence ; some, lacking the means and skill to cope with it, left the dying of Aix to their fate ; and, at last, most of the others, panic-ridden by the ghastly thing that clammily had enveloped the town, fled.

And so the grim angel swept on his way, touching with uncleanness strong men, who in an hour became weak, in a day welcomed death ; touching babes in their mothers' arms and distorting their frail bodies with that venomous touch ; seizing upon the weeping mothers as they bent over the little sufferers, and stretching them agonized beside their babies. Such was the Plague.

The Comité of the town assembled—a fearful gathering, for no man knew if his neighbour were stricken, no man knew if he himself were clean. It was decided unanimously to send a deputation to wait upon Nostradamus and to beg of him to assist them in their hour of need.

He delayed not an instant. Leaving his wife and family, the great physician hurried to the scene of the contagion. Despair was written upon every face; hope was banished from this ancient and opulent town, now sorrowful and desolate.

Fearlessly, the famous doctor passed through the hospitals, remaining for hours beside the afflicted people that he might study the causes and progress of the disease. Having assured himself of the nature of the plague, he devised remedies by the aid of which he snatched back to life many who had stood upon the very threshold of death. It is a golden name in the annals of Provence, that of Michel de Notre Dame, called a sorcerer.

Astruc, in his *Mémoires*, says on the subject of the plague of 1546 and of the deliverer of the town of Aix : " Nostradamus accepted any work that was offered to him, however dangerous ; and so long as the plague lasted, he neglected nothing in his efforts to relieve the sufferings of its victims." It was on this occasion that he made great use of a certain powder to disperse the pestilential odours, of which he has given the composition in his *Traité des Fards*.

In gratitude for the services rendered by the ex-professor of Montpellier to its citizens, the town of Aix voted him, not only thanks, as in the modern fashion, but an annual pension, which was maintained until the end of his days. The artists of the district painted portraits of their saviour ; the notable inhabitants offered him rich presents ; and these he accepted only to distribute them among the widows and orphans.

The seal was set upon his fame in the following year, when the same pestilence which had ravaged Aix laid its deathly hold upon Lyons, and Michel Nostradamus once more left Salon in order to place his services at the disposal of the stricken.

Jean Antoine Sarrazin, a prominent member of the Faculty of Montpellier, together with other doctors of the district, had journeyed to Lyons with the object of ridding the country of the plague without assistance from outside. Jealous of the fame of Nostradamus, Sarrazin and his colleagues thought that now was their opportunity to establish for themselves a reputation at least as great as that of the doctor of Salon.

But factors beyond their control had to be reckoned with. If they possessed the devotion of Nostradamus, they lacked his scientific knowledge, although Sarrazin in particular was regarded by the chroniclers of Lyons and Montpellier as one of the most accomplished physicians of the period. Nostradamus, although by no means blind to his own abilities, was a very modest man ; and he imparted to Sarrazin the observations which he had made at Aix, and advised his colleague to adopt a certain method, if he wished to stay the progress of the plague.

Sarrazin, however, paid no heed to the wise counsels of Nostradamus, and killed, or left to die, those whom he had told himself he would save. The Lyonnais sought out the Salon physician (who cured in secret, in order that he might not offend Sarrazin). They threw themselves at his feet and beseeched him not to abandon them.

He answered :

"I wish to succour you, but must proceed after my own fashion. I honour greatly," he added, "the celebrated doctor, Antoine Sarrazin, my colleague, but as my methods differ from his, I desire that you choose him who shall remain. Shall it be I or Sarrazin?"

"Nostradamus!" cried the deputation. "Nostradamus, the preserver of Aix!"

A month later joy was seen in every face, for the devastating plague existed no longer, and Nostradamus, overwhelmed with honour and with presents, returned in triumph to Salon, escorted by the authorities of the town which his science and devotion had saved.

All this has been attested by the historians Astruc and Bouche, and by the Provençal chronicles.

IV. PUBLICATION OF THE "CENTURIES"

No great man is without enemies, and if we are to judge of Nostradamus's greatness by the number of his foes and the venom of their onslaughts, then was he great indeed.

We know that about the middle of the sixteenth century alchemists and sorcerers often came to the stake, although astrologers were tolerated. Nostradamus, since early boyhood, had studied the planets, and by means of certain calculations based upon the teachings of the ancient astrological books had succeeded in predicting several events which duly came to pass.

But now Jean Antoine Sarrazin spread abroad the rumour that Nostradamus devoted himself to sorcery; whereupon, it is characteristic of the times and of the people, his once zealous partisans became his bitter opponents. Despite the almost daily cures which he affected, he was attacked upon the ground that he departed from the ordinary (and murderous) methods of the Faculty. Very soon the saviour of Aix and Lyons found himself shunned by all. The ignorant peasants made the sign of the cross and averted their eyes when they met him ; for he was reputed to derive his powers from Satan !

Keenly affected by the cowardly betrayal of his old friends and colleagues, Nostradamus retired from the world. He communicated with no one, but passed his time in study ; neither did he deign to take part in the fierce discussions which seethed concerning him. Some few men of spirit and understanding espoused his cause, and Nostradamus was content to leave his defence in the hands of these, and to posterity.

Respecting the nature of his studies at this time, the following quatrain from his first *Century* is of interest :

> *Étant assis, de nuit, secrète étude,*
> *Seul reposé sur la selle d'airain,*
> *Flambe exiguë sortant de solitude*
> *Fait proférer que n'est à croire vain.*

> (Alone, on brazen tripod, when the night
> My studies doth all secretly enfold,
> From out the darkness dawneth astral light,
> Revealing what Futurity doth hold.)

All the predictions of Nostradamus seem to have been made by night ; for in a letter to Henri II he says :

" I address myself to one, not like unto the Kings of Persia, whom it was forbidden to approach, but unto a very prudent and wise Prince to whom I have consecrated my nocturnal and prophetic vigils."

His famous *Centuries*, according to the "janus français," he kept a long time before he would publish, estimating that the novelty of the matter would bring upon him infinite persecution. At last, however, on March 1, 1555, the light of day shone upon his *Centuries*, dedicated to his son, César Nostradamus.

In his *Histoire de Provence*, César speaks of the dedication :

"The year after (*i.e.* 1555) Michel Nostradamus dedicated to me, whilst I was yet in the cradle, and published the *Centuries*, which, rendering his name immortal, taught me to follow the path of virtue which had been traced out for him by his fathers."

In the dedicatory epistle, which one only understands with great difficulty, Nostradamus tells his son how he attained to a knowledge of the future : "Thy late advent, César Nostradamus, my son, has made me give much time to nocturnal vigilance," etc.

This is not very clear, as will be seen ; but that which did him more harm was that he dared, in this epistle, to write that calculations alone do not suffice in predicting the future ; that one must also be inspired, and possessed of a supernatural and prophetic gift which Providence accords only to certain privileged beings.

In his letter to Henri II, Nostradamus claims that he knows exactly at what epoch the events which he predicts shall come to pass, but that he fears to give utterance frankly to his thoughts on account of displeasing the many.

Note that this letter was written on June 27, 1558 :

"A greater persecution shall befall the Christian Church than has ever been in Africa, and will last until the year 1792, when there will be a revision of centuries. Afterward will commence various reforms by the people, the dispersing of some obscure shadows, receiving a little of their pristine splendour, but not without great divisions and continual changes."

"If we examine closely this prophecy," says a French commentator, "we are astonished at the accuracy of the prediction of Nostradamus. In effect, did not this year commence with the Revision? Did not the year 1792 see the palace of the Tuileries, hitherto inhabited by the Kings, fall into the hands of the people? Was it not in 1792 that a monarch (Louis XVI) was thrown into prison by his own subjects? Was it not in 1792 that the ancient costumes were changed, and the title ' citoyen français ' was accorded to Schiller and to all those philosophers who in their writings had defended the principles of Liberty? Was it not in 1792 that the nobles and priests were slaughtered, even those of families respected for fifteen centuries? Lastly, was it not in 1792 that the National Convention abolished royalty, and this year that saw the commencement of the Republican era, the Republic reforming the calendar ; the birth of the factions of the mountains and the plains; and was it not in 1792 that the terrible guillotine emerged bloody from the brain of Guillotin? "

The first selection of *Centuries* had an extraordinary success. Everybody wished to read the predictions, and everybody did read them. A revulsion of feeling took place. From all the corners of Provence, from all the French towns, and even from foreign countries, came those who would seek to learn the future from the seer of Salon. Nobles and commoners, men of learning, scoffers and believers—everybody visited the ex-professor of Montpellier. Nostradamus, who detested these demonstrations, excited only by the insatiable curiosity of ignorant humanity, frequently gave no replies; or, if he replied at all, it was in terms so ambiguous, so obscure, that the majority of the interrogators understood nothing at all.

After the individual curiosity of townspeople came the less egotistical curiosity of the inhabitants of the countryside. Labourers, gardeners, housewives, went to consult Nostradamus—the diviner, the prophet, the man of God, as the greater number now chose to call him. Some asked him if the year would prove a rainy year; others whether the spring would be fine or whether there would be many storms; and a host of similar petty questions. Nostradamus, then, to rid himself of these troublesome visitors, composed a little book under the title of the *Almanac of Nostradamus*.

The predictions which he set forth in the Almanac proved so accurate that the work was no sooner published than the edition became exhausted; and such was the profit made by the printers that these decided to issue a new and enlarged edition of their own under the same title as that which had met with so great a success. The reason for ascribing this to Nostradamus was, of course, that they might reap a rich harvest; but, although based upon the original and genuine work, it now contained an enormous number of deliberate inaccuracies which the enemies of the seer were not slow to write about, for they afforded them an opportunity of attacking him with success.

Even some of his supporters, ignorant of the truth, began to waver, and he was named throughout the country a charlatan and a rogue. His denials availed him nothing, but the small circle of friends that re-

mained to him eagerly and with energy took up the
fight on his behalf.

The poet, Jodelle, author of *Cléopâtre Captive* and of
Didon le Sacrifiant, left his tragedies and his comedies
and wrote among other things a Latin distich upon
Nostradamus, towards whom he was fiercely antago-
nistic.   It enjoyed great success:

> *Nostradamus cum falsa damus, nam fallere nostrum est ;*
> *Et cum falsa damus nil nisi Nostradamus.*

As will be seen, there is considerable play upon the
word *damus*, and it is consequently difficult to explain
by direct translation ; but the following may be taken
as the jibe conveyed :

Nostradamus is made to speak : " We give that
which belongs to us when we give those things that
are false ; and when we give those things that are false
we do nothing but give to ourselves that which belongs
to us."

The friends of Nostradamus lost no time in replying,
which they did in these terms :

> *Vera damus cum verba damus quæ Nostradamus dat ;*
> *Sed cum nostra damus, nil nisi falsa damus.*

This we may explain in the following manner :

The adversaries of Nostradamus speak : " We say
that which is true when we give the words of Nostradamus ; but when we give our own they are nothing
but lies."

V. THE COMMAND TO THE LOUVRE

Although the publication of his *Centuries* increased
the number of his enemies, Nostradamus, on the other
hand, added to his friends, and had the good fortune

to attract to his side men of intelligence and reason.
These defended him so well that they imposed silence
upon calumny, and introduced with honour his name
into the Court of France. Many reasonable men regarded Nostradamus as one of those privileged beings
who appear from time to time by the will of Providence, in order that they may avert those calamities
which otherwise would befall mankind ; and highly-
placed people reported to the King and Queen his work
and devotion during the plagues at Aix and Lyons,
and the new reputation he had gained by the composition of his *Centuries*.

According to the Princess de Clèves, Henri II had
but a poor opinion of prophets and prophecies ; for
by her he is reported as saying :

" At one time I had a great curiosity as to the
future ; but so many of the things that were told me
proved false that I am convinced it is impossible to
foretell the truth. Some years ago a man came here
(one Luc Gauric) who enjoyed a great reputation as
an astrologer. Everybody went to see him ; I went
like the others, but without telling him who I
was, taking with me M. de Guise and Descars. I
gave precedence to my two companions, but the
astrologer addressed me as if he regarded me as the
master of the others. I thought perhaps he knew me ;
but then he told me something which proved that
he was ignorant of my identity, in predicting that I
should be killed in a duel.

" He then said to M. de Guise that he would be
killed from behind, and to Descars that his head would
be broken by a kick from a horse. M. de Guise was
annoyed at this prediction, as if he had been accused
of cowardice. Descars was not at all satisfied to find

that his career would end through so miserable an accident. However, we quitted the astrologer, all three very annoyed with him. I do not know what happened to M. de Guise and to Descars, but there is not the slightest chance of my being killed in a duel. We have concluded peace with the King of Spain ; had we not done so I doubt not that we should have fought, and that I should have challenged him as the King, my father, challenged Charles V."

It will be readily understood that Henri II, in saying that there was not the slightest chance of his being killed in a duel, meant that, although he might have fought with the King of Spain in person, he could not, as sovereign, accept a challenge to single combat from one inferior in rank, although he himself might challenge whomsoever he pleased.

Henri and Catherine de Médicis, having heard, then, of the medical science and astrological knowledge of the celebrated physician of Salon, wrote to Claude de Savoie, Count de Tende, governor of Provence, with instructions to invite Nostradamus to visit the Court. The Count de Tende duly performed this mission, conveying the royal command to Salon. Nostradamus at once hastened to obey the summons, and, on July 14, 1556, the new prophet quitted Salon to present himself at Paris. The incidents connected with his arrival at the capital are curious, if without significance ; but even regarded merely as coincidence, they are worth relating.

Nostradamus arrived before the walls of Paris on August 15, 1556. He himself regarded this as of happy augury, for the citizens were celebrating the Feast of Notre Dame. Entering the city, he dismounted at the first hotel he reached, and the name of this hostelry completed the coincidence, for it hung out the sign of St. Michel. Happening upon the occasion of his first journey to the French Court, Michel de Notre Dame may be forgiven if he regarded this combination of curious circumstances as significant of a happy culmination of his life's work.

We will now read of the reception accorded to Nostradamus by the King and Queen, and by the Court at large.

It was with a light heart that the seer of Salon made his way towards the Louvre to be received by his most Christian Majesty. What thoughts must have pursued one another through his mind! Frequently he must have compared the virulent attacks made upon him by men of his profession, of no mean standard of intelligence, his erstwhile friends and companions, with the honour which he now was receiving from the highest in the land. Had these paid heed to the calumnies without giving ear to the truth concerning him, he must long since have suffered the penalty imposed upon all who were convicted of sorcery, and been burnt at the stake as a wizard. But he still lived, and, more, was about to be honoured by his sovereign. Nostradamus had triumphed, indeed.

Arriving at the Louvre, in the company of M. le Connétable, this high dignitary presented Nostradamus to the King and Queen. He was received with great kindness by the sovereign and his consort, both of whom heaped upon their guest presents innumerable. The Constable of France, during the sojourn of the famous doctor in the capital, had intended to lodge Nostradamus at his residence, but His Majesty commanded that he should be the guest of the Cardinal de Sens.

Whilst residing at the hotel of this prince of the Church—truly a singular host for one who, even now, was accused of communicating with the devil—Nostradamus suffered from a severe attack of gout, which detained him some ten or twelve days. The King showed great solicitude in the illness which had so suddenly attacked his eminent subject, and daily sent to inquire as to his progress. He also sent him a further present, this time one hundred écus d'or in a purse of velvet.

"No sooner had he recovered from these violent pains," says his son, César, "than he was invited to Blois to see the young princes of France, an invitation of which he readily availed himself. As to the honours, regal and magnificent presents, which he received at the hands of their Majesties, of princes, and of the high dignitaries of the Court, I would rather let them remain at the end of my pen than name them here."

Presenting himself anew before their Majesties, he was asked to erect the horoscopes of the young princes, and in obedience to this desire he found it necessary to proceed warily, and made use of a diplomatic talent worthy of a Minister of the Crown. He did not speak at all of any dangers that the young princes would incur.

Interrogated by Henri and Catherine, his replies were wrapped up in generalities which "could compromise neither himself nor science," and he contented himself with answering that the three princes would mount the throne. It is of interest at this point to recount briefly that which befell each of these princes.

The eldest son of Henri and Catherine of France, who, in 1558, had married Mary, Queen of Scots, suc-

ceeded his father in 1559, ascending the throne as
François II.   His reign, however, lasted but one year,
and he was followed by his brother, Charles IX, whose
accession took place in 1560 at the age of ten.   His
mother, Catherine de Médicis, was appointed Regent
during his minority, and that bloody stain upon the
fleur-de-lis, the Massacre of St. Bartholomew, occurred
during his tenure of the reins of government.   Remorse for this act hastened his death, which took
place in 1574.   Henri III succeeded to the throne, and
his reign was marked by religious dissensions.   Allied
with Henri de Navarre against the League, he besieged
Paris in the year 1589, and it was during these operations that he met his death at the hands of the assassin,
a crazy friar named Jacques Clément.

For the peace of mind of Henri II and Catherine,
and also perhaps in the interests of his own safety,
Nostradamus, when erecting the horoscopes of their
three sons, had placed the best complexion he could
upon their future ; but that he knew what should take
place during the reign of each, and the manner in which
each should meet his end, is proved by the fact, say
contemporary chroniclers, that he had already announced these things in his *Centuries*.

Mr. Charles A. Ward, in his *Oracles of Nostradamus*,
selects Century V, Quatrain 67, as predicting the death
of Henri III :

> *Quand chef Pérouse n'osera sa Tunique,*
> *Sans au couvert tout nud s'expolier,*
> *Seront prins sept, faict aristocratique :*
> *Le père et fils mort par poincte au colier.*

To my mind this quatrain has no bearing whatever
upon the death of the monarch in question, and I am

entirely at a loss to understand how the learned author reconciles it with history. I must confess that, despite contemporary statements, I have failed to find any other more suitable, either in regard to Henri III, Charles IX, or François II ; but nevertheless I cannot accept Century V, Quatrain 67.

Following his journey to Paris, Nostradamus published in 1558 a new and augmented edition of the *Centuries*, prefaced by a letter to Henri II, the reigning King. On the death of this monarch, in 1559, there was a great demand for the new issue of his work, for those courtiers who were acquainted with the quatrains of the physician of Salon saw this melancholy event predicted in the 35th quatrain of the first *Century*, and written in the year 1555 :

> *Le lion jeune le vieux surmontera.*
> *En champ bellique par singulier duel,*
> *Dans cage d'or les yeux lui crevera,*
> *Deux playes*[1] *une, puis mourir mort cruelle.*

To the explanation of the foregoing must be added for guidance a few facts concerning the tournament in the Rue Saint-Antoine.

Henri II, desiring to celebrate the nuptials of his daughter, the Princess Elizabeth of France, caused it to be announced publicly by the heralds, in the streets of the capital, that a tournament would be held on the first day of July 1559, near to the Bastille Saint-Antoine. He further commanded that it be made known that he would attend the tourney and himself break lances with the foremost knights of his kingdom.

[1] In the edition of 1588, this reads " Deux *classes*." I find the same reading also (*classes*) in Bareste's edition of the quatrain published in 1840.

The chivalric contests opened, and the King indulged in jousts with a few of his gentlemen, each of whom gave way to his sovereign. Whether the excitement of combat had seized him, or whether he flattered himself upon having disposed of such valiant antagonists, it is now impossible to say; but toward sundown he announced his intention of once more entering the lists, this time challenging a young Scottish nobleman of his bodyguard, the Comte Gabriel de Montgomery.

We know that the Duc de Savoie remonstrated with His Majesty, pointing out that he had risked his life already more than once during the day, and that he had gained sufficient honour in consequence. The King, however, was adamant, and paid no heed to the wise counsels of the Duc. Montgomery, on his part, was unwilling to engage his sovereign, and repeatedly prayed him that he should not fight. Henri, however, persisted in his challenge, and there was nothing left to Montgomery but to accept.

Accordingly they took up their respective positions, closed their vizors, and prepared for the charge.

At the given signal they rode against each other. The young Scottish captain endeavoured to avoid the King, but in this he failed, and nearly unhorsed the monarch. In spite of the anxious requests of several gentlemen there that he should now abandon the tourney, the King decided once more to ride against Montgomery.

This final charge justified the advice previously proffered him by Henri's attendants; for, failing to turn aside his antagonist's weapon, he received the full force of the blow on the head. The lance penetrated the helm, and the head of Montgomery's weapon pierced the right eye of the King.

> The young lion vanquisheth the old.
> When on the field he duelleth,
> His eyes destroyed in cage of gold,
> Two wounds are his—then cruel death.[1]

The King indeed suffered cruelly during ten days—as Nostradamus had predicted : " Deux playes une, puis mourir mort cruelle." By " the old lion " we understand the King, and " the young lion " the Comte de Montgomery, the latter having triumphed (surmontera). The expression " en champ bellique " (field of battle) is also justified. But " single combat " or " duel " is still more extraordinary, since the tournaments served for single combats. " In cage of gold his eyes will be destroyed " was also realized—Montgomery destroyed the eyes of the King in piercing the latter's helm, which was gilded.

Beyond doubt this prophecy is very curious, but it nearly brought its author to the stake. The enemies of Nostradamus, finding that they could not successfully denounce him in any other manner, caused it again to be noised abroad that he was a magician, a sorcerer, and possessed of the devil.

But whilst the populace busied itself in burning in effigy the celebrated doctor, the Duc and Duchesse de Savoie turned from their route and hastened to Salon to render homage to the genius of the astrologer of this town. The calumnies concerning Nostradamus

---

[1] Another version reads :
> The young lion will conquer the old one
> In a single duel upon the field of battle.
> He will pierce his eyes in a gilded cage.
> This is the first of two blows, after which
> Will come a cruel death.

It has been suggested that the " second blow " refers to the murder of the King's son, Henri III, by Jacques Clément,

did not prevent even the high personages of the Court from consulting him.

For instance, Madame de Lesdiguières having consulted him upon the future of her son, Nostradamus told her, in clear terms, that the young man would become one of the first in the kingdom. And this descendant of the Lesdiguières was made Constable. Trone de Condoulet, a wealthy bourgeois of Salon, who was intimately acquainted with Nostradamus, records a fact of which he was witness:

" One evening," he says, " Michel having seen the Prince of Béarn, who was yet a child, said to those to whose care he was entrusted, ' This young prince will ascend the throne of France, and the title of " Great " will be added to his name.' "

The dignitaries laughed, and would not believe this prediction of Nostradamus.   But this Béarnais became, as is well known, King of France, under the name of Henri IV, or, which accords more closely with the prophecy of Nostradamus, under that of Henri le Grand.

On another occasion, having met a young Franciscan, named Felix Peretti, he saluted him by bending before him on one knee ; and those who accompanied the monk, surprised at this deference, on asking of Nostradamus the reason for it, received the following reply :

" Because I must bow the knee to holiness."

This Franciscan monk became, in 1585, Pope Sixtus V.[1]

---

[1] It is interesting to note that the Roman Church condemned the prophecies of Nostradamus in 1781, as they were supposed to contain a prediction of the fall of the Papacy.

VI. DAWN: JULY 2, 1566

In 1564, Charles IX, when visiting Provence, accompanied by Catherine de Médicis, desired to go himself and visit Nostradamus. The notables of Salon gathered before the gate of the town to receive with dignity their King ; but Charles contented himself with replying to the usual complimentary speeches by saying, " I am come to Provence only that I may see Nostradamus."

The latter, who was amongst the knot of magistrates, was immediately presented. The King, taking him by the hand, made him mount the horse of one of his suite, and rode through Salon engaged in animated conversation with Nostradamus at his side.

So gracious and honourable a reception aroused such feelings of joy within this great man that he could not refrain from comparing his treatment with that which he had received at the hands of the people, and could not suppress the exclamation against his ungrateful country, " *O ingrata patria!* "

On leaving Provence the King made him a present of two hundred pieces of gold, and appointed him physician-in-ordinary and counsellor to his person. The Queen-Mother, Catherine de Médicis, added to this gift another of two hundred pieces of gold, in recognition of his double science of medicine and astrology.

And now the people, easily moved by such events, yet again changed their opinion, and Nostradamus passed for a man of genius ; for martyr ; for diviner ; for a god ! In the streets some knelt before him, nor was he ever forgotten in public prayers ; and when he attended church, every one rose and bowed to him with respect.

I need scarcely add that his accusers were hunted from the town, and that after this period no one dared to speak a word against the prophecies of Nostradamus.

But age, sorrows, work, and illness undermined the constitution of the astrologer. He never went out, and received at his house only a few intimate and devoted friends, such as Chavigny, Palamèdes, and Condoulet. He knew that his end was approaching, and in his own hand wrote the following : " *Hic propre mors est* " (" My death is not far off ").

Never, perhaps, did he give so exact a prediction ; for ten or twelve days later, his illness having developed into dropsy, he expired on July 2, 1566, at the age of sixty-two years. Before he died he called for Père Vidal, to whom he confessed sincerely, with contrite heart and with tears in his eyes.

Upon June 30, 1566, that is, two days before his death, he called Maître Roche, notary in Salon, and to him dictated his testament. On July 1 he said to Chavigny, who was leaving him in order to obtain some repose : " To-morrow, at dawn, I shall be no more." In the morning, when his friends entered his room, he was found seated upon a bench near his bed, but life was extinct. What makes this death yet more surprising is that it was predicted a year previously by Nostradamus, in a collection of " presages " which he was then composing. I give this famous quatrain :

> *Du retour d'ambassade, don du roy, mis au lieu*
> *Plus n'en fera ; sera allé à Dieu*
> *Proches parens, amis, frères de sang*
> *Trouvé tout mort, près du lit et du banc.*

By this quatrain Nostradamus predicts that on his
return from his visit to the King at Arles, where His
Majesty would bestow gifts upon him, he would no
more practise the science of astrology, but would await
the divine call; finally, that he would be found quite
dead near to his bed, seated upon a bench.

Janus Gallicus relates that a few hours after his
death his friends entered the house to inquire after
the condition of the seer, and, as he had predicted,
they found him in a sitting position, near the bed,
and quite dead. His body was swollen as the result
of dropsy ; and, finding it impossible to lie upon his
bed in this state, he had crawled to the bench, and,
seating himself upon it, patiently awaited his end,
which occurred at dawn.

When the death of Nostradamus became known, his
friends, and those who still remembered the devotion
to the afflicted, during the plagues, displayed by this
good man, were stricken with grief. Crowds gathered
before his house, many dressed in mourning attire ;
and at his funeral, which took place in the Eglise des
Cordeliers of Salon, the church of the Frères Mineurs,
many were the orations that were delivered. Nostradamus was buried in the left wall. The following
epitaph is inscribed on his tomb :

RELIQVIÆ MICHAELIS NOSTRADAMI IN HOC SACELLVM
TRANSLATÆ FVERVNT POST ANNVM MDCCLXXXIX
EPITAPHIVM RESTITVTVM MENSE IVLIO ANNO MDCCCXIII.
D. O. M.
CLARISSIMI OSSA MICHAELIS NOSTRADAMI VNIVS OMNIVM
MORTALIVM IVDICIO DIGNI CVIVS PENE DIVINO CALAMO
TOTIVS ORBIS EX ASTRORVM INFLVXV FVTVRI EVENTVS
CONSCRIBERENTVR. VIXIT ANNOS LXII MENSES VI DIES XVII
OBIIT SALONE ANNO MDLXVI. OVIETEM POSTERI NE INVIDETE
ANNA PONTIA GEMELLA SALONIA CONIVGI OPTAT V. FELICIT.

VII. SOME REMARKABLE QUATRAINS

Nothing like a complete examination of the *Centuries* thus far has been attempted in the language. The task would be one of peculiar difficulty for many reasons, but here I may give one or two examples of quatrains which, without distortion, seem certainly to synchronize with history. I have availed myself of some licence in translating, and I have not attempted to parallel the metre of the original French.

CENTURY III, QUATRAIN 30

Celuy qu'en luitte et fer au faict bellique
Aura porté plus grand qui luy le pris,
De nuict au lict six luy feront la pique,
Nud, sans harnois, subit sera surpris.

To him who, armour'd, on the field of fight,
  Did snatch the laurel from a greater brow ;
Six foes do wound him, in the still of night.
  Surpris'd, alone, unarmour'd is he now.

Montgomery, the gentleman so unfortunate as to vanquish his King, Henri II—and to cause his death—" carried off the prize," or, as I have expressed it, " the laurel," on that lamentable occasion. Montgomery is clearly indicated in the first two lines, I think ; and the third and fourth predict that six men will surprise him in bed at night, naked and unarmed.

Although, according to some accounts, the King, dying, freely pardoned the man who had brought about his death, others aver that Montgomery fled to England for safety. He certainly came to England and espoused the Protestant cause. On his return to France he placed himself at the head of the Norman Huguenots, and was beseiged in Domfront by the Marshal de

Matignon and a numerous force, to which he ultimately surrendered.

The terms guaranteed his life, but at express command of Catherine de Médicis he was arrested in his own castle of Domfront on the night of May 27, 1574, by six gentlemen of the Royal forces, and carried to the Château de Caen and thence to the Conciergerie at Paris, where he was imprisoned.

I next shall quote a quatrain which Garencières believed to relate to Charles II, but which more closely corresponds with the fate of his father:

> *Du règne Anglais le digne dechassé,*
> *Le conseiller par ire mis à feu,*
> *Ses adhérans iront si bas tracer,*
> *Que le bastard sera demy receu.*

When heir of England's crown shall—driven from the throne—
His counsellor on Demos' altar immolate ;
So base shall prove those friends he call'd his own,
The upstart, now Half-king, shall grasp the State.

The counsellor abandoned to the rage of the people ("par ire") we may regard as the unhappy Strafford, whose harshest reproach upon Charles was his heart-wrung cry, "Put not your trust in princes!" The Covenanters' bloody bargain ("si bas tracer") and the accession of Cromwell ("le bastard") to the Protectorship ("sera demi receu") make up a sufficiently extraordinary sequence.

In conclusion I append the following quatrain, said to point to the execution of Charles I, January 30, 1649:

> *Gand et Bruxeles marcheront contre Anvers,*
> *Sénat de Londres mettront à mort leur Roy ;*
> *Le sel et vin luy seront à l'envers*
> *Pour eux avoir le regne en desarroi.*

'Gainst Antwerp, Brussels and Ghent combine,
The Senate of London their monarch slay ;
Wine serves for salt and salt serves for wine
In this kingdom of chaos and disarray.

Bouys says that this quatrain alone is sufficient to prove that Nostradamus had true prophetic insight. He points out the fact that until the execution of Charles I no King had ever been condemned to death by a Senate.

DR. JOHN DEE

I. THE BLACK SKULL-CAP

THE life of John Dee is a tragedy. It offers us the spectacle of a wise man courting folly, of a philosopher duped by knaves. Had Dr. Dee been born not in 1527 but in 1827, it is possible, it is probable, that his name would generally be known and revered ; whereas now he lives but in the annals of alchemy, endures only in the laboratory of the hermetic researcher and in the study of the curious. What he actually accomplished we shall see in due time, and it was little enough ; but in futile research John Dee lost his youth and what the world had to offer to youth ; immolated his peace, his reputation ; ruined his body and seared his mind ; finally, in the height of his scientific frenzy, he prostituted his wife upon the altar of alchemy, and passed unmourned to a pauper's grave.

John Dee was born in London on July 13, 1527, and in his earliest youth, in London and at Chelmsford, he displayed a marked inclination for study. Proceeding to St. John's College, Cambridge, at the age of fifteen, he became so absorbed in his reading that eighteen hours of every twenty-four were spent among his books. Since of the six remaining hours he devoted only four to repose, his was evidently that type of constitution which enables its possessor to dispense entirely with physical exercise and almost to dispense with sleep.

A brilliant scholar, and one of the original Fellows of Trinity, 1546, he early found himself a man shunned —a social pariah.   Sinister rumours began to circulate, and we can readily imagine that the midnight lamp shining out from Dee's window often enough became the focus of fearful glances.   His mechanical beetle, presented in a performance of Aristophanes' *Peace*, added to the reputation already attaching to the youthful student ; and when, about 1547, he returned from a visit to the Low Countries with much bulky luggage in the shape of strange instruments, a whisper disturbed the peace of the colleges—" Sorcery ! "— when morning after morning dawn came to dim the philosopher's lamp.

We can see men taking the wall as Dee passes and retracing their steps in preference to meeting him on the stair.   Groups melt at his coming ;   silence falls upon the room in which he appears.   But always there are nervous movements and sidelong glances.   Conversation, hushed and ominous, springs up anew as the young mystic departs.

Such environment becoming intolerable, and covert accusation developing into open persecution, Dee quitted Cambridge and sought a more congenial abode at the University of Louvain, where, surrounded by kindred spirits, he found every encouragement in his strange studies, which now had led him out upon the hazardous path to the philosopher's stone.

At the age of twenty-four, however, he returned to England, and was successful, through the kindly offices of his friend, Sir John Cheek, in securing presentation at the Court of Edward VI, where he was well received, and had bestowed upon him a pension of one hundred crowns. In London he remained for several years, practising as an astrologer, when an event occurred which very nearly terminated his career : this was a charge of heresy and conspiracy against the life of Queen Mary.

He was imprisoned at Hampton Court, " even in the weeke next before the same Whitsuntide that Her Majesty " (*i.e.* Elizabeth, prior to her accession) " was there prisoner also." In one of the documents printed for the Chetham Society in 1851, Dee speaks of " false information given in by one George Ferrys and Prideaux, that I endeavoured by enchantments to destroy Queene Mary."

Accused of being " a conjuror, a caller of devils, a great doer therein, and so (as some would say) the arche conjuror of this whole kingdom," Dee retorted that it was " a damnable slander, utterly untrue, on the whole, and in every word and part thereof, as (before the King of Kings) will appere at the dreadful day."

Suffice it that he was acquitted of attempting the life of the Queen by enchantments, but was committed to prison on the charge of heresy and required to clear himself of that charge to the satisfaction of Edmund Bonner, Bishop of London. Considering Dee's reputation, the beliefs and superstitions of the times, and the fierce bigotry of his judge, I regard it as one of the most notable points in a singular career that Dee convinced the Bishop of the orthodoxy of his faith. Probably no man ever came nearer to a Smithfield stake and escaped the burning.

Follows a period of comparative placidity. With Elizabeth's ascent to the throne Dee's fortunes im-

proved, a circumstance which, viewed side by side
with the charges that so nearly had wrought his end,
is not without significance.

Elizabeth, during her retirement at Woodstock,
had apparently consulted Dee as to the time of Mary's
death, which interview seems to have led to his trial.
Dudley, Earl of Leicester, was also sent by Elizabeth
to inquire of Dee the day of her coronation ; and the
philosopher enjoyed so great a favour that a few years
afterwards the Queen paid him a visit in person at
his home at Mortlake. Indeed, when later he became
ill, it was Elizabeth's own physician who attended him.

But although his livelihood was earned by the
practice of astrology, the dream of Dee's life was to
bridge the gulf and explore the mystic borderland.
He had studied deeply the mysteries of the Cabala and
Talmud, and these had impressed him with the belief
that it would be possible for him to hold converse
with spirits and angels, and to learn from them the
secrets of the universe.

He relates how, one day, when engaged in fervent
prayer, the window of his museum, which looked towards
the west, suddenly glowed with a dazzling light, in
the midst of which, in all his glory, stood the angel
Uriel. Stricken with awe and wonder, Dee looked
upon this vision, and the angel, smiling graciously,
placed in his hands a crystal of convex form, telling
him that if he wished to communicate with beings in
another sphere, he had but to gaze intently into it,
and they would appear and disclose to him all the
secrets of futurity ; the past and the future should
be as the present.

Here, then, we find ourselves face to face with the
first real problem in regard to our subject. Had con-

DR. JOHN DEE

FROM A PAINTING IN THE ASHMOLEAN MUSEUM, OXFORD

tinuous brooding upon mystic lore terminated in obses-
sion ?   Was the story of Uriel's appearance with the
crystal a mere fabrication ?   Or must we seek a third
solution to the enigma ?

I recognize that the point is one of importance ; for
upon this vision, and with the convex crystal for
foundation, was built up the whole amazing structure
of John Dee's after-life.   Hence, here lies the clue by
means of which we may determine whether he was a
madman, an impostor, or that type of being to this
day imperfectly classified and comprehended—a clairvoyant.   That he was no impostor with regard to
crystallomancy will appear later ; but the final verdict
in the case of John Dee cannot fairly be pronounced
until the bewildering mass of documentary material
bearing upon the career of this extraordinary man has
been properly examined.

Dee has recorded that, although his early experiments with the crystal were partially successful, he
was unable afterwards to recall anything of the revelations thus made to him.   He decided, then, to confide
his secret in another, one who might gaze into the
crystal and converse with the spirits, whilst Dee, in
another part of the room, noted down these revelations.

Enters Edward Kelly, the man in the black skull-
cap.   His appearance at this point in Dee's life has
about it something Mephistophelean ; his personality
harmonizes with such infernal origin.   He became
Dee's shadow, and that shadow lies black upon the
name of the doctor of Mortlake to this day.   Let us
consider what little is known of the early life of Edward
Kelly—perhaps the most sinister figure in the annals
of alchemistical philosophy.

According to Anthony à Wood, he first saw the

light on August 1, 1555, the third year of the reign of
Queen Mary, at Worcester. Educated in his native
city until the age of seventeen, he is supposed to have
gone up to Oxford. The registers of that University,
however, contain no record of any Edward Kelly
being entered at the period, and it has been suggested
that his real name was Talbot. Three persons of the
latter name were entered about this time at Gloucester
Hall. In any case, the evidence of Kelly's residence at
Oxford is of a very slender character ; but if his study
at the University be doubted, there is no reason to
doubt that he had occasion to change his name, as will
be seen later.

Certain authorities state that he was trained as an
apothecary, and thus acquired some skill in chemistry ;
but this is doubtful, for he entered the legal profession
and became a notary, practising in London (or, according to another account, in Lancaster). It was at any
rate in the latter town that he came under official
notice.

A skilful penman, Kelly had been at great pains to
acquaint himself with, and to become proficient in,
archaic English, and, as a native of Worcester, he had
also studied Welsh. By the aid of these accomplishments he was accused of forging title deeds (a dreadful
crime in those days), but it must be granted that the
evidence upon which he was indicted was of a very
unsatisfactory nature. Despite this, it is almost certain that he was pilloried in Lancaster, and suffered
the loss of both ears—a mutilation degrading enough
in any man, but fatal to a philosopher.

Hereafter, then, we meet Edward Kelly arrayed in
a black skull-cap which, fitting closely over his head
and descending over his cheeks, not only conceals his

loss, but lends him an appearance at once oracular and sinister. So well did he preserve his disgraceful secret that even Dee, with whom he lived for so many years, never discovered it.

II. THE IVORY CASKETS

The adventures and intrigues of Edward Kelly, his imprisonments, his abrupt transition from utter poverty to opulence, his yet more amazing leap from the state of a hunted fugitive to that of a noble of Bohemia— lastly, his disgrace, final incarceration, and dramatic death, make up a real life-story unsurpassed by anything in sensational fiction.

Following the trial which resulted in the loss of his ears, he evidently fled to Wales where, adopting a nomadic life, he successfully concealed himself from the ferocious law of the land, which he seemingly had good reason to dread. Let us follow his furtive, black-capped figure through the Welsh wilds, for his wanderings are to lead him to a wondrous discovery.

What emotions must have claimed the lonely shepherd, tending his flock upon a mountain side, when, along the harsh and stony path below, he perceived a weird, repellent stranger making his way! Wrapped in his long cloak, his head so covered by his closely fitting skull-cap that only a small part of his features remained visible, this furtive figure must have struck awe and dread into the heart of such a simple peasant, have persuaded him that he looked upon an evil thing—an envoy infernal.

Closely enwrapped, and with more substantial fears

than these for company, Edward Kelly, making his way to the neighbourhood of Glastonbury Abbey, came to a lonely inn and there sought shelter for the night. We are indebted to Louis Figuier for an account of what befell him there.

Finding himself temporarily in safety, Kelly evidently shook off the incubus of dread which rarely left him, and engaged the innkeeper in conversation. Growing confidential—and the passage of the ages has not vastly changed the temperament of mine host— the latter exhibited to his guest an old manuscript which local erudition had shown itself inadequate to decipher.

Kelly, we have seen, was no stranger to the ancient writings, and a glance sufficed to convince him that the MS. was in the old Welsh language and treated of the transmutation of metals. Upon inquiry he learnt that it had been brought to light during one of those outbursts of religious fanaticism so common in the reign of Elizabeth.

The sepulchre of a deceased bishop in a neighbouring church had been violated ; but this sacrilege was only rewarded by the discovery of the manuscript, which the despoilers were not even able to read, and by that of two small ivory caskets, containing respectively a red and white powder, to their eyes equally valueless. The casket containing the red powder they broke, and some of its contents was lost ; but the powder which remained, the second casket, and the manuscript they disposed of to the innkeeper for a flagon of wine.

How the eyes of the saturnine visitor must have gleamed when the whole of this treasure-trove was laid before him ! Few people of education, at that day, were ignorant of the red and white tinctures which were essential instruments for the performance of the *magnum opus*. Alchemy, indeed, claimed the attention of the learned throughout the civilized world, and Kelly promptly offered one guinea for the entire collection, an offer which the innkeeper as promptly accepted.

In this manner, then, Kelly became the possessor of the book of St. Dunstan and the alchemical powders of which it treated. I hope, in a later chapter, to quote some fragments of St. Dunstan; for the present my purpose will be served if I explain that St. Dunstan, who died Archbishop of Canterbury, is by some supposed to have been an alchemist, and has been regarded as the patron saint of goldsmiths; but an anonymous authority says that this prelate " had no other elixir or philosopher's stone than the gold and silver, which, by the benefit of fishing, was obtained, whereby the King's plate and bullion was procured. For the advancement of the fishing trade, he did advise that three fish days be kept in every week, which caused also more abstinence, and hence the proverb that St. Dunstan took the devil by the nose with his pincers."

With his hermetic treasures, Edward Kelly, in whom ambition must have silenced fear, next appears in London, where we definitely hear of him in partnership with Dr. Dee. In what way and at what time these two became acquainted is a debatable point; but we soon find Kelly assisting Dee in his experiments with the crystal.

Shortly after commencing their mystical operations, certain spirits appeared to Kelly, and held extraordinary discourses with him, all of which were duly taken down by Dee.

The latter, convinced that his colleague was an excellent and devout medium, with the growing success of their joint experiments took Kelly more and more into his confidence. Their conversation was constantly upon the subject of the hermetic mysteries, each giving the other accounts of his inquiries into the various sciences, and discussing the possibilities offered of a great reputation and future by the successful transmutation of base metal into pure gold. Kelly claimed that he could do this, and, as dramatic evidence, put before the amazed doctor the Glastonbury manuscript and the caskets containing the red and white powders.

We have seen that Dee practised astrology, which brought him great profits. According to one authority, his fame as an astrologer had spread over the country, and even to the Continent. From all points of the compass came people anxious to have their nativities cast by the doctor of Mortlake, and to behold the man who, claiming, as one authority says, to possess the elixir of life, asserted that he would never die. The same writer also states that Dee carried on a most profitable trade, but spent so much in drugs and metals, to work out some peculiar process of transmutation, that he never became rich. On the other hand, we read from a different source that :

" Dr. Dee has been popularly regarded as an alchemist with about as much reason as he has been regarded a magician. No doubt he knew something of alchemy before he became acquainted with Kelly, and . . . he conducted a phenomenal series of experiments in artificial lucidity through the medium of his celebrated crystal ; but he was not an alchemist on the one hand, nor a necromancer and a dealer with devils on the other. He was actually a learned mathematical philosopher, who was to some extent absorbed by the physics and metaphysics of the hermetic traditions."

Dee, then, was drawn headlong into the consuming science by the glamour of the ivory caskets of St. Dunstan ; for he readily and eagerly financed the schemes of his ambitious and sordid-minded partner.

They lost no time in getting to work, and soon were surrounded by their crucibles, retorts, and furnaces. Much labour was spent in experiments ; much gold, not the manufactured metal, but Dee's own coin of the realm, was expended in efforts to produce it by artificial means. Eventually, we are told, they "successfully accomplished a transmutation of metals which proved the richness of Kelly's tincture to be 1 upon 272,230 ; but they lost much gold in experiments before they knew the extent of its power."

I shall ask you, here, to glance at one or two entries in Dr. Dee's "private diary," for they serve to show that he was convinced of Kelly's success in transmutation, and that he regarded his companion as an adept alchemist.

Thus :

"May 10, 1588. E. K. did open the great secret to me. God be thanked."

And :

"Dec. 14th. Mr. Edward Kelly gave me the water, earth, and all."

It should be mentioned, as no other opportunity may present itself, that according to John Weever, the Lancashire author, an accusation of necromancy was levelled against Kelly ; so that he may, as a well-known modern authority points out, in occult matters have acted in good faith, and believed that there was efficacy in those magical processes of which crystallomancy formed a part.

The charge was to this effect : " That he caused a poor man who had been buried in the yard belonging to Law Church, near to Wotton-in-the-Dale, to be taken out of his grave (that is, evoked the spirit of the departed) and to answer to such questions that he then propounded to him." (A Bodleian MS. states that Weever's authority was an accomplice of Kelly and actually present at the unholy transaction.)

But despite his enthusiasm at this time regarding the *magnum opus*, Dr. Dee's profound interest in crystal-gazing remained, and grew greater with the passage of each year. His alchemical notes are scanty, whilst those dealing with planetary spirits and other invisible intelligences, summoned through the mediation of Kelly and the crystal, are exhaustive. Selections alone from them fill a large folio volume, and they are admitted to constitute the most extraordinary account extant in the language of intercourse with the borderland. Respecting these communications of Kelly, a well-known English authority says :

" In the present state of psychological knowledge, imperfect as it still is, it is, on the one hand, too late to deny that a state of lucidity can be frequently induced by the mediation of crystals and similar transparent substances ; whilst it is evident, on the other hand, from the history of the subject, that beyond the bare fact and such possibilities as may be reasonably attached to it, nothing of real moment has resulted from any such experiments. Edward Kelly may have lost his ears for forgery, or he may have deserved to be deprived of them, and he may still have been a genuine clairvoyant, for the faculty does not suppose an advanced or even tolerable morality in its possessor. He may equally have been guiltless of any otherwise illegal practices, and yet may have shamefully imposed upon his friend. There is only one fact of importance— that Edward Kelly, apparently by no desert of his own, came into possession of the two tinctures of hermetic philosophy. Convict or martyr, seer or cheating conjurer, knave or saint, matters nothing in comparison. He may further have accounted for his possession of the tinctures by a romantic fiction, but this itself is trivial. At the same time, with regard to his visions, it must be admitted that either he was a clairvoyant of advanced grade, or he was a man of most ingenious invention."

III. COUNT LASKI, AND THE JOURNEY TO POLAND

At about the time that Dee and Kelly were commencing their experiments with the two hermetic tinctures, the doctor made the acquaintaince of a wealthy Polish noble, Albert Laski, Count Palatine of Siradz. This was in May 1583. The distinguished foreigner, whilst making a tour of the learned centres of the kingdom, informed the Earl of Leicester that he should not have visited Oxford, had he not anticipated meeting Dr. Dee there.

The earl promised that he would introduce the count to the renowned doctor of Mortlake on their return to London ; and in accordance with this promise he brought the two together a few days later. The meeting took place in the ante-chamber of Queen Elizabeth, whilst both were awaiting audience of Her Majesty.

We are told by Krasinski that Count Albert Laski was received in England by Queen Elizabeth with great distinction ; and the honours which were accorded him during his visit to Oxford, by special command of the Queen, were such as are usually reserved for reigning princes. This Polish nobleman was one of the delegates sent to France, in order to announce to Henri de Valois, later Henri III of France, his election to the throne of Poland. The extraordinary prodigality of Count Laski rendered even his own enormous wealth insufficient to defray his expenses, and he therefore threw himself into the study of alchemy.

Laski found the society of Dr. Dee extremely congenial, and he became a frequent visitor to the house at Mortlake. Fitting entertainment of the Pole and his retinue was a costly matter, and we find Dr. Dee, in the *Autobiographical Tracts*, writing the following :

" Her Majesty (An. 1583 *Julii ultimo*) being informed by the Right Honourable Earl of Leicester, that whereas the same day in the morning he had told me that his honour and the Lord Laski would dine with me within two daies after, I confessed sincerely unto him that I was not able to prepare them a convenient dinner, unless I should presently sell some of my plate or some of my pewter. . . ."

Elizabeth listened to the favourite, and immediately sent to Dr. Dee a present of twenty pounds.

On the day appointed for the visit Count Laski arrived, attended by a numerous and magnificent retinue. He expressed his warm admiration at the wonderful accomplishments and attainments of his host ; and so profuse was he in compliments to Dee that the latter, being a very modest man, was almost speechless in his embarrassment. The wealthy Pole no doubt appealed to Kelly in quite a different manner ; and already the brain beneath the black skull-cap was at work upon a scheme whereby profitable use could be made of the stranger's enthusiasm.

During the days which followed, the Count was a constant visitor at Mortlake, and much of his time was taken up in the company of Dr. Dee. Now and again Kelly would point out to his friend the necessity of interesting this man in their experiments ; and he suggested that Dee, during one of his conversations with the visitor, should throw out hints of the philosopher's stone and the elixir of life, and if Laski displayed deep interest in the subject, should turn their discussions to the spirits, telling him that by their means they were able to look into the book of the future.

After much debate Dee decided to approach the Count in the manner suggested by Kelly, and Laski, on being informed of the results attained both in alchemy and in communion with the spirits, fell an easy victim to the lure of the Unseen. He inquired with much eagerness if he might be allowed to be present at one of their séances, or, better still, be admitted himself into conversation with the angel Uriel.

Dee, possibly prompted by Kelly, did not at first agree to the desire of his new acquaintance ; it may be that the earless notary desired to whet the appetite of the Pole. He explained that it was difficult and even dangerous to summon the spirits in the presence of a stranger ; for how could they know whether he was really sincere, or whether he had no other motive than that of gratifying idle curiosity ? Dee himself relates :

" I and E. K. (Edward Kelly) sat together, conversing of that noble Polonian Albertus Laski, his great honour here with us obtained, and of his great liking among all sorts of the people."

(He adds a note, which, considering what we have seen of the doctor's character, is at least extremely curious :)

" Suddenly there seemed to come out of the oratory a spiritual creature, like a pretty girl of seven or nine years of age, with her hair rolled up before and hanging down behind, attired in a gown of silk, of changeable red and green, and with a train. She seemed to play up and down, and seemed to go in and out behind the books ; and as she seemed to go between them, the books displaced themselves and made way for her."

In the dark places which abound throughout these records, we find ourselves looking, not to Dee, but to Kelly, for the key to the labyrinth ; and rarely do we look in vain. Whatever the scene, his shadow lies upon it ; from somewhere in the background peers out the malignant face. Be our subject deep in his books, bending to his retorts, studying the heavens above, always over the shoulder of the doctor of Mortlake we may catch a glimpse of the black skull-cap.

But the apparition recorded above sets us looking toward Kelly, and looking, it would seem, in vain. He may have deceived Dee respecting the spirits, and lied to him concerning the Glastonbury manuscript and the ivory caskets, but, short of hypnotic suggestion, how may we satisfactorily account for the " spiritual creature " ? That it was a fabrication of Dee's I am not prepared to admit ; for I can find nothing in the character of the man to justify such an assumption. Therefore, I shall invite you to seek your own solution.

At last the Pole was admitted to their mysteries. During the séances Kelly would place himself at some distance from the magic crystal and gaze steadily and intently into it, whilst Dee, as the recorder of the revelations, took his place in a far corner of the room.

Kelly, having worked himself into a state of great excitement, would again become quiescent, and, after a time, utter the prophecy. On occasions he is represented as predicting to the Pole that he should become the fortunate possessor of the philosopher's stone ; that he should live for centuries, and be elevated to the throne of Poland ; that, having become King, he would gain many great victories over the Saracens, and cause his fame to spread throughout the world.

That he urged Laski to take himself and Dr. Dee back to Poland ; that the two fastened, octopus-like, upon the Count, and plundered him mercilessly, is the view of more than one biographer : but I doubt if it can be justified. Certainly, a very short time later we find Dee and Kelly, together with their wives and families, *en route* for Poland.

Four months were occupied in the journey to the neighbourhood of Cracow, where were situated the Pole's estates. During the journey they denied themselves no pleasure, and spent money in a most lavish and extravagant fashion. Once, however, settled in the Count's palace, they immediately commenced the great hermetic operation of the transmutation of base metal into pure gold. Of course, Laski bore the enormous expense involved in these experiments ; and although their hopes always were disappointed at the very moment when it seemed that success was assured —failures which only impelled them in recommencing their work upon a larger and still more extravagant scale—the Count never lost hope. His lands brought him a rich revenue, and he had recovered from the terrific expenses he had incurred during his stay in England ; so he was not afraid in these early stages to sink his thousands in the venture, firmly believing as he did that he would be repaid a hundred-fold.

Weeks passed, months flew by ; and still they toiled in vain. Even Laski's purse began to feel the strain, and, in order to keep the ravenous furnaces going, he was compelled to raise money on his estates. Matters then went from bad to worse, and ruin actually stared him in the face. The families of Dee and Kelly had to be maintained, which constituted no small item of his expenditure.

It was during his sojourn in Cracow that Dr. Dee had news of the destruction of his library at Mortlake by a fanatical mob, which, raising the cry of " Wizard," had wrecked his house. In the August of the same year, 1584, the party left Cracow. Hostile critics have represented that, like satiated leeches, they dropped off from the unfortunate Laski and proceeded in quest of a fresh victim.

Since there is no record of the circumstances of their parting—save that it was not unkindly, for they bore letters of introduction to the Emperor Rudolf—I cannot accept that view as fair and unprejudiced. I prefer to think that Count Laski, though remaining confident of Dr. Dee's good faith, found Edward Kelly's overbearing temper and ill-veiled roguery no longer supportable, and determined, moreover, to abandon the quest of the great hermetic secret ere absolute financial ruin overtook him.

At any rate, accompanied by their wives and Dee's family, our alchemistical nomads set out upon their journey to Bohemia, whither I shall ask you to follow them.

IV. THE EXCHANGE OF WIVES

Alchemy was the one topic of Prague. Men spoke of it in the market-place, in the highways and the byways. By day, this process and that furnished subject for debate ; by night, the glow of a thousand furnaces told of the quest pursued. It was even said that an apartment of the Imperial palace was fitted up as an alchemical laboratory.

We can imagine the reception here accorded to the possessor of St. Dunstan's powders !

Very shortly, indeed, all Prague was burning with a fever of excitement ; for it was noised abroad, indeed was accepted as verity from palace to hovel, that the great English Adept, Edward Kelly, was transmuting with absolute success.

One of these operations is reported to have taken place at the house of the Imperial physician, Thaddeus de Hazek, and Kelly also is said to have initiated high officers of State into the secret. Whatever of truth be discoverable in all this, there certainly remains one outstanding fact. The whole party was suddenly translated from abject poverty to extraordinary affluence. Their extravagance became unbounded, and wherever they went they were attended by magnificent retinues.

In fact, this phase of our subject's career must always be an enigma and a stumbling-block in the path of inquiry. Contemporary authorities speak of Kelly's experiments, certainly, but with a halting voice for the most part, and in terms which conflict one with another.

There seems to be little doubt, however, that they were invited to the Court of Rudolf II, but in what measure the kindly offices of Count Laski served them here we cannot hope to learn. Whereas there seems to be good evidence to show that Kelly was created a Marshal, one authority actually tells us that Dee and Kelly met with but little consideration during their sojourn in Prague, and that the Emperor Rudolf, at the end of a few months, gave orders that they should quit Bohemia within twenty-four hours; this, as an alternative to a dungeon or the stake.

From the same source we learn that both families now suffered the utmost privation until chance threw in their path a new and wealthy patron in the shape of King Stephen of Poland. From the Court of Stephen, their dealings with whom are but poorly substantiated, they proceeded to Trebona, where they were sumptuously entertained by one Count Rosenberg.

According to a frankly hostile historian, their stay at the palace of this new patron lasted nearly four years. Rosenberg appears to have been more ambitious than avaricious, for he was an extremely wealthy man and allowed his guests an almost unlimited command of his money. He cared little for the amount of gold which the philosopher's stone would pour into his coffers, but desired its possession on account of the new and extensive lease of life which would thereby be assured to him. Kelly told him, says our authority, that he would become King of Poland, and promised that he would attain to the age of five hundred years to enjoy this dignity, provided that he supplied them with sufficient money to carry on their experiments!

Whatever was the nature of the dealings between Dee, Kelly, and the Count Rosenberg of Trebona, it was during their stay under the roof of this nobleman that quarrels between the two philosophers became frequent, resulting finally in complete rupture. The success which rewarded the schemes of Kelly so stimulated the arrogance of his nature that his manner towards Dr. Dee became overbearing to an intolerable degree. Even Dee's pacific soul was compelled to revolt against the man who once had been his assistant only, but who now asserted, and asserted with unspeakable insolence, his superiority over his partner, and over all who engaged in alchemical research.

Whilst full credit is due to the doctor of Mortlake for his conscientious and honest attempts to leave and work independently of his knavish partner, he seems at this time to have fallen so completely under the influence of the latter as to lack the courage to sever the knot. In fact, the sinister Kelly was so persuaded of his hold upon Dee as to threaten his colleague that he would forsake him entirely ; and whenever this threat was uttered poor Dee seems to have been brought to his knees.

We come to the most singular episode in the history of the pair, an episode which reveals the character of Dr. Dee in all its fixity and all its weakness, and which illuminates the mind beneath the black skull-cap, enabling us to study its libidinous activity, as a torch might cast its light into some noisome dungeon.

Kelly's wife was an ill-natured and far from prepossessing person, apparently, while Dee's was attractive and amiable. What other traits were hers events will show. And now Kelly determined to gratify a passion long nurtured in secret—in secret from Dee, as I understand the matter, but that Kelly had preserved his secret from Madame Dee I cannot believe. In fact, I find it impossible to doubt, despite the " fasting, vows, and prayers for enlightenment "—*Faithful Re-*

lation, pp. 16, 17, " Acta Tertia "—that a liaison existed between these two ; and the difficulty of conducting such a guilty amour under the very eyes of the wronged husband probably led Kelly to adopt the plan which I am about to mention. Its unparalleled audacity is such that for all time it must remain a mystery why Dr. Dee did not strike down the man who conceived it.

One day, whilst consulting the crystal, Kelly declared to Dee that he could not acquaint him with the message because of the nature of the suggestions being made by the mysterious beings. He remained stanch in his refusal to impart their words to his companion, but Dee, whose curiosity was thus naturally aroused, insisted, and at length Kelly, who had carefully and patiently awaited favourable opportunity, told him that a naked woman had appeared to him and directed that in future they were to have their wives in common !

At first Dee, in view of the numerous quarrels which had already taken place between them, thought that the message was in the nature of an exhortation to cease their useless squabbles and live together in harmony and goodwill. But he was soon disillusioned by the sinister being in the skull-cap, who, having questioned the naked spirit anew, declared that she insisted upon a literal interpretation of her words.

The unfortunate Dee no longer doubted ; but it formed no part of Kelly's plan to insist at present upon carrying out the dictates of the spirit. He even gave it as his conviction that the phantom being who had made the extraordinary suggestion could have been none but a satellite of the Evil One, and

Two Holy wax Lights used in the Invocation by the Chrystal.

The true size & form of the Chrystal which must be sett in pure Gold, & the same names & characters as in the model here given.

Michael
Uriel
Gabriel
Raphael

The Magic Wand to be used in Invocations by the Chrystal

Agla
On
Tetragrammaton
write or engrave on the other side Ego, Alpha et Omega.

The magic Circle of a simple construction in which the operator must stand or sit when he uses the Chrystal.

Tetragrammaton
ADONAI
Elohim

The Tripod on which the perfumes are put, & may be either held in the hand or sett in the earth.

מיכאל

El Elohim Elohe Zabaoth Elion Escerchie Adonai Jah Jehovah Vanadriel Tetragrammaton Iuday Ied Ehciti

Michael

The Lamen, or Holy Table of the Archangel Michael.

Pub by Lackington & Allen

MAGICAL IMPLEMENTS AND CIRCLES
FROM *THE MAGUS*

that in consequence he refused to give ear to such instructions.

After this we are led to believe that a further quarrel took place, for Kelly was sorely displeased that on all occasions when eminent persons came to consult them Dee was accorded by far the larger share of homage and consideration. Kelly, then, abruptly left his associate, telling him that he would see him no more.

Dee was now thrown upon his own resources, and in his unsettled state of mind could not decide upon which way to look for a suitable person to act as " skryer " in the place of Kelly. Ultimately, he fixed upon his own son, Arthur, then a boy of about eight or nine years of age, and impressed upon the child's mind the awful nature of the duties he was to perform.

As a medium, Arthur Dee proved a hopeless failure, for he had neither the imagination nor understanding for so mysterious a subject. Obedient to his father's instructions, he looked deeply and intently into the crystal, but nothing could he see, and nothing could he hear. Dee's disappointment was genuine and intense, for he really believed, after the results attained by and through Kelly, that it was possible to hold intercourse with the angels, and that his son was imbued with the same mystic sense as his late colleague, though perhaps not in the same degree. The boy, however, could only tell his father that he perceived a vague, indistinct shadow—an experience common to us all after long, fixed staring at a particular object.

In ever-increasing despair, Dee's thoughts constantly turned to Kelly. Keenly did he regret the rupture between them ; he was utterly miserable now that he found it impossible to commune with intelligences of the other world, for these experiments had become a part of his life. His shrewd partner had foreseen this, and, having allowed sufficient time to elapse, he suddenly and unexpectedly returned, to Dee's amazement and genuine relief.

Kelly entered the room where the séances usually took place and found the doctor's son gazing in vain into the crystal for something to appear. In his journal Dee remarks the welcome return of Kelly as a " miraculous fortune " and a " divine fate," adding that, having taken the place of his son Arthur, his colleague was immediately able to communicate with the spirits which had refused to appear to the boy. Such now was the fatuity of Dee, that when Kelly reported that the spirit which had previously appeared to him repeated the command that they should use " their two wives in common," the unfortunate philosopher bowed to the unkind fate which could insist upon so cruel an arrangement.

As the result of this " revelation " a solemn covenant was drawn up between Dr. Dee, Edward Kelly, Jane Dee, and Joan Kelly, as may be read in the *Faithful Relation*. Further comment upon this amazing incident could serve no useful purpose ; but I may add that the original rough draft, much interlineated, of this unique document, in Dee's own handwriting, is still extant.

V. THE LAST ACT OF THE DRAMA

We now find the party established once more in Prague, and engaged in desperate experiments with the red and white powders of St. Dunstan. These, however, were seriously diminished by excessive pro-

jection, indeed were almost exhausted. In their
efforts to increase the quantity of the tinctures they
merely succeeded in destroying that which remained.

It is evident that the Emperor had believed the
claims of Kelly (though he may nevertheless have
thought him a rogue), who had everywhere boasted
that he was an Adept—not merely the heir of the Stone,
but an enlightened and proficient master. So great
was Rudolf's faith in the ability, if not in the honesty,
of the man now become his guest—and whom he had
promoted to the dignity of a Marshal of Bohemia—
that the failure of Kelly to produce the alchemical
powders was attributed, not to impotency, but to
obstinacy.

The Royal alchemist became so furious with the
wearer of the black skull-cap as to cast him into a
dungeon of the Castle of Zobeslau ; but, always a
man of resource, he regained his liberty by undertaking to manufacture the Stone, on condition that he
was allowed to return to Prague and consult Dr. Dee,
who, throughout this time, appears to have been
left unmolested, and, indeed, to have been regarded
with much respect.

Kelly returned to Prague—under escort. The house
in which he stayed was practically turned into a
prison, for he was never for one moment unguarded.
All further experiments in manufacturing the powder
were as futile as his earlier attempts, and the alchemist,
at last, gave up in despair and made a desperate effort
to escape. In his fury he succeeded in murdering
one of his guards, but was eventually overpowered,
and sent to the Castle of Zerner.

Leaving the man in the black skull-cap alone in his
cell and occupied in the compilation of the *Stone of*

the Philosophers, which was begun and completed in captivity, I shall ask you to follow Dr. Dee, now for ever separated from the evil companion whom, despite all, he had loved.

It is believed that at this time the doctor returned to England. He set out from Bohemia with a magnificent retinue, and travelled with three coaches for himself and family and three wagons to carry his luggage. Each coach was drawn by four horses, and the whole party was escorted by a guard of twenty-four soldiers. One wonders if he had resumed friendly relations with his wife.

Some time before, when Kelly had first threatened to leave him, Dee had decided, should this desertion come about, to return to England, and had accordingly written to Elizabeth requesting that he might be granted a favourable reception on his return home. At the same time he sent to the Queen, as it is alleged, a round piece of silver, which he claimed to have transmuted from a piece of a brass warming-pan. Later, he also sent her the warming-pan, so that she might see for herself that the piece of silver fitted exactly into the hole which was cut in the brass. This was not without its effect, and he received the desired invitation to return to England.

On his arrival in his native country Elizabeth immediately granted him an audience, receiving him very kindly, promising and giving orders that he must suffer no interference in his experiments in alchemical research.

Very soon he had squandered what was left of the money with which he was enabled so sumptuously to travel from Bohemia; but Elizabeth could not believe that he was in want. She very reasonably argued that a man who claimed to be able to manufacture gold from baser metal could never fall into straitened circumstances, and the only marks of favour bestowed upon him were occasional audiences and her protection.

Poor Dee struggled manfully with his crucibles and retorts, and seriously affected his health by his existence amongst the poisonous fumes ever present in his laboratory. Now and again he turned his attention to his magic crystal, but could find none to replace the invaluable Kelly.

The pathetic impotency of Dee, now that he was once again and finally thrown upon his own resources, in his efforts to obtain the stone of the philosophers, or elixir, brought him to his knees. His repeated attempts in this direction, expensive and fruitless as they were, soon saw him on the verge of starvation. In great distress he applied to the Queen for relief. In stating his deplorable case, he wrote that, having left his library and the valuable contents of his museum behind him when he travelled to the Continent in the company of Count Laski and Kelly, the mob, aroused into fury by the exaggerated untruths which had been circulated regarding him, had broken into his house at Mortlake and destroyed everything they could lay their hands upon.

He denied the charges levelled against him of necromancy and wizardry, and, informed Her Majesty that his library, which consisted of four thousand volumes—rare and ancient—together with his philosophical instruments and other paraphernalia, having been wantonly and ruthlessly destroyed, he considered that he should be compensated for his loss ; for research was impossible in the circumstances, and his means of livelihood was taken from him.   He added that, as he had by the Queen's command returned to England, she should defray the expenses incurred by the journey.

Elizabeth, still kindly disposed towards the unfortunate doctor, at intervals sent him small sums of money. At last, another commission having sat to consider his claims, he received an appointment as Chancellor of St. Paul's Cathedral, transferring later to the college of Manchester, where he was appointed Warden. His troubles, however, were by no means at an end, for at Manchester he was subjected to continued persecution by the Fellows of the college, and suffered other indignities, which he endured with the patience characteristic of his whole career. His appointment to Manchester took place in 1595 ; and as this was the year which saw the dramatic and tragic end of Kelly, we must now return to the latter and see what befell this heir of St. Dunstan.

Whilst Kelly remained in durance, Dee had not been idle in making representations on behalf of his erstwhile companion. The doctor had forgiven the man who had ruined his whole career, and his generous nature impelled him to beseech Elizabeth to secure his release by the Emperor Rudolf and propose his return to England under safe conduct.

The Queen acceded to the requests made by Dee, and wrote to the Emperor, claiming Kelly as her subject. The Bohemian monarch, however, explained that, his prisoner being guilty of murder, he could not release him. By this time Kelly had completely given up all further experiments to produce the powders, although it would appear that he was afforded ample opportunity for continuing his researches within the prison walls. Instead, he set himself to compile a treatise on the stone of the philosophers, and in this way employed the remaining months of his miserable existence. His book he dedicated to his " most gracious master, Rudolfus II," extracts from which, together with excerpts from two of his letters to the Emperor upon the subject of transmuting metals, will be found upon a subsequent page.

His volatile temperament at last revolted against his enforced retirement from the world, and he resolved upon a desperate attempt to escape. It is stated on good authority that one stormy night, in February 1595, he made a rope of his bedclothes and proceeded to let himself down from the window of his dungeon, which was situated at the top of a very high tower. His weight, however, for he was a corpulent man, proved too great a strain upon the improvised rope, which broke, and, falling from a considerable height, he sustained such severe injuries, breaking two ribs and both legs, that he died a few days afterwards, at the age of forty-two.

We have it on the authority of another, John Weever, that Queen Elizabeth sent in secret Captain Peter Gwinne, with some others, to persuade Kelly to return to his native country. It is said that he then decided to escape, but from his own house in Prague—which was virtually his prison, since it was under strict guard ; and in descending from a wall, the rope he had made gave way and he was precipitated to the ground.

Whereas the reports differ as to the place from which he tried to escape, they are agreed upon the actual manner in which he met his death.

What must have been the thoughts of Dee when the news reached him of the end of the man with whom he had shared many dangers and privations ;

who had wronged him, yet whom he had loved, and whose behest, in his enthusiasm, he had blindly obeyed? His fanatic soul refused to admit that the great secret, to the solution of which he had devoted his whole life, was beyond the grasp of man. But now that Kelly was no more he felt himself abandoned in the wilderness of unbelief, the desert of persecution; and grieved, not that his learning had been wasted in useless research, but that his intellect, not being allowed to expand further, was starved.

Kelly's death, and the continued persecution to which he was subjected at Manchester, had an enormous effect upon the mind of Dee. Old age, too, began to tell its inevitable tale, and about the year 1603, his health having broken down and his mind become enfeebled, the philosopher was compelled to resign his chair at the college of Manchester.

He retired to Mortlake, but soon again found himself almost penniless, and was driven to eke out a miserable existence by fortune-telling. Frequently he was forced to sell some of his books in order that he might procure a meal, and more than one appeal on his behalf was made by influential persons to King James I.

This monarch, unlike Elizabeth, turned a deaf ear to the requests that John Dee's learning should be rewarded with a pension, so that the philosopher might spend the evening of his days in comfort and be relieved of the fear of want. James refused, and there was nothing left to John Dee but patiently to await his end. He died in 1608, and was laid to rest near his riverside home.

VI. THE BOOK OF ST. DUNSTAN AND SOME KELLY FRAGMENTS

In the diaries of Dr. Dee we find several references to the *Book of St. Dunstan* in connection with the " powder found at the digging." It is reasonable to suppose that the work referred to was the Glastonbury manuscript, and the powder that which lay in the ivory caskets. Arthur Dee, too, the son of Dr. Dee, refers more than once to this book.

It has been inferred that the bishop whose sepulchre was violated must have been none other than St. Dunstan himself, but this inference is evidently wrong, since Dunstan, dying in 988, was buried in Canterbury. He is said to have founded Glastonbury Abbey, but this, too, is incorrect ; for he was himself educated at the Abbey, of which he became abbot in later years, then to commence the great work of reformation which made Glastonbury a centre of learning famed throughout the kingdom.

As a young man he seems to have practised alchemy, and the old fascination apparently reasserted itself in later years, at Canterbury ; but whether, justly, the mysterious Glastonbury manuscript may be attributed to him is very doubtful. A number of extant manuscripts have been ascribed to his pen, including some metrical treatises which might perhaps with greater justice have been credited to Edward Kelly. However, I transcribe some metrical fragments selected at random from Mr. A. E. Waite's compendium of the writings of Edward Kelly, which (it is at least possible) may be from the *Book of St. Dunstan*, and append some Kelly selections from the same source :

No, no, my friends, it is not vauntinge words,
Nor mighty oaths that gaines that sacred skill ;
  It is obteined by grace and not by swords,
Nor by greate reading, nor by long sitting still,
Nor fond conceit, nor working all by will,
But, as I said, by grace it is obteined ;
Seek grace, therefore, let folly be refrained.

  It is no costly thing, I you assure,
That doth beget Magnesia in hir kind ;
  Yet is hir selfe by leprosis made pure.
Hir eyes be cleerer being first made blind,
And he that can earth's fastnes first unbind
Shall quickly know that I the truth have tould
Of sweete Magnesia, wife to purest gold.

  I doubte as yet you hardly understand
What man and wife doth truly signifie,
  And yet I know you beare your selves in hand
That out of doubt it Sulphur is and Mercury ;
And so it is, but not the common certainly ;
But Mercury essentiall is trewly the trew wife
That kills hir selfe to bring hir child to life.

  For first and formest she receives the man,
Her perfect love doth make her soone conceive,
  Then doth she strive with all the force she can,
In spite of love, of life him to bereave,
Which being done, then will she never leave,
But labour kindly like a loving wife
Untill againe she him have brought to life.

  Take then this Stone, this wife, this child, this all,
Which will be gummous, crumbling, silken, soft ;
  Upon a glasse or porphire beat it small,
And, as you grinde, with Mercury feed it oft,
But not so much that Mercury swim aloft,
But equal parts nipt up their seed to save ;
Then each in other are buried within their grave.

Mercury crude in a crucible heated
Presently hardeneth like silver anealed,
    And in the high throwne of Luna is seated.
Silver or gold as medecine hath sealed,
And thus our greate Secret I have revealed,
Which divers have seene, and myself have wrought,
And dearly I prize it, yet give it for nought.

Yet will I warne thee, least thou chaunce to faile,
Sublyme thine earth with stinkeking water erst ;
    Then in a place where Phœbus onely tayle
Is seene att midday, see thou mingle best ;
For nothing shineth that doth want his light,
Nor doubleth beames unless it first be bright.

(The following is from the treatise written by Kelly, whilst imprisoned in the Castle of Zerner :)

St. Dunstan of the Stone of the Philosophers.

(1) Take of the best red transparent ore of gold as much as you can have, and drive its spirit from it through a retort ; this is the Azoth and the Acetum of the Philosophers, from its proper minera, which openeth radically Sol that is prepared.

(2) Take the minera of Venus or Saturn, and drive their spirits in a retort ; each of these dissolveth gold radically, after its purification.

(3) Take pulverized ore of Saturn, or vulgar Saturn calcined ; extract its salt with Acetum or its antinæ (? anima) ; purify it in the best manner, that it may be transparent as crystal, and sweet as honey, and be fluid in heat like wax, and brittle when cold. This is the tree which is cut off, of unwholesome fruits, on which must be inoculated the twigs of Sol.

(4) Take of that earth which lieth waste in the field, found everywhere in Moorish grounds, into which the astrals ejaculate their operations, being adorned with

all manner of colours, appearing like a rainbow ; extract from it its purest and subtilest. This is the universal menstruum for all ; and is all in all.

(5) Take of the ore of Sol and Mercury a like quantity ; grind each very well ; pour on it the spirit of Mercury, that it stand over three fingers deep. Dissolve and digest it in a gentle warmth.

(6) Take of the best vitriol, or of the vitriol of Venus ; drive their spirits in a retort, white and red. With this red spirit, being rectified and sweetened, you may ferment and imbibe the subtle gold calx, and with the white spirit you may dissolve it after it hath been purified.

(9) Take of the rank poisonous matter or stone, called kerg swaden, exuviæ, or husk of the metals ; drive its spirit very circumspectly ; receive it so that it may turn unto water ; it reduceth all metals to a potableness.

(10) Take of the air or heavenly dew, being well purified, ten parts, and of subtle gold calx one part ; set it in digestion, dissolve and coagulate it.

(12) Take the best ore of gold ; pulverize it very well ; seal it with Hermes his seal ; set it so long into the vaporous fire till you see it spring up into a white and red rose.

(13) This last experiment he calleth the Light. Take, in the name of the Lord, of Hungarish gold, which hath been cast thrice through antimony and hath been laminated most thinly, as much of it as you will, and make with quick Mercury an amalgam ; then calcine it most subtily, with flowers of sulphur and spirit of wine burnt, so often till there remaineth a subtle gold calx of a purple colour. Take one part of it and two parts of the above mentioned red matter ;

grind it very well together for an hour on a warmed marble ; then cement and calcine well by degrees for three hours in a circle fire.   This work must be iterated three times ; then pour on it of the best rectified spirit, that it stand over it three fingers deep ; set it in a gentle and warm digestion, for six days to be extracted ; then the spirit of wine will be tinged as deep as blood ; cant off that tincture, and pour on another as long as it will tinge it ; put all these tinged spirits of wine into a vial so that the fourth part only be filled, and seal it hermetically ; set it on the vaporous fire of the first degree ; let it be of that heat as hot as the sun shineth in July ; let it stand thus for forty days—then you shall obtain your wish.

The author recommendeth this last experiment very highly, affirming upon his experimental practice that this Aurum Potabile is the highest medicine next unto the universal, and, being taken in appropriated vehicles, cureth all diseases without causing any pains at all.

Item.—With this Aurum Potabile is Antimony prepared, so that it purgeth only downward, and carrieth forth all ill humours without molestation, and is called the purging gold.

TO THE MOST POTENT
LORD OF THE HOLY ROMAN EMPIRE

RUDOLFUS II

KING OF HUNGARY AND BOHEMIA, ETC.
HIS MOST GRACIOUS MASTER,
THIS BOOK IS DEDICATED BY EDWARD KELLY

(From a letter of Edward Kelly, dated June 20, 1587.)

" As you are willing to take my advice, I will partially reveal to you the Arcanum, so that the field may not disappoint the hopes of the husbandmen.   Open your

ears. Our gold and silver, Sun and Moon, active and
passive principles, are not those which you can hold
in your hand, but a certain silver and golden Herma-
phroditic water ; if you extract it from any perfect
or imperfect metallic body, you have the Water of
Life, the Asafœtida, and Green Lion, in which are all
colours, ending in two—white and red. The earth
does not so much matter, only let it be fixed, for the
Elixir must above all be fixed. If you are in earnest
all your thoughts must be concentrated on the fixed
earth and the indestructible metallic water ; nor need
you seek these in gold and silver, or in any determinate
compound. It is true, however, that after the separa-
tion of this tincture from the gold, that indestructible
water is fixed in its white earth ; but it is foolish to
do by much what you can do by little.''

(From a letter dated November 15, 1589.)

" I have given you both luminaries and the best
instruction concerning these things, if you can bear it
in mind. To sum it all up in a few words : ' Mix
water with water ; digest with a vaporous cloud, and
you will not easily make a mistake.' ''

(From " The Humid Path," by Edward Kelly.)

" The Sages have, indeed, purposely concealed
their meaning under a veil of obscure words, but it is
sufficiently clear from their writings that the substance
of which they speak is not of a special, but a general
kind, and is therefore contained in animals, vegetables,
and minerals. It would, however, be unwise to take
a round-about road when there is a shorter cut ;
and they say that whereas the substance can be found

in the animal and vegetable kingdoms only with great difficulty and at the cost of enormous labour, in the bowels of the earth it lies ready to our hands. It is the matter which the Sages have agreed to call Mercury or Quicksilver. Our quicksilver, indeed, is truly a living substance, so-called not because it is extracted from cinnabar, but because it is derived from the metals themselves. If common Mercury be freed by fixation from its crude, volatile, and watery super-fluities, it may with the aid of our Art, attain to the purity and virtue of the substance of which we speak. And as *this* Mercury is the metallic basis and first substance, it may be found in all metals whatsoever. . . . Nothing contributes so much to a ready apprehension of our secret as a knowledge of our first substance, and after that of the distinctive species of minera which is the subject of investigation by the Philosopher."

CAGLIOSTRO

I. GIUSEPPE BALSAMO

IN appearance he was below medium height and inclined to be stout; he had a neck such as appears in busts of Nero, a brown complexion, and a low, bald forehead. His large eyes—the most striking features of a countenance otherwise somewhat gross—were aglow with a mystic fire. He had the deep chest and distended nostrils which indicate unusual virility; and the lines of his mouth, if we may judge from Houdon's bust, suggest that he may have taken himself less seriously than would appear to be the case from documentary evidence.

The majority of those who came in contact with him—friends and enemies alike—admitted him to possess a very imposing presence. He spoke fluent Italian, but almost incomprehensible French. Yet he never failed to fascinate his listeners. He is described as appearing, on one occasion, arrayed in a coat of blue silk, with braided seams, his hair powdered and gathered up in a net. His shoes were fastened with buckles of precious stones; his stockings studded with gold buttons; rubies and diamonds glittered on his fingers and on his shirt-frill. He wore a diamond watch-chain, from which depended six larger diamonds, a gold key set with diamonds, and an agate seal. To crown all he wore a musketeer's hat wherefrom floated huge white feathers.

" Who are you, monsieur ? " was a question to which he was well used, and to which, pointing heavenward, he was wont to reply :

" I am he who is."

Such was Alessandro, Comte di Cagliostro, at the height of his fame, about 1780. In the Memoir compiled by himself during his incarceration in the Bastille, he speaks of his infancy in mysterious and romantic terms :

" I am ignorant," he tells us, " not only of my birthplace, but even of the parents who bore me. All my researches on these points have won for me nothing but vague and uncertain, though, frankly, exalted notions. My earliest infancy was passed in the town of Medina, in Arabia, where I was brought up under the name of Acharat—a name by which I was known during my Asiatic and African travels—and where I was lodged in the palace of the mufti. I distinctly recollect four persons who were continually about me —a tutor, between fifty-five and sixty years of age, named Althotas, and three slaves, one of whom was white, whilst the others were black. My tutor always led me to believe that I had been left an orphan at the age of three months, and that my parents were noble, and were Christians ; but he preserved an absolute silence respecting their name and the place of my birth, although by certain chance words I was led to infer that I first saw the light at Malta. Althotas was pleased to cultivate my inherent taste for the sciences ; he himself was proficient in all, the profound and the trivial alike. It was in botany and physics that I made most progress. My instructor and I wore the dress of Moslems, and outwardly we professed the Moslem law. The principles of the true religion were, however, established in our hearts. I was frequently visited by the mufti, who treated me with great kindness, and who exhibited a profound respect for my instructor, from whom I acquired proficiency in most Oriental languages . . ."

From the proceedings published by the Inquisition at Rome, however, we learn that his origin was invested with little romance, and that his early history was chiefly notable for brawls, frequent visits to prison, and a precocious debauchery quite unnatural. Between the several accounts, more than one biographer has come to grief ; but it is generally believed that he was the son of Pietro Balsamo and of Felice Braconieri his wife.

Balsamo the elder was of Jewish extraction and a tradesman of Palermo. In this city, on June 8, 1743, Giuseppe was born. At the age of thirteen, his father being no more, he was placed at the Seminary of St. Roch di Palermo, from which he promptly ran away. Recaptured, in evil company, and sent to a Benedictine convent (or a convent of the Misericordia Brothers) he remained there long enough to acquire some knowledge of pharmacy and medicine.

He ultimately quitted the monastery, apparently by climbing the wall, and fled back to Palermo, vested with those rudiments of science later to be developed with such astonishing results.

For some years he abandoned himself to a life of riotous debauchery, during which period he is said to have indulged in such petty crimes as forging orders of admission to theatres and rescuing prisoners from

"THE GRAND COPT"—CAGLIOSTRO

FROM AN OLD PRINT

the police. From this it is recorded that he proceeded to the counterfeiting of a will (his uncle's) and to a Palermo gaol.

Upon regaining his freedom, he is next brought to our notice in the character of an intermediary in the amorous intrigue of a pretty cousin with one of his own associates. He is represented as appropriating the gifts of the lover and blackmailing his mistress. But it is all but impossible to say with certainty which of the many crimes imputed to him were justly imputed, or in what chronological order they occurred. Therefore I shall dismiss them and proceed to the most notorious and best authenticated exploit of Giuseppe Balsamo's early days. The Italian account of the episode, though possibly the more accurate, is certainly the less picturesque ; so that I turn to that of Louis Figuier, who tells a similar story, but clothes it in a pleasing vesture of French imagery.

A certain goldsmith, Marano by name, resided in Palermo, and he found himself fascinated by the aroma of mystery which, even thus early, distinguished the doings of Balsamo from the deeds of other men. Balsamo, in fact, already proclaimed himself an initiate of the occult sciences, in which claim he was assisted by his striking personality and a certain command of will which thralled those with whom he came in contact. In short, if we are to believe that these twain indeed were one, this was the period of transition when Balsamo the ne'er-do-well was merging into Cagliostro the master thaumaturgist.

The first interview, says Figuier, took place in Balsamo's lodging ; the goldsmith fell on his knees before the youthful sorcerer, and, Balsamo, having accepted his homage, raised him condescendingly from the ground, and demanded solemnly why he was come to him.

"Thanks to your daily communion with spirits, you must already know," answered Marano, "and you should have no difficulty in assisting me to recover the money which I have wasted among false alchemists, or even in procuring me more."

"I can perform this for you, provided you believe," answered Balsamo.

"Provided I believe!" cried the goldsmith; "I believe, indeed!"

An appointment accordingly was made for the next day, in a meadow beyond the town, and the interview ended without another word.

At the appointed time they met, Balsamo, in dignified silence, motioning the goldsmith to follow him, and proceeding, but in a preoccupied manner, along the road to the chapel of St. Rosalia, for the space of a whole hour. They stopped at length in front of a grotto, before which Balsamo extended his hand, solemnly declaring that a treasure was buried within it which he himself was forbidden to touch and which was guarded by devils from the hells. These demons, he added, might be bound for a time by the angels who obeyed his magical invocations.

"It only remains to be ascertained," he said in conclusion, "whether you will fulfil scrupulously the conditions which must be imposed; upon which terms the treasure shall be yours."

The credulous goldsmith implored him to name them.

"They cannot be learned from my lips," answered Balsamo. "On your knees!"

He himself had already assumed a kneeling posture;

and Marano hastened to imitate him, when immediately a clear voice pronounced the following words :

" Sixty ounces of pearls, sixty ounces of rubies, sixty ounces of diamonds, in a coffer of chased gold, weighing one hundred and twenty ounces. The infernal *ginn* who protect this treasure will place it in the hands of the worthy man whom our friend has brought, if " . . . and several conditions were stipulated to which Marano found no difficulty in conforming—even to the last, which was this : " And if he deposit at the entrance of the grotto, ere setting foot therein, sixty ounces of gold to propitiate the guardians."

" You have heard," said Balsamo, who, already on his feet, began to retrace his steps, completely ignoring the stupefaction of his companion.

" Sixty ounces of gold ! " ejaculated the miser with a dismal groan, and torn by an inward conflict of avarice and cupidity ; but Balsamo heeded the exclamation as little as the groan, and they regained the town in dramatic silence.

When they were on the point of separating, cried Marano :

" Grant me one instant ! Sixty ounces of gold ? Is that the irrevocable condition ? "

" Undoubtedly," said Balsamo, carelessly.

" Alas ! alas ! and at what hour ? "

" At six o'clock in the morning, and at the same spot."

" I will be there."

Such was the parting speech of the goldsmith, and it marked his victory over the demon of petty avarice. On the morrow, punctual to the appointment, they met as before, Balsamo reserved and nonchalant, Marano clutching his gold. They arrived in due course at the grotto, where the spirits, invoked as on the previous day, made the same responses. Marano then, groaningly, deposited his gold and prepared to cross the threshold. He took one step forward, then started back, inquired if it were dangerous to penetrate into the depths of the cavern, and, being assured of his safety, entered with more confidence, only to return again. These manœuvres were repeated several times, under the eyes of the Adept, whose expression indicated complete indifference.

At length Marano took courage and proceeded so far that return was impossible; for three black, muscular devils started out from the shadows and barred his path, at the same time uttering most dreadful cries! They seized him, whirled him round and round for a long time, and then, whilst the unhappy goldsmith vainly invoked the assistance of Balsamo, proceeded to cudgel him lustily, until he dropped almost insensible to the ground, where a voice bade him to remain, absolutely silent and motionless, warning him that he would be instantaneously dispatched if he stirred hand or foot.

The wretched man did not dare to disobey; indeed, he swooned. Upon recovering consciousness, the complete stillness encouraged him to raise his head; he dragged himself as best he could to the mouth of the terrible grotto, and looked around him—to find that the Adept, the demons, and the gold alike had vanished.

On the morrow, the goldsmith, fortunately discovered by muleteers, was carried home, and forthwith denounced Balsamo to the law. The strange story spread everywhere, but the magician had sailed for Messina.

II. ALTHOTAS, THE MYSTERIOUS

Although one author avers that it was at Medina, in Arabia, that Balsamo first became acquainted with the alchemist Althotas, and although Cagliostro himself, as we have seen, represents him as the Oriental instructor of his infancy, it would appear that the encounter really took place in Messina.

As he was promenading one day near the jetty at the extremity of that port, he encountered a person most singularly dressed, and possessed of a countenance remarkable anywhere. This person, who was apparently of about fifty years of age, seemed to be an Armenian, or, according to other accounts, a Spaniard ; probably he was a Greek. He wore a kind of caftan, or long-sleeved gown, a silk turban, and the extremities of his Eastern trousers disappeared within a pair of wide boots. In his left hand he held an umbrella, and in his right the end of a cord, by which he led an Albanian greyhound.

Probably out of curiosity, Cagliostro saluted this grotesque being, who bowed slightly, but with dignity.

" You do not reside in Messina, signor ? " he said in Sicilian, but with a marked foreign accent.

Cagliostro replied that he was only remaining for a few days ; whereupon they began to converse upon the beauty of the town and upon its advantageous situation, a rich Oriental imagery characterizing the stranger's discourse. He evaded inquiries regarding his own identity, but offered to unveil Cagliostro's past, and to reveal what was actually passing in his mind at that moment. Cagliostro hinting at sorcery, the Armenian smiled somewhat scornfully, and dilated on the ignorance of a nation which confused science with witchcraft, and prepared faggots for discoverers.

His hearer, much interested, ventured to ask the address of the eccentric stranger, who graciously invited him to call. They walked past the cathedral and halted in a small street shaded by sycamores, and having a pleasant fountain in the centre.

" Signor," said the wearer of the caftan, " yonder is the house I inhabit. I receive few visitors ; but since you are a traveller, young and courteous, since, moreover, you have a passion for the sciences, I ask you to visit me. I shall be at home to you to-morrow a little before midnight. You will rap twice "—he pointed as he spoke to the door of a small house— " then three times more slowly, and you will be admitted. Adieu ! Hasten at once to your inn. A Piedmontese is about to rob you of the thirty-seven ounces of gold that are in your valise, shut up in a press, the key of which lies in your pocket ! "

Cagliostro, we learn, returning in all haste, discovered the thief in the act, and forthwith delivered him to justice.

On the morrow, at the time appointed, he knocked at the door of the little house inhabited by the mysterious stranger. It was opened at the fifth blow without any visible agency, and closed as soon as the visitor had entered.

Cagliostro advanced cautiously along a narrow passage, illuminated by a small iron lamp in a niche of the wall. At the extremity of the passage a big door swung open, giving admittance to an apartment which was illuminated by a four-branched candelabra, containing tapers of wax, and was, in fact, a laboratory furnished with all the apparatus in use among alchemists.

The man of mystery, issuing from an adjoining cabinet, greeted the visitor, inquired after the safety of the gold, and learnt that his prescience had led to the apprehension of the thief. He silenced the expressed astonishment and admiration of Cagliostro by declaring that the art of divination was simply the result of scientific calculation and close observation.

" What are your plans ? " he asked Cagliostro.

" I intend to seek riches."

" That is, you would rise superior to the common herd, the imbecile mob—a laudable project, my son ! Do you propose to travel ? "

" Certainly, so far as my thirty-seven ounces of gold can take me."

" You are very young," said the other ; then, abruptly : " How is bread manufactured ? "

" With flour."

" And wine ? "

" From the grape."

" But gold ? "

" I come to inquire of you."

" We will solve that problem hereafter. Listen to me, young man. I am about to depart for Grand Cairo, in Egypt. 'Will you accompany me ? "

" With all my heart ! " cried Cagliostro, overjoyed ; and they sat down in tall oaken chairs, at either end of the table whereupon stood the candelabra.

" Egypt," began the mysterious host, " is the birthplace of human science. Astronomy alone had Chaldea for its fatherland. There the shepherds first studied the courses of the stars. Egypt availed itself of the astro-Chaldean initiations, and soon surpassed the methods and increased the discoveries of the shepherds. Since the reign of Menes " (probably Mena, the first

historic Pharaoh), " Egyptian knowledge has advanced
with giant strides. Joseph the dream-reader established the basis of chiromancy ; the priests of
Osiris and Isis invented the Zodiac ; the priestesses
of Ansaki unveiled the secrets of philtres ; the priests
of Serapis taught medicine. I might proceed further,
but to what end ? Will you follow me to Egypt ?
I hope to embark to-morrow, and we shall touch at
Malta on the way—possibly at Candia also—reaching
the point of Phare in eight days."

" 'Tis settled ! " cried Cagliostro, delighted. " I
have my thirty-seven ounces of gold for the journey."

" And I not a single crown."

" The devil ! "

" What matters it ? What need to have gold when
one can make gold ? What need to possess diamonds
when one can extract them from carbon more readily
than from the mines of Golconda ? Go to, simpleton ! "

But he extended his hand, the bargain was sealed,
and their departure fixed for the morrow.

This Althotas, says Figuier, in his sprightly account,
was no imaginary character. The Roman Inquisition
collected many proofs of his existence, without, however, ascertaining where it began or ended, for the
mysterious personage vanished like a comet. According to the Italian biography of Joseph Balsamo, Althotas was in possession of several Arabic manuscripts,
and had great skill in chemistry ; but according to
Figuier, he was a sorcerer as well.

They embarked on board a Genoese vessel, sailed
along the Archipelago, landed at Alexandria, and
remained there for forty days, performing several
operations in alchemy, by which they are said to
have produced a considerable sum of money, but

whether by transmutation or by imposture is not evident.

Althotas claimed to be in complete ignorance as to his birth and parentage.

" This may surprise you," he said, " but science, which can enlighten us on behalf of another, is almost invariably impotent to instruct us concerning ourselves."

He declared himself to be much older than would appear, and to be in possession of certain secrets for the conservation of health and strength. He had discovered the scientific methods of producing gold and precious stones, spoke ten or twelve languages fluently, and was acquainted with almost the entire cycle of human sciences.

" Nothing astonishes me," he averred, " nothing grieves me, save the evils which I am powerless to prevent ; and I trust to reach in peace the term of a protracted existence."

He confessed that his name, Althotas, was assumed. His early years had been passed on the coast of Barbary, near Tunis, where he belonged to a Moslem privateer, who was a rich and humane man, and who had purchased him from pirates, by whom he had been stolen from his family. At twelve years of age he spoke Arabic like a native, read the Koran to his master, who was a true believer, studied botany under his direction, and learned " the best methods of making sherbet and coffee." A post of honour awaited him in the household of his master ; but Kismet decreed that when Althotas was sixteen the worthy Moslem should be visited by " the Terminator of delights." In his will he gave the young slave his liberty, and bequeathed him a sum equivalent to six thousand livres, wherewith Althotas quitted Tunis, to indulge his passion for travelling.

Cagliostro later claimed to have followed his instructor into the heart of Africa and to Egypt, to have visited the pyramids, making the acquaintance of the priests of several temples, and penetrating to their inner sanctuaries. Moreover, he declared himself to have visited, during the space of three years, all the principal kingdoms of Africa and Asia.

At Malta, they had letters of introduction to the Grand Master, Pinto, and remained for some time to work in his laboratory; for Pinto, after the fashion of the period, indulged in alchemical experiments.

In Malta, the Count relates in his memoir :

" It was my miserable misfortune to lose my best friend, the most wise, the most illuminated of mortals, the venerable Althotas. He clasped my hands shortly before his death.

" ' My son,' he said, in a failing voice, ' keep ever before thine eyes the fear of the Eternal, and the love of thy neighbour. Thou shalt ere long learn the truth of all that I have taught thee.' "

With every mark of respect on the part of the Grand Master, and accompanied by the Chevalier d'Aquino, of the illustrious house of Caramania, and himself a Knight of Malta, Cagliostro repaired to Naples, where he supported himself for some time with the money which had been presented to him by Pinto.

From Naples, after a number of adventures, Cagliostro proceeded to the Papal States, where he is said to have assumed several different characters, including that of a monk. According to one account, he visited all the churches, fulfilling the Roman religious duties, and frequenting the palaces of cardinals. By means of letters of recommendation, he obtained access to several persons of distinction, among others to the Seneschal de Breteuil, at that time Maltese Ambassador to Rome, who, hearing of his former connexion with the Grand Master, received him with much warmth, and procured him entrée to other aristocratic houses.

Figuier relates, then, that he was soon firmly established in the Holy City, retailing wonderful recipes and specifics for all the weaknesses which flesh is heir to. He lived extravagantly, but refrained from outraging the proprieties.

III. LORENZA FELICIANI

In Rome it was that Giuseppe Balsamo ceased to exist—henceforth we have to deal with Comte di Cagliostro ; and in Rome he met the young and beautiful Lorenza Feliciani. Although some authorities tell us that Lorenza was of noble birth, the fact would seem to be that he met her in the workshop of a *batadore*, or coppersmith, in Pellegrini Street. At this time Cagliostro was lodging at the sign of the " Sun " in the Rotunda, and, according to the biography inspired by the Holy Office, selling copies, manufactured by himself, of " Rembrandt etchings."

Lorenza had eyes like the transparent shadows of a lagoon, hair of prisoned sunlight, and lips to have exhausted the similes of an Arabian poet—so she is painted for us. And she was barely fifteen.

We read of assignations at the house of an old Neapolitan woman, and we can picture the lovely Lorenza listening spellbound to the eloquence of her lover, hugging to her heart his wild, romantic declarations, whilst her very soul looks out from the wonderful eyes. Despite parental opposition, in April 1769 the marriage was celebrated at the church of San Salvador in Campo.

I shall now draw your attention to the discordant views of Madame di Cagliostro held by two different authorities. Says one:

"Amid all the incense that was offered at her shrine, Madame was ever faithful to her spouse. She encouraged hopes, it is true, but she never realized them; she excited admiration, yet kept it within bounds; and made men her slaves, without ever granting a favour of which the vainest might boast."

But, according to another testimony, although Lorenza was not only ravishingly beautiful, but " rich in every quality of the heart, being tender, devoted, honest, and modest, her husband conceived the diabolical design of advancing his fortunes at the expense of her honour, and in private conversation took occasion to rally her notions of virtue, which he sought to undermine. The first lesson which the young bride received from her husband was intended to instruct her in the means of attracting and gratifying the passions of the opposite sex. The most wanton coquetry and the most lascivious arts were the principles with which he endeavoured to inspire her. The mother of Lorenza, scandalized at his conduct, had such frequent altercations with her son-in-law that he resolved to remove from her house, and in other quarters found it a simpler task to corrupt the mind and morals of his wife."

Then, says the Italian author (it must be remembered that he sought to justify the Inquisition), he

presented her to two persons " well qualified for the
exercise of her talents, having instructed her to entangle
them both by her allurements.   With one of these she
did not succeed, but over the other she acquired a
complete victory.   Cagliostro himself conducted her
to the house destined for the pleasure of her lover,
left her alone in his company, and retired to another
chamber."

The offers made to her during the interview were
regarded as entirely satisfactory by the husband, but
the wife on this occasion did not find conjugal obedience
and personal inclination to march together, and
consequently she received most bitter reproaches and
most violent and dreadful menaces.   He repeatedly
assured her that adultery was no crime when committed by a woman to advance her interests, and not
by reason of affection for lovers.

His wife, hearkening at length to his evil instructions, was conducted several times to the place where
she had formerly proved disobedient.   She sometimes
received, avows the same prejudiced witness, either
clothes or trinkets, and sometimes a little money as
the price of her condescension.   On one occasion her
husband wrote a letter, in his wife's name, in which
he begged the loan of a few crowns ; these were for-
warded immediately.   " In return for them an interview was promised during the course of the next day
—and the lady was faithful to the appointment."

Mr. Arthur Edward Waite, probably the least biased
and certainly the most conscientious and erudite
English authority, says that all biographers agree
that Cagliostro corrupted the morals of his wife ; but
that the verdict is not entirely unanimous we have
seen.   He adds : " Whatever were her natural virtues

or failings, it is highly improbable that she sold her uncommon attractions for such paltry and miserable advantages."

His meaning I take to be that the foregoing stories are of dubious authenticity ; that being so, why should we attach any greater importance to those that follow, wherein the beautiful wife of Cagliostro is represented as abandoning herself to lover after lover ? For are not all these defiled streams of anecdote traceable to a common source ?

Even granting that Cagliostro was capable of this loathsome infamy, is it credible that a tactician so accomplished as he, that a man about to embark upon those tremendous projects which presently engaged the attention of Europe, should have descended to the petty and filthy intrigues of a bawd ?

Following some doubtful adventures, then, the Comte and Madame di Cagliostro proceeded to Venice, accompanied by a certain Sicilian marquis. Here Cagliostro again found himself in prison, but he was very soon set at liberty, apparently owing to the efforts of the marquis ; for " Donna Lorenza," says a chronicler, " was one of the beauties of Europe." The innuendo is scarcely veiled.

From this moment the life of the Comte di Cagliostro was for several years one of incessant wandering. According to the same Italian writer, as mendicity proved unprofitable, Lorenza was again forced by her husband to augment their resources by the sale of her charms. In this way they arrived at Barcelona, where they stayed for six months, " the same course of infamous prostitution, followed by Lorenza with the most manifest reluctance, contributing in the main to their support."

Casanova seems to have met them as they journeyed through Aix in Provence. They were habited as pilgrims. "They could not but be people of high birth," he relates in his monumental and astounding *Mémoires*, "since on arriving at the town they distributed alms widely."

Later, he visited them at their inn. He writes :

"We found the female pilgrim seated in a chair, looking like a person exhausted with fatigue, and interesting by reason of her youth and beauty, singularly heightened by a touch of melancholy, and by a crucifix of yellow metal . . . which she held in her hands. . . . This young woman, far from flaunting the airs of libertinage, had all the outward bearing of virtue."

They ultimately settled for a time in Barcelona, but at the end of some few months they departed, "because the viceroy," Lorenza relates, "had taken a fancy for me, wanted to amuse himself with me, and, when I repulsed him, conceived much ill humour against us. . . ."

From Barcelona they went on to Madrid, where they seem to have spent the year 1771, and then proceeded to Lisbon. Throughout this time, according to the chronicles published by the Italian Chamber, Cagliostro continued to traffic in the person of Lorenza.

They next appear in London, Cagliostro setting up as a designer. We are told that he joined a congregation of Quakers, one of whom found his austerity no armour against the burning glances of Lorenza. We read how a meeting was arranged between the two frail ones, whereat "the conversation grew so warm that the Quaker had stripped off his hat and wig and coat—when Lorenza gave a scream, the door flew open," and Cagliostro burst in, accompanied by a witness. The episode concluded, says our author, with the transference of a note for one hundred pounds from the Quaker to Cagliostro !

In 1772 Cagliostro and his wife returned to France, accompanied by a M. Duplessis. Lorenza and M. Duplessis drove together by post-chaise to Paris, we learn, Cagliostro following on horseback. This delightful arrangement led to a scene in the chaise, it would appear ; for Lorenza avows, " I was several times tempted to stop and leave M. Duplessis, in order to escape the solicitations and even the actual violence he showed me in the carriage. . . ."

However, Paris was come to at last ; and, according to a chronicle before me at the moment, " apartments were taken for Lorenza by M. Duplessis ; . . in the Rue Saint-Honoré."

But Cagliostro was insatiable, says St. Felix. He sold his honour at a high price, and the fortune of Duplessis melted in the crucible of another's follies and extravagances. According to one account Lorenza endeavoured to return to her parents, but another says that she sought refuge from incessant prostitution with M. Duplessis himself. Whatever the facts, Cagliostro had recourse to the authority of the King ; and, obtaining an order for her arrest, she was imprisoned in the penitentiary of Sainte Pélagie, and was detained there for several months, which episode, in my humble opinion, alone constitutes a case for the defence of Cagliostro ; particularly since the imprisonment of Lorenza did not prevent a reconciliation with her husband immediately after her release, which occurred on December 21, 1772.

SERAPHINIA FELICHIANI,
COMTESSE DE CAGLIOSTRO.

FROM A RARE FRENCH PRINT

IV. ADVENTURES IN LONDON

In July 1776 Cagliostro paid a second visit to London. It was at this time that he was initiated into masonry at the " Esperance " Lodge, attached to the " Rite of the Strict Observance," meeting at the " King's Head " in Gerrard Street, Soho, and composed mainly of French and Italians. At this time, no doubt, he also conceived his project of establishing a great rival brotherhood of which he should be supreme master.

The Comte and Comtesse di Cagliostro rented apartments in Whitcomb Street ; and a certain Vitellini, a teacher of languages, was employed in the capacity of interpreter. This man was a ruined gamester, who in the endeavour to repair his crumbled fortunes had left few stones unturned. Immediately that he became acquainted with Cagliostro's labours in the laboratory, he seems to have taken it for granted that the Comte's pretensions had solid foundation. Within a remarkably short space of time it was common knowledge throughout London, if not throughout England, that a true Adept, of immense fortune, who could transmute into purest gold as much base metal as he pleased, was lodged in Whitcomb Street.

Thereupon we find the house invested with a gaping horde of idle, credulous, and avaricious sycophants ; and first among the besiegers to effect a breach— through treachery of one of the garrison, Vitellini— is a pretended Scottish noble, " Lord Scot."

This person, who shortly presented a woman named Fry as " Lady Scot," was one of a gang of sharpers ; and " his lordship's " first achievement (since his effects had not arrived from the North and he had no

London banker) was to borrow two hundred pounds from the Comte. What a wondrous lever is flattery !

Scot had in his possession a Cabalistic manuscript, which he submitted to Cagliostro, begging him to point out therefrom a lucky number in the lottery or at the roulette tables. The Comte, in his English memoirs, tells us that he obeyed, but with little confidence ; he predicted 20 as the successful number for the following November 6.

Out of the borrowed two hundred pounds, Scot ventured a small sum, and won. Cagliostro selected 25 for the next drawing ; and Scot won a hundred guineas. We are informed that the numbers 55 and 57 now being announced, with equal success, for the 18th, Cagliostro declined to predict further. No doubt he was determined to challenge fortune on his own behalf in future.

At about this time he discovered, too, that the pretended peer was a mere swindler, and forthwith he closed his doors to Scot and company. The gang was very shortly reduced to sore straits. The sharpers' faith in Cagliostro remained unshaken ; they alternately implored and threatened, so fully persuaded were they that the Count's unkindness alone stood between them and fortune.

Finally, the woman Fry gained access to Lorenza, begging her to intercede with her husband. Cagliostro, probably hoping to rid himself of them all, named the number 8 for the next lottery. We read with great astonishment that number 8 was awarded the first prize, and that Scot and company thus cleared fifteen hundred guineas.

In this way the Comte became involved in the mysterious affair of the necklace—the true facts of which defy research. As one author says, " Necklaces were evidently fated to bring him misfortune "—a reference to the notorious case of the diamond necklace.

It was out of the lottery proceeds that Mrs. Fry purchased a handsome necklace at a pawnbroker's for ninety guineas. She is said to have ordered a richly chased gold box at a jeweller's, and to have concealed the necklace in it. Seeking another meeting with Lorenza, she urged her to accept the casket as a token of esteem, without mentioning that it contained the necklace.

This according to one account ; but both Figuier and d'Almeras state that the necklace was handed to Cagliostro by Mrs. Fry owing to his having persuaded her that by burying the diamonds he could cause them to become soft and grow to double their size ; then, by the application of a rose-coloured powder which he showed her, he could recover their pristine hardness, and thus increase their value a hundredfold ; d'Almeras naïvely adds, " Cagliostro mit les diamants non pas dans la terre, mais dans sa poche."

Then once more the vultures descended upon the Comte ; until at last, exasperated beyond endurance, Cagliostro seems to have forcibly ejected Fry from the house. Very promptly that lady caused his arrest and instituted an action for the recovery of the neck-lace ! Furthermore, Fry accused both Cagliostro and Lorenza of sorcery and of foretelling lottery numbers by the aid of the devil !

This charge actually came up before Mr. Justice Miller, and the necklace case was tried before the Lord Chief Justice of the Common Pleas. In the mean-time, Cagliostro having been released from prison on bail, he was waited upon by a knavish attorney,

Reynolds, who offered to compromise the actions upon
certain onerous conditions. Whilst these were under
discussion, in upon the Comte rushed Scot, covering
him with a pistol and promising him instant death
unless he revealed the secret of predicting winning
numbers and of transmutation !

Cagliostro, however, whatever his moral lackings,
did not lack spirit ; he was not the man to succumb
to this kind of coercion. He defied Scot and Reynolds,
and invited them to depart. This, perforce, they did,
swearing vengeance against him, and shortly afterwards the Comte was called upon to surrender to his
bail.

London now had become an uncomfortable abode
for Cagliostro ; when at last he escaped from English
law, and from Scot and company, poorer by some two
thousand nine hundred pounds, he quitted the land
which had treated his wisdom so unkindly.

V. AUDIENCE WITH THE COMTE DE SAINT-GERMAIN

We shall now accompany Cagliostro to Holstein, and
to the famous interview from which dates the rise of
his fortunes. It was in Holstein that he prostrated
himself before the renowned man of mystery, his
immediate and distinguished predecessor in the Cabalistic arts—Saint-Germain (reputed to be the issue of
an Arabian princess by a *ginn*).

According to the author of the *Mémoires authentiques pour servir à l'Histoire du Comte de Cagliostro*,
published in 1785, he demanded an audience with the
man of inscrutable mystery, in order that he might
prostrate himself before the *dieu des croyants* or " god

of the believers." The Comte de Saint-Germain appointed two in the morning as the hour for the interview, which moment having arrived, say the *Mémoires*, Cagliostro and his wife, clothed in white garments clasped about the waist with girdles of rose-colour, presented themselves at the temple of mystery, which was the abode of the " god " whom they had come to adore.

The drawbridge was lowered, and a man six feet in height, clothed in a long grey robe, led them into a dimly lighted chamber. Therein some doors sprang suddenly open, and they beheld a temple illuminated by innumerable wax lights, with the Comte de Saint-Germain enthroned upon the altar ; at his feet two acolytes swung golden thuribles, which diffused sweet aromatic perfumes. The divinity bore upon his breast a diamond pentagram of almost intolerable radiance. A majestic white statue upheld on the steps of the altar a vase inscribed " Elixir of Immortality," whilst a vast mirror was upon the wall, and before it a living being, majestic as the statue, paced to and fro. Above the mirror were the singular words—" Store House of Wandering Souls." The most solemn silence prevailed in this retreat, but at length a voice, yet scarcely that of any one man, pronounced these words :

" Who are you ? Whence come you ? What would you ? "

The Comte and Comtesse di Cagliostro prostrated themselves, and the former answered, after a long pause :

" I come to invoke the god of the believers, the father of truth. I come to demand of him one of the fourteen thousand seven hundred secrets which are treasured in his breast ; I come to proclaim myself his slave, his apostle."

The god did not respond, but after a long silence the same voice asked :

"What does the partner of thy long wanderings desire ? "

" To obey and to serve," answered Lorenza.

Coincident with her words, profound darkness succeeded the glare of light, uproar followed on silence ; terror descended upon the visitors to the shrine, and a loud and menacing cry came :

" Woe to those who cannot pass the tests ! "

Cagliostro and his wife were immediately separated to undergo their respective trials ; which, we are told, they endured with exemplary fortitude, and particulars whereof may be found in the *Mémoires*.   When the romantic initiation was over, the two postulants were led back into the temple, with the promise of admission to the divine mysteries. There a man draped in a long mantle cried to them :

" Know ye that the *arcanum* of our great art is the government of mankind, and that the one means to rule mankind is never to tell mankind the truth. Do not foolishly regulate your actions in accordance with the precepts of common sense ; rather outrage reason and indomitably maintain every incredible absurdity. Remember that reproduction is the primary power in nature, politics, and society alike; that it is a madness with mortals to be immortal, to know the future although they fail to comprehend the present, and to be spiritual whilst grovelling in the grossly material ! "

After this harangue the orator genuflected before the divinity of the temple and retired. At the same moment a man of gigantic stature led the Comtesse to the feet of the immortal Comte de Saint-Germain, who addressed her modestly thus :

" Marked out from my tenderest youth for greatness, I employed myself in ascertaining the nature of true glory. Politics appeared to me nothing but the science of deception; war the art of assassination; philosophy the ambition of imbecility; physics quaint conceits about nature and the habitual mistakes of persons suddenly translated to a country utterly unknown to them; theology the science of misery born of human pride; history the contemplation of perpetual perfidity and blundering. Thence I concluded that the statesman was a skilful liar, the hero an illustrious idiot, the philosopher an eccentric creature, the physician a pitiable and blind person, the theologian a fanatical pedagogue, and the historian a wordmonger.

" Then did I hear of the divinity of this temple. I cast my cares upon him, with my doubts and my aspirations. When he took possession of my soul he enabled me to perceive all objects in a new light; I began to read futurity. This universe so limited, so narrow, so desert-like, was now bordered only by infinity. I abode not only with those who are, but with those who were. He united me to the loveliest women of antiquity. . . ."

To illustrate the spiritual character of the ladies with whom Saint-Germain claimed acquaintance, I append the whole passage in the original French of Figuier : " Il me fit connaître les plus belles femmes de l'antiquité—cette Aspasie, cette Leontium, cette Sapho, cette Faustine, cette Semiramis, cette Irène, dont on a tant parté ! "

When the service was finished, the costume of ordinary life was resumed. A superb repast terminated the ceremony. During the course of the banquet the two guests were informed that the Elixir of Immor-

tality was merely Tokay coloured green or red according
to the necessities of the case. Several essential precepts were enjoined upon them; among others that
they must detest, avoid, and calumniate men of understanding, but flatter, encourage, and blind fools;
that they must spread abroad with much mystery the
report that the Comte de Saint-Germain was five
hundred years of age; that they must make gold, but
dupes above all.

The facts of this singular encounter unfortunately
are not available from any reliable source. If it occurred
as above narrated, it served beyond doubt to confirm
Cagliostro in his ambitious projects; and certainly
a marked change had taken place in the adventurer
since his second visit to England, as is described by
Figuier:

" His language, his mien, his manners, are all transformed. His conversation turns only upon his travels
in Egypt, to Mecca, and to other remote places, upon
the secret sciences into which he was initiated at the
foot of the pyramid, on the *arcana* of nature which
he has discovered. At the same time, he talks little,
and more often envelops himself in mysterious silence.
When interrogated, he only deigns, for the most part, to
draw his symbol—a serpent with an apple in its mouth
and pierced by a dart—meaning that human wisdom
should be silent respecting the mysteries which it has
unravelled. . . ."

VI. THE HEALING ART OF CAGLIOSTRO

From this time onward the Comte takes the stage
in the character of a new Æsculapius. Louis Figuier
says—*Histoire du Merveilleux*, tome iv.—that as

Cagliostro came into prominence at the time when Mesmer was engaging much attention, each was regarded as the rival of the other, and it was asserted that they both drew their powers from the same source. Cagliostro, less restrained in the application of his knowledge of the use of the common agent, more catholic than Mesmer, seems to have generalized the employment of magnetism.

It is known that Cagliostro cured quite as successfully as Mesmer, although he was without title and without other mission than that which he gave to himself ; but he cured without passes, without iron wands, without manipulations, and by a mere touch ; which approached more to Gassner and Greatrakes than to Mesmer. Another difference : Cagliostro did not exploit his patients. On the contrary, in all the towns that he visited, medicines were prepared by his agents at his own expense, and all those who came to him to be cured received these palliatives at his hands, with relief for their wants and even for the needs of their families.

Cagliostro was lavish, and he proved it by the generous alms which he distributed in his path. For the rest, profoundly silent on the origin of his fortune, he maintained the same silence as to the nature of his agent, and betrayed nothing to savants, doctors, or academicians. He proceeded with audacity, operated with authority, and everywhere produced an astonishment which occasioned, without any doubt, a great part of his success. Louis XVI, who ridiculed Mesmer, pronounced guilty of *lèse-majesté* (or something similar) whomsoever should injure or cast reflection upon Cagliostro.

But the medical cures of Cagliostro were merely a

hors-d'œuvre in his career of a universal magnetizer, and served only as a means of obtaining popularity with the masses.

His imposing figure and haughty manner, his numerous suite, and the extensive train that accompanied him on his journey, naturally attracted all eyes and caused the vulgar spirits to regard him with an admiration almost idolatrous. He seems, moreover, to have exercised a fascination over all who approached him. All sorts of sciences and marvellous faculties were attributed to this latest man of mystery. The following is a description by a contemporary who claimed to have been intimately acquainted with Cagliostro:

" He is a doctor initiated in the Cabalistic art ; in that part of the art which consists of communication with the dead and absent. He is a Rosicrucian ; he is possessed of all the human sciences and is an adept in the transmutation of base metal into gold. He is a good Samaritan, who treats the poor without thought of gain, and sells, for a consideration, immortality to the rich. . . ."

Bordes, in his *Lettres sur la Suisse*, describes Cagliostro as an admirable man :

" His face," he says, " indicates spirit, discloses genius, and his eyes of fire search the depths of the soul. He knows nearly every language of Europe and Asia ; his eloquence astounds, entrances even those of whom he speaks lightly."

I append other descriptions of him. Carlyle says : " A most portentous face of scoundrelism ; a fat snub abominable face ; dew-lapped, flat-nosed, greasy, full of greediness, sensuality, ox-like obstinacy ; the most perfect quack face produced by the eighteenth century ! "

Madame d'Oberkirch in her *Mémoires* writes : " He was not, strictly speaking, handsome, but I have never seen a more remarkable face. His glance was so penetrating that one might almost be tempted to call it supernatural. I could not describe the expression of his eyes ; it was, so to speak, a mixture of flame and ice. It attracted and repelled at the same time, and whilst it inspired terror it aroused along with it an irresistible curiosity."

The *Gazette de Santé* completed the painting of this personage :

" M. le Comte de Cagliostro is the possessor, it is said, of the marvellous secrets of a famous Adept who has discovered the Elixir of Life. . . . M. le Comte is painted in an Oriental garb, his portrait is always to be seen at Medina, at the house of the *Grand Seigneur* ; he never sleeps but in an arm-chair ; he satisfies himself with a meal of macaroni. He is learned in the medicine and chemistry of Egypt, and suggests fifty thousand écus to found an Egyptian hospital. He does not hold communication with others of the art, but, to distinguish himself from them, he cures gratuitously. He is named M. le Chevalier de I . . . It is said that his remedy is the same as that of a famous operator who had watches for buttons, like the wife of another who carried chimes in her ear-rings."

From their initiation by the Comte de Saint-Germain the Comte and Madame di Cagliostro proceeded into Courland, where they established Masonic lodges, according to the sublime rite of Egyptian Freemasonry. Madame was an excellent preacher to captivate hearts and enchain imagination, and her beauty fascinated a large number of the Courlandaise nobility.

At Mittau, Cagliostro attracted the attention of

persons of high rank, who were led by his conversation to regard him as an extraordinary person. By means of his Freemasonry he began to obtain an ascendancy over the minds of the nobles, some of whom, discontented with the reigning duke, are actually represented as offering him the sovereignty of the country !

The Comtesse, at this time, was about five-and-twenty years of age, and radiant with grace and beauty ; indeed, she looked like an incarnation of immortal loveliness, a very goddess of love ; " and it is possible that the crowds of young men and old, who at all convenient seasons haunted the perfumed chambers of this enchantress, were attracted less by their belief in her occult powers than from admiration of her languishing bright eyes."

In St. Petersburg they soon became the one topic of conversation. The miraculous cure of a nobleman's child exalted Cagliostro to the pinnacle of popularity ; but the extraordinary beauty of Madame, which thus far had powerfully contributed to his success, now brought about Cagliostro's banishment.

The Prime Minister, Potemkin, says one authority,[1] then at the outset of his favour, goes to see him, and has his reasons for going again, reasons to which the fair and fascinating Lorenza is no stranger. According to one of the thousand reports which were then in circulation, Catherine herself intervenes in order to get rid of this rival, offering her thirty thousand roubles, which the lady refuses in favour of twice the amount on the part of the favourite. The story is highly improbable. Catherine had better means than that of getting rid of her rivals, and she has given too amusing

[1] Waliszewski.

an account, in a letter to Grimm, of the prowess of Cagliostro in her capital :

" He came here calling himself a colonel in the service of Spain, and Spanish by birth, pretending to be a sorcerer, having spirits at his beck and call. When I heard that, I said : ' This man has made a mistake in coming here ; nowhere will he succeed so badly as in Russia.'

" We do not burn sorcerers here, and for twenty years there has only been one single affair in which there were supposed to be any sorcerers, and then the Senate asked to see them, and, when they had been summoned, they were found to be quite stupid and perfectly innocent.

" M. Cagliostro, however, has come just at the right moment for himself, when several lodges of Freemasons, which had taken up Swedenborg's principles, were anxious at all cost to see spirits ; they therefore ran to Cagliostro, who declared he had all the secrets of Dr. Falk, an intimate friend of the Duc de Richelieu, and who formerly sacrificed to the black goat in the midst of Vienna. . . . M. Cagliostro then produced his marvellous cures ; he pretended to extract quicksilver from a gouty man's leg, and he was taken in the act of pouring a teaspoonful of quicksilver into the water in which he put the gouty man. Then he produced dyes which would dye nothing, and chemical preparations which would not work. . . . After which, it has been discovered that he could hardly read or write.

" Finally, overwhelmed with debts, he took refuge in the cellar of M. Ielaguine, where he drank as much champagne and English beer as he could. One day, apparently, he exceeded the usual measure, for, on leaving his repast, he hooked himself on to the wig of the secretary of the house, who boxed his ears, whereupon there was a free fight ; M. Ielaguine, tired alike of his cellar-rat and of the expenditure of the wine and beer, as well as of his secretary's complaints, politely persuaded him to take his departure in a *kibitka*, and not in the air as he threatened ; and in order that his creditors should put no hindrance in the way of this brisk means of conveyance, he gave him an old soldier to accompany him and Madame la Comtesse as far as Mittau. There is the whole story of Cagliostro, in which there is everything but the marvellous. I never saw him, even at a distance, nor had any inclination to."

Madame Cagliostro, adds this chronicler, seems to have had no share after all in the failure of the expedition ; "Catherine of Russia always had, as we know, an exceptional allowance for the amorous caprices of the most capricious and amorous of her favourites."

She had, also, the tact which selects ridicule as the most potent weapon to slay romance. Her letter, in which there is no mention of Lorenza, except that of her departure, has no historical value.

According to another account, obliged to quit Russia by reason of the jealousy of the chief physician of the Empress, M. le Comte di Cagliostro proposed to this official that each should make up four pills of the most violent poison.

" I will take yours," he said to the Russian doctor, " and I will afterwards swallow a drop of my elixir, which will cure me. You will take mine, and cure yourself if you can."

This reasonable challenge was not accepted.

VII. NO. 1, RUE SAINT-CLAUDE

With Cagliostro's arrival in Paris, we reach the most extraordinary part of his career. Paris, no doubt, had for long been the Mecca of his dreams, and, well aware that the capital was already overfull of magnetic healers and mesmerists, he attacked Parisian society in the guise of a practical sorcerer, at the same time proclaiming himself the restorer of Egyptian Freemasonry and the founder of a new philosophy.

He claimed to possess the science of the priests of Ancient Egypt, and his conversation usually turned upon three points : (*a*) the Universal Medicine, the secret of which was known to him ; (*b*) Egyptian Freemasonry, which he had come to restore, and of which he had already established lodges ; (*c*) the Philosopher's Stone, which he proposed to obtain by means of the solidification of quicksilver.

Furthermore he claimed, as Saint-Germain had claimed before him, to have a process for giving to cotton the appearance and properties of silk, and one for softening marble and afterwards restoring it to its pristine hardness—of great interest to sculptors; another was that for increasing the size of rubies, emeralds, and diamonds ; fourth, a means of feeding a pig upon arsenic, and from its carcass manufacturing a fulminating poison.

(It is interesting to compare this process with that whereby—according to a contemporary historian— the Borgias procured their liquid poison—as distinct from the notorious *Contarella*. Their method, then, was to administer arsenic to a boar, and, so soon as the poison began to take effect, hang the animal up

by the heels. Convulsions supervened ; and a froth,
deadly and abundant, ran out from his jaws. It was
this froth, collected into a silver vessel and subsequently transferred to a bottle hermetically sealed,
which constituted the liquid poison.)

But perhaps the most curious of Cagliostro's claims
was that of being able to render sea-water as com-
bustible as oil. On his last visit to London he
asserted that he could light the Metropolis by such
means.

Cagliostro's task, according to himself, was to
restore the knowledge of God in all its purity. The
delegates of the French lodges, having considered his
pretensions, declared in their report that they had
seen in him " a promise of truth which none of the
great Masters had so completely developed before,
and perfectly analogous with the blue masonry of
which it seems to be a sympathetic and sublime
interpretation."

No doubt the Cardinal de Rohan was in some
measure instrumental in securing Cagliostro's admission to Parisian society, but Madame's beauty played
its part as well. Paris went into rhapsodies about
the seductive Lorenza.

Says one author, " Her lips, arched in the antique
manner, of a carmine which seemed very bright in
contrast with the whiteness of her complexion, were
always motionless, as if they were never to be awakened
but by the caresses of love." " She had nobility,"
declares Casanova, " modesty, naïveté, sweetness, and
that blushing timidity which gives so much charm to
a young woman."

Accordingly, when she passed by on Djérid, her
black mare, with set figure, with animated bust, men

followed her with their looks. They fell in love with her at a distance, without having seen her.

" Her warmest partisans, her most passionate admirers were precisely those who had never looked upon her face. There were duels about her, duels proposed and accepted as to the colour of her eyes, which neither of the adversaries had ever seen, as to whether a dimple was on her right cheek or her left."

The hôtel of the Marchioness d'Orvillers, No. 1, Rue Saint-Claude, on the corner of the Boulevard Beaumarchais, to-day—for it still exists—fills one with that kind of gloom experienced in an empty theatre. This was the house that Cagliostro rented in Paris.

" And one can imagine," says Lenôtre, " without great effort, the effect which the house would produce at night, with its angular pavilions, at that time concealed by ancient trees, its deep courtyards, its wide terraces, when the flames—the live flames from the crucibles of the alchemist—showed themselves through the high window-blinds."

At the back of the house (the carriage entrance opens on to the Rue Saint-Claude), beneath a frowning porch, may be seen a stone staircase with railings of forged iron. Here once blazed in the torchlight the liveries of noble houses ; the courtyard, now so dreary and grey, was crowded with fine carriages ; there was a stamping of hoofs, a cracking of whips—a scene of the greatest animation. And how many women boasting ancient names have mounted that stone stair, with hearts thudding wildly in their breasts, to consult the mysterious Cagliostro ! How many nobles of France have passed the same way, seeking a glance from the bright eyes of Madame ! Like Dr. Dee, the Count summoned the angels to reveal the future ; he called up the mighty departed. Says the *Biographie des Contemporains* :

" There was hardly a fine lady in Paris who would not sup with the shade of Lucretius in the apartments of Cagliostro ; a military officer who would not discuss the arts of war with Cæsar, Hannibal, or Alexander ; or an advocate or counsellor who would not argue legal points with the shade of Cicero."

Cagliostro received in a vast and sumptuously appointed apartment on the first floor, whilst Lorenza lived a comparatively retired life, only being visible at certain hours before a select company, " and in a diaphanous and glamorous costume."

Indeed, fortune smiled upon the thaumaturgist. The fast friendship existing between him and the Cardinal de Rohan was no doubt a powerful factor in his success, and it had been strengthened by a marvellous cure which Cagliostro effected. One of the brothers of the great Cardinal—the Prince de Soubise— being dangerously ill, certain doctors had pronounced that he was suffering from a wasting disease, others that he had contracted scarlet fever ; but all were agreed that it was a desperate case.

The Cardinal, who had unbounded faith in the great empiric, prayed him earnestly to visit his brother, and one day took him in his coach and conducted him to the Hôtel de Soubise, where, without mentioning any name, he announced " a doctor."

As the faculty had declared the patient incurable, the family had left the Prince to die ; a few servants only were to be seen in the sick-room when the Cardinal and Cagliostro entered. The latter requested to be left alone for a time with the patient, and all withdrew.

" What," inquires Figuier, " did Cagliostro do,

closeted with the Prince ? Did he hypnotize him, or did he himself fall into a state of somnambulism ? "

None can say, since none ever knew ; but eventually this man of mystery summoned the Cardinal and said :

"If my prescriptions are followed, in two days Monseigneur le Prince de Soubise will leave his bed, and will walk in this room ; in eight days he will ride in a coach ; in three weeks he will attend the Court at Versailles ! "

"When one has consulted the Oracle one can do nothing but obey." The Cardinal hastened to place himself at the disposal of Cagliostro, who, the same day, returned with him to the Hôtel de Soubise, this time provided with a little phial of liquid, of which he administered ten drops to the patient.

"To-morrow," he said, "we shall give the Prince five drops less ; the day after he will take only two drops of this elixir, and he will be up in the evening."

The event surpassed the prediction of the Oracle ; for the same day, following this visit, the Prince found himself well enough to receive a few friends. In the evening he rose, walked around his room, talked with animation, and eventually seated himself in an arm-chair.

He even felt well enough to ask for a wing of chicken. But this was refused, as the prescription of the doctor—still unknown—did not allow of that diet.

From the fourth day he was convalescent, but it was not until the evening of the fifth that he was allowed to partake of his wing of chicken.

No one in the Hôtel de Soubise as yet was aware that Cagliostro was the anonymous physician who had given his attentions to the Prince. He was only named at the moment of the cure, and this name, already so famous, was from that time never again referred to as that of a charlatan. Ennobled by this miraculous cure, his fame was noised throughout the city and at the Court, amid unbounded enthusiasm.

Some little time afterwards, as many as two hundred coaches stationed themselves along the Rue Saint-Claude. At Versailles, the King and Queen, having heard of the good news concerning this wonderful and unexpected recovery, openly gave evidence of their great joy, and sent messengers to compliment the Prince de Soubise upon his return to health, which amounted to an official consecration of the glory of Cagliostro.

His bust was executed in marble by Houdon and cast in bronze, and beneath his portrait, after the bust, was engraved the following poetic inscription :

> De l'ami des humains reconnaissez les traits,
> Tous ses jours sont marqués par de nouveaux bienfaits.
> Il prolonge la vie, il secourt l'indigence ;
> Le plaisir d'être utile est seul sa récompense.

He was now referred to as the " divine " Cagliostro. His portraits could be seen everywhere on snuff-boxes, rings, and upon the fans of the women. Paris was set wondering at his enchantments and prodigies. At Versailles, and in the presence of several distinguished nobles, he is said to have caused the apparition in mirrors, vases, etc., not merely of the spectra of absent or deceased persons, but animated and moving beings of a phantasmal description, including many dead men and women selected by the astounded spectators.

But Cagliostro was no longer young, whereas Lorenza was in the flower of her beauty ; and he is said " for the first time to have experienced the pangs of jealousy, on account of a certain Chevalier d'Oisement, with whom Madame had had several assignations."

Nevertheless, he prosecuted his plans to reform Freemasonry according to the Egyptian rite, with unabated vigour. He had cases filled with statuettes of Isis, Osiris, Anubis, and other deities, covered with mystic hieroglyphics ; and these he distributed among his disciples. The lodge of Isis, whereof Madame di Cagliostro was Grand Mistress, counted in 1784, among its Adepts, some of the most prominent women of title in France.

Among the many anecdotes bearing upon this phase of his career, the following is worthy of citation, if only because so many versions exist, and for the reason that an episode almost identical is related of the celebrated Comte de Saint-Germain.

One day, then, whilst passing along the picture-gallery in the Louvre—so one account tells us—Cagliostro halted before the picture by Jouvenet, " The Descent from the Cross," and began to weep. Several of his companions questioned him as to the cause of his emotion.

" Alas ! " he replied, " I shed tears for the death of this great moralist, for this man so good with whom I have had intimate intercourse. Indeed, we dined together at the house of Pontius Pilate."

" Of whom do you speak ? " inquired the Duc de Richelieu, stupefied.

" Of Jesus Christ. I knew him well ! "

Cagliostro is said, too, at this time (again in imitation of Saint-Germain) to have had in his service a valet who, by his mysterious silence, considerably added to the impression created by his master.

M. d'Hannibal, a German noble, one day seized this fellow by the ear, and in a tone half jesting and half angry cried :

"Rascal! You will tell me now the true age of your master!"

But the valet was not to be bullied ; and after a few moments of earnest reflection he replied :

"Listen, monsieur—I cannot tell you the age of M. le Comte, as it is unknown to me. He has always been to me as he appears to you ; young, gay, *buvant sec*. All I can tell you is that I have been in his service since the decline of the Roman Republic ; for we agreed upon my salary on the very day that Cæsar perished at the hand of the assassin in the Senate!"

VIII. THE BANQUET OF SPIRITS AND INITIATION OF ISIS

I shall now invite you to attend one of Cagliostro's magical banquets at No. 1, Rue Saint-Claude.

According to the *Mémoires authentiques pour servir à l'Histoire du Comte de Cagliostro*, the great thaumaturgist announced that at a private supper, given to six guests, he would evoke the spirits of any dead persons whom they named to him, and that the phantoms, apparently substantial, should seat themselves at the banquet.

Mr. A. E. Waite says, "The repast took place with the knowledge, and, it may be supposed, with the connivance of Lorenza" ; but Louis Figuier states that it took place *unknown* to Madame : "Le souper eut lieu rue Saint-Claude, où demeurait Cagliostro, et à l'insu de Lorenza."

At midnight the guests were assembled : a round

"THE MAGICIAN'S STAIRCASE"—No. 1 RUE ST. CLAUDE

table, laid for twelve, was spread, with extraordinary luxury, in a dining-room where all the appointments were in harmony with the approaching Cabalistic operation. The six guests, with Cagliostro, took their seats, and thus thirteen were designed to be present at table.

The supper was served, the servants were dismissed with threats of instant death if they dared to open the doors before they were summoned. Each guest demanded the deceased person whom he desired to see. Cagliostro took the names, placed them in the pocket of his gold-embroidered vest, and announced that with no further preparation than a simple invocation on his part, the evoked spirits would appear in flesh and blood, for, according to the Egyptian dogma, there were in reality no dead.

These guests of the other world, asked for and expected with trembling anxiety, were the Duc de Choiseul, Voltaire, d'Alembert, Diderot, the Abbé de Voisenon, and Montesquieu. Their names were pronounced slowly in a loud voice, and with all the concentrated determination of the Adept's will ; and after a moment of intolerable doubt, the evoked guests appeared very unobtrusively, and took their seats with the quiet courtesy which had characterized them in life !

The first question put to them, when the awe of their presence had somewhat abated, was as to their situation in the world beyond.

"There is no world beyond," replied d'Alembert. "Death is simply the cessation of the evils which have tortured us. No pleasure is experienced, but, on the other hand, there is no suffering. I have not met with Mademoiselle Lespinasse, but neither have I seen

Lorignet. Some deceased persons who have recently joined us inform me that I am almost forgotten. I am, however, consoled. Men are unworthy of the trouble we take about them. I never loved them, now I despise them."

" What has become of your learning ? " asked M. de —— of Diderot.

" I was not learned, as people commonly supposed. I merely adapted all that I read, and in writing I borrowed right and left. Hence the disconnected style of my books, which will be unheard of in half a century, *The Encyclopædia*, with which I am credited, does not belong to me. The duty of an editor is simply to set in order his subjects. The man who showed most talent was the compiler of the index, yet no one has dreamed of recognizing his claims to honour ! "

" I praised the enterprise," said Voltaire, " for it accorded with my philosophical opinions. Talking of philosophy, I am none too certain that I was in the right. I have learned strange things since my death, and have conversed with a half-dozen Popes. They are good to listen to. Clement XIV and Benedict, above all, are men of infinite intelligence and good sense."

" That which rather annoys me," said the Duc de Choiseul, " is that there is no sex in our present habitation. Whatever may be said of this fleshly envelope, 'twas by no means so bad an invention."

" That which has afforded me great pleasure," said the Abbé Voisenon, " is that amongst us one is cured of the folly of intelligence. You cannot imagine how I have been jeered at about my absurd romances. I expiate almost daily the mistakes of my mortal existence."

.   .   .   .   .

Throughout these days, however, Cagliostro proceeded with the dearest of all his projects, viz. the spread of his Egyptian Masonic rite, into which women subsequently were admitted, a course of magical instruction being conducted for the purpose by Madame di Cagliostro.

The postulants admitted to this course were thirty-six in number, and all males were excluded. Lorenza was the Grand Mistress of Egyptian Masonry, as her husband was himself the grand and sublime Copt. The neophytes were required to contribute each of them the sum of one hundred louis, to abstain from all intimacy with mankind, and to submit to everything which might be imposed on them. A big mansion was hired in the Rue Verte, Faubourg Saint-Honoré, at that period a lonely part of the city, as lonely as was the Rue Saint-Claude. The building was surrounded by gardens and magnificent trees. The ceremony of initiation took place shortly before midnight on August 7, 1785.

On entering the first apartment, says Figuier, the ladies were obliged to disrobe and to endue a white garment, with a coloured girdle. They were divided into six groups, distinguished by the tint of their girdles. A large veil was also provided, and they were conducted to a temple lighted from the roof, and furnished with thirty-six arm-chairs upholstered in black satin. Lorenza, clothed in white, was seated on a kind of throne, supported by two tall figures, so habited that their sex might not be determined. The light was lowered by degrees until surrounding objects could scarcely be distinguished, when the Grand Mistress commanded the ladies to uncover their left legs as far as the thigh, and raising the right arm, to rest it upon an adjoining pillar.

Two young women then entered sword in hand, and with silken ropes bound all the ladies together by the arms and legs. Then, after a period of impressive silence, Lorenza pronounced an oration which I shall not quote at length, but which advocated fervidly the emancipation of womankind from the shameful bonds imposed on them by the lords of creation.

These bonds were symbolized by the silken ropes from which the fair initiates were released at the end of the harangue, when they were conducted into separate apartments, each opening on the garden. Here they met with most incredible experiences.

Some were pursued by men who unmercifully persecuted them with barbarous solicitations; others encountered less ferocious admirers, who sighed in languishing postures at their feet. More than one discovered the double of her own lover; but the oath they had all taken rendered them inexorable, and all faithfully fulfilled what was required of them. The new spirit infused into regenerate woman triumphed throughout the six-and-thirty initiates, who re-entered, palpitating but triumphant, the twilight of the vaulted temple, to receive the congratulations of the high priestess.

When they had breathed a little after their trials, the vaulted roof opened suddenly, and, on a sphere of gold, there descended a man, naked as the unfallen Adam, holding a serpent in his hand, and having a flaming star upon his head.

The Grand Mistress announced that this was the genius of Truth, the immortal, the divine Cagliostro, issued without procreation from the bosom of our father Abraham, and the depositary of all that hath been, is, or shall be known in the universe. He was there to initiate them into the secrets of which they had been fraudulently deprived.

Thereupon the Grand Copt commanded them to dispense with the profanity of clothing, for if they would embrace truth they must be as naked as itself. The high priestess, setting the example, unbound her girdle and permitted her drapery to fall to the ground, and the fair initiates, following her example, exposed themselves, in all the nudity of their charms, to the glances of the Grand Copt, who then commenced his revelations.

He informed his beloved daughters that the much-abused Cabalistic art was the secret of doing good to humanity. It was initiation into the *arcana* of nature, and the power to make use of her occult forces. The visions which they beheld in the garden, where so many had seen and recognized those who were dearest to their hearts, proved the reality of hermetic operations. They had shown themselves worthy to know the truth ; he undertook to instruct them by gradations. It was sufficient at the outset to inform them that the sublime objective of that Egyptian Freemasonry which he had brought from the secret heart of the Orient was the happiness of mankind. This happiness was illimitable in its nature, including material enjoyments as well as spiritual peace.

Cagliostro concluded his harangue by bidding his hearers renounce a deceiving sex, and let the kiss of friendship symbolize the purity of their hearts. The high priestess instructed them in the nature of this Platonic embrace.

Thereupon the Grand Copt seated himself again upon the sphere of gold, and was borne away through the roof. At the same time the floor opened, lights blazed into being, and a table, splendidly adorned and luxuriously spread, came up through the floor. The ladies (despite their abjuration of the deceiving sex) were joined by their lovers *in propria persona*, and the supper was followed by dancing and various diversions, which continued until the small hours of the morning.

IX. THE SECRET OF ST. ANGELO

It was at about this time that Madame de la Motte, the adventuress, one day surprised Lorenza, under compromising circumstances, with the Chevalier d'Oisement—a gentleman whom I have already mentioned. At any rate, so it is averred ; and the price of Madame's silence is measurable by the sudden intimacy which sprang up between the Cagliostros and the la Mottes. This intimacy later was to implicate the Count in the astounding affair of the diamond necklace ; was to bring him, in company with Cardinal de Rohan, to the Bastille.

Beugnot, who met the thaumaturgist in the salon of Madame de la Motte, speaks of his " paying very tender compliments to the mistress of the house." In addition, Beugnot says that he spoke " of heaven, the stars, the great *arcanum*, Memphis, hierophancy, transcendental chemistry, giants, immense animals, and a town in the interior of Africa ten times as great as Paris." Madame de la Motte he called his fawn, his gazelle, his swan.

How different was his language a short time later, when, standing his trial for complicity in the necklace case, he said of the same lady that " she was *mentiris impudentissime*, which two words he begged her counsel to translate for her, as it was not polite to tell her so in French."

After his acquittal, Cagliostro, in obedience to a *lettre de cachet*, lost little time in leaving Paris. He returned again to London, where he was well received and from whence he addressed his " Letter to the French People," dated June 26, 1786. This letter created a profound sensation ; it is impossible to deny that it struck a shrewd blow against the ancient fortress of the Bastille—a blow that shook those gloomy towers to their foundations—the sound of which penetrated, though it might be but as a whisper—to the very deepest and very darkest cell of the dreadful place—which echoed boomingly throughout France— which, I verily believe, was the first tocsin heralding the Terror.

" Are all State prisons like the Bastille ? . . . A barbarous silence is the least of the crimes there committed. For six months I was within fifteen feet of my wife without knowing it. Others have been buried there for thirty years, are reputed dead, are unhappy in not being dead, having, like Milton's damned souls, only so much light in their abyss as to perceive the impenetrable darkness that enwraps them. I said it in captivity, and I repeat it a free man : there is no crime but is amply expiated by six months in the Bastille. . . .

" You have all that is needed for happiness, Frenchmen. . . . All you want, my good friends, is one little thing : to be sure of lying in your own beds when you are irreproachable. To labour for this happy revolution is a task worthy of your *parlements*. It is only difficult to feeble souls. . . .

" Yes, I declare to you . . . your States-General

will be convoked, your Bastille shall become a public promenade, you . . . will achieve glory in the abolition of *lettres de cachet*. . . ."

But now it was that Morande, editor of the *Courrier de l'Europe* (published in London) attacked Cagliostro unmercifully. The articles ran through several numbers of the paper, commencing September 1 and ending November 1, 1786. Although the attack proved fatal to its subject, the Count's retort at least served to call down ridicule upon the journalist; for he challenged the latter to a duel of arsenicated sucking pig (cochon de lait)! This original mode of conflict Morande declined to essay.

Against this man, Morande, a recent inquirer—Trowbridge—makes a strange charge. In short, he attempts to prove (rightly or wrongly) that Balsamo and Cagliostro were two distinct personages, who had no connexion with one another beyond the fact of having married Italian wives bearing the same surnames. He writes:

" As late as the date of his trial in the affair of the diamond necklace no suggestion of the identity of the two characters was ever mooted. The story appears to owe its origin to the fertile brain of one of the greatest scoundrels of whom European history holds record, the notorious blackmailer Theveneau de Morande."

He goes on to say that the editor of the *Courrier de l'Europe* was a spy and subsidized journalist in the pay of the French Government. The latter, fearing that Cagliostro's acquittal in the necklace trial would reflect unfavourably on the Queen, instructed Morande to ruin Cagliostro's reputation, which he forthwith attempted to do in his journal. It may be mentioned, too, that Cagliostro, in *Une Lettre au Peuple anglais*,

1786, denied having been in London in 1771, and asserted that he was not Balsamo.

But the Count's reputation was damned. The following advertisement was inserted by him in the *Morning Herald* for November 1786 :

To all True Masons

In the Name of 9, 5, 8, 14, 20, 1, 8 ; -9, 5, 18, 20, 18.[1]
The Time is at hand when the Building of the New Temple, or New Jerusalem 3, 8, 20, 17, 8, must begin ; this is to invite all True Masons in London to join in the Name of 9, 5, 18, 20, 18 (the only one in whom is a Divine 19, 17, 9, 13, 9, 19, 23) to meet to-morrow Evening, the 3d. instant, 1786 (or 5790) at Nine o'clock at Riley's, Great Queen Street ; to lay a plan for the laying the first stone of the foundation of the True 3, 8, 20, 17, 8 ; in this visible world, being the material representative Temple of the Spiritual 9, 5, 17, 20, 18, 11, 5, 12.

A Mason, and Member of the new 3, 8, 20, 17, 8.

It is an interesting advertisement, too, because it would appear that Cagliostro had the intention of forming a lodge of the Swedenborgian rite. The wording is suggestive ; and we know that he consorted

---

[1] The cipher is a very simple one ; A = 1, B = 2, and so on, the letters I and J being treated as one letter ; also U and V.

Line   1.—Jehovah ;—Jesus.
　　　,,   3.—Churh, *i.e.* church.
　　　,,   5.—Jesus.
　　　,,   6.—Trinity.
　　　,,   10.—Churh, *i.e.* church.
　　　,,   11.—Jerusalem.
　　　,,   13.—Churh, *i.e.* church.

for some time with the Swedenborgians during his last visit to London.

But Morande had done his work too well. D'Almeras adds : " Vox clamans in deserto ! No one came to Reilly's tavern [1] to lay the foundation stone of the true Temple, and Jehovah, that night, did not pay expenses ! "

The last mention made by Morande of Cagliostro occurred in the issue of his journal dated August 14, 1787, when he boasts of having succeeded in driving Cagliostro from England.

Figuier points out that, despite the persecution to which he was there subjected, Cagliostro committed a great error in leaving England, as he did, and in taking up an abode in Rome.

But that which brought about his downfall was the temerity with which he practised the principles of Freemasonry in the capital of the Catholic world ; and although Lorenza advised him against this, he obstinately pursued his work, and ultimately founded a lodge after the Egyptian rite. He had only three members, but amongst them was found one false brother.

Denounced by this spy, Cagliostro was arrested on September 27, 1789, by command of the Holy Office.

His papers, including the MS. entitled *Maçonnerie Égyptienne*, were seized and placed under the seals, and the inquiry was commenced which lasted for no less than eighteen months. If one considers Cagliostro's history, and admits his identity with Balsamo, there

---

[1] Reilly's tavern was the " Hercules Pillars " in Great Queen Street, and is yet standing opposite Freemasons' Hall. Reilly, Riley, or O'Reilly as his name is variously spelt was formerly proprietor of the " King's Head " in Gerrard Street, where Cagliostro was initiated.

were several episodes which could not have borne scrutiny ; but the majority of his misdeeds were committed outside Rome, and the others were covered by prescription.

On March 21, 1791, the case, conducted at such wearisome length, was taken to the General Assembly of the Holy Office, and in accordance with custom, before the Pope, on the 7th of the following April. Judgment was rendered, and Cagliostro was condemned to death.

Pope Pius VI, to whom was reserved *definitive* judgment, pronounced it in the following terms :

" Giuseppe Balsamo, accused and convicted of many crimes, and of having defied the censures and penalties pronounced against heretics, dogmatists, masters, and disciples of superstitious magic, as well as the apostolic laws of Clement XII and Benedict XIV against those who, in any way whatsoever, support and form Societies of Freemasons . . . in Rome or in any other place in the Pontifical dominions : now, by special grace, the penalty which delivers the culprit into the secular arm is the committal to prison for life in a fortress, where he will be closely guarded, without hope of grace ; and, after he has abjured heresy in the actual place of his detention, he will be absolved, and salutary penances will be prescribed, to which he must submit himself."

These " penances " (I shall be more clearly understood if I term them tortures) were of so cruel a nature in the Castle of St. Angelo, where Cagliostro was confined, that in case the people, among whom he had many partisans, should commence a movement in his favour, the report was spread abroad that he had conspired to burn Rome as Nero had done.

The still beautiful Lorenza was treated with less severity; she was condemned to perpetual seclusion in a convent, and beyond its gates she, whom so many had loved, vanished for ever from the ken of man.

All Cagliostro's papers were burned by the Holy Office; which institution, or what remains of it, preserves to this day the secret of its victim's end. A rumour was circulated that, having become insane, he had endeavoured to strangle a confessor; later, that he had strangled himself.

Meanwhile, the Revolution, which the great thaumaturgist seems, evidently enough, to have divined, was an established fact. Approaching the Italian borders, the forces of the red bonnet, like an encroaching sea, burst upon the walls of the Eternal City and swept around the Castle of St. Angelo.

Several officers of the first battalions that advanced upon Rome had scarce entered the city ere they were seeking the dungeon of Cagliostro. They had hoped to release the man, prophet or charlatan, sorcerer or saint, who had cried " Frenchmen ! . . . your Bastille shall become a public promenade ! "

They were too late. They were told that Cagliostro was dead. In what manner did he meet with his death, and at what time ? The Holy Office was dumb, and no man can ever hope to know.

" At this news," says Figuier, " our officers realized that there was no comparison to be made between the former *Parlement* of France and the tribunal of the Inquisition of Rome; and although none regretted the destruction of the Bastille, they were forced to admit that it yielded up its prey far more readily than did the Château de Saint-Ange."

So passed Cagliostro from an overcrowded stage. Of him a sound commentator has said :

That "he was a powerful mesmerist, that he could induce clairvoyance with facility in suitable subjects, that he had dabbled in Arabic occultism, that he had the faculty of healing magnetically, are points which the evidence enables us to admit, and these genuine phenomena supported his titanic impostures, being themselves supplemented, wherever they were weak or defective, by direct and prepared fraud. Thus his miraculous prophecies, delineations of absent persons, revelations of private matters, etc., may to some extent be accounted for by the insatiable curiosity and diligence which he made use of to procure knowledge of the secrets of any families with which he came into communication."

With this the opinion of Lavater may profitably be compared. The great physiognomist had several opportunities of studying Cagliostro in the course of interviews which he had with him when at Strasburg. He formed the opinion that the " Grand Copt " was a man of wonderful endowments, possessed of mediumistic powers, but untruthful and a trickster. He writes, " So long as Cagliostro retains his forehead, and I mine, we shall never here below be confidential friends." He says further : " I believe that nature produces a form like his only once in a century, and I could weep blood to think that so rare a production of nature should, by the many objections he has furnished against himself, be partly so much misconceived, and partly, by so many harshnesses and cruelties, have given just cause for offence."

Lorenza declared upon oath during her examination that many of the pupils had been prepared beforehand by her husband, but that some had been brought to him unawares, and that in regard to them she could only suppose that he had been assisted by the marvels of magical art.

To this I have nothing to add, save that, whatever his crimes, I pity from my very soul this man of undoubtedly great accomplishments who ended his days in the dungeons of the Holy Office.

MADAME BLAVATSKY

I. THE WISDOM RELIGION

IN the realm which those characters already dealt with had professedly set out and devoted their lives to explore, no one has claimed to have penetrated more deeply (I had almost said, so deeply) as Helena Petrovna Blavatsky.

Our conception of a priestess of the higher mysteries (which, by an automatic mental process, must be based upon classic ideals) will lead us wildly astray from the reality, as represented by this singular woman. The many stories current of the adventures of her stormy and wandering life ill prepare us for the H. P. Blavatsky who, her wanderings ended, was submitted to the soul-searching scrutiny of the Society for Psychical Research.

The strange being who attracted to herself such men as Crookes and Flammarion was no imposing, queenly figure, but a stout, plain woman, having a great frizzy-haired head—the hair thick and bright and splashed with grey. Her complexion was muddy to a marked degree ; but her large, pale blue eyes were wonderful eyes, eyes wherein burned the fires of a secret, hidden power.

Homely and coarse, ill-dressed, her puffy hands overloaded with jewellery, Madame H. P. Blavatsky more nearly corresponded in appearance with a seaside fortune-teller than with all one might have imagined the author of *Isis Unveiled* to be.

I have drawn your attention to the magnetic attractions of the beautiful Comtesse di Cagliostro. It is not difficult to imagine the salon of the Italian sorcerer in the Rue Saint-Claude filled with men of fashion, since it boasted an ornament so lovely. But this modern mouthpiece of the gods, lacking wholly those physical qualities which are, and have ever been, a loadstone, yet surrounded herself with men of learning and women of culture.

Wherein lay the attraction ? In the golden promise of the Secret Doctrine, in the written word, or in the *phenomena*? Evidence goes to show that the latter were, at least, extensively contributory.

The justice or injustice wherewith Madame is included in this present gallery of historical portraits affords stimulating matter for debate ; but having defined sorcery—which I did in an early chapter—I hold myself justified in classing H. P. Blavatsky amongst those who have practised it ; and I propose to deal with the events—or with some of them—which bear upon this phase of her activity. Her youth, her married life, do not concern us ; the Madame Blavatsky with whom we have to deal was created out of the ashes of that earlier woman.

In the preface to the second edition of *The Occult World*, by A. P. Sinnett, the following certificate appears :

" I certify by the present that Madame H. P. Blavatsky, now residing at Simla (British India), is from her father's side the daughter of Colonel Peter Hahn, and grand-daughter of Lieutenant-General

Alexis Hahn von Rottenstern-Hahn (a noble family of Mecklenburg, Germany, settled in Russia). And that she is from her mother's side the daughter of Helene Fadeeff, and grand-daughter of Privy-Councillor Andrew Fadeeff and of the Princess Helene Dolgorouki ; that she is the widow of the Councillor of State, Nicephore Blavatsky, late Vice-Governor of the Province of Erivan, Caucasus.

"(Signed) MAJOR-GENERAL ROSTISLAV FADEEFF
(" of H.I. Majesty's Staff,
" Joint Secretary of State at the Ministry of the Interior).

" ST. PETERSBURG, 29, LITTLE MORSKAYA,
     " September 18, 1881."

Helena Petrovna Blavatsky claimed to be the chosen priestess of the " Wisdom Religion "—the most ancient cult in the world. In order fully to appreciate her pretensions, as set forth in The Secret Doctrine, Isis Unveiled, Key to Theosophy, and Voice of the Silence, it is necessary to come to some understanding upon the point : what is this Wisdom Religion, or Secret Science ?

Firstly, and comprehensively, it numbers among its initiates the Rishis Manu, Narada and others, Buddha, Confucius, Zarathustra, Pythagoras, Plato, Apollonius of Tyana, Christ, and other world-teachers. In the sixteenth century Paracelsus was its exponent, in the nineteenth Madame Blavatsky, who was initiated in Tibet. Her teachers were the Mahatmas Morya and Koot Hoomi.

The existence of such a secret knowledge, inaccessible, because dangerous, to the ordinary mortal, but portentous and supremely potent, has been acclaimed by every mystic, from the most remote to the most

modern. Éliphas Lévi defined *Magic* as the traditional science of nature's secrets which has come down
to us from the wise men of old.

But the term Wisdom Religion, apparently, was
applied to this great science by Madame Blavatsky, in
Isis Unveiled, that is to say, in the year 1877, when
the book first saw the light in America. The world
was then asked to accept the existence of certain higher
intelligences, incarnate, but constrained by none, or by
few, of the common bonds of humanity; was introduced to the Adepts, or Masters, who had chosen
Madame to be their mouthpiece.

Later, Mr. A. P. Sinnett, in *The Occult World* and
Esoteric Buddhism, enlarged upon the subject, showing
how, whilst the Western world—by divine design—had
devoted its genius to the physical sciences, the East
had been conducting inquiries in the science of the soul,
and had made progress at least parallel with that
accomplished by the West.

In Europe, Asia, Africa, and America are branches
and lodges of the Wisdom Religion; few large centres
are without lesser Adepts. But the earthly residences
of the Super-Adepts or Masters are set far from the
hives of busy humanity. Thus, one centre from whence
radiates the arcane illumination is said to be some
remote spot in the Tibetan highlands; and, according
to Mr. Sinnett, the oldest lodge in the world is situate
in, or near to, the silent, swamp-bound temples of
Yucatan. The head-centre I understand to be the
great White Lodge, but I am without other information respecting it.

The Masters are not exclusively Orientals; all
distinctions of race and of creed have ceased to exist
among them. For the most part, they are unseen,

although they have from time to time manifested themselves to the initiate. They possess the power of translating themselves from place to place, as did Apollonius of Tyana, and are products of many generations of searchers, who have so refined the fleshly envelope as to have transcended the phenomenal.

Death has no meaning to them, and whilst some are said to have lived, in the same incarnation, for several centuries, others, discarding one carnal mantle, have endued another and thus remained in the sphere which required their continuous ministration.

In India, the existence of such beings, known there as Rishis or Mahatmas, is an article of popular faith, and Gautama Buddha is regarded as the greatest Adept in the world's history and in the history of the Secret Doctrine.

What may be learned, then, of the Wisdom Religion by direct inquiry into Indian tradition remains to be established by experiment, but, so far as can be determined by the ordinary student, who relies almost wholly upon written records, all our knowledge of the Masters comes to us through the mysterious Madame Blavatsky.

II. COLONEL OLCOTT AND THE THEOSOPHICAL SOCIETY

It is in the year 1874 that we first hear definitely of Madame Blavatsky. Her wanderings, covering I know not where, led her to America and to the village of Chittenden, Vermont, celebrated by reason of the mediumship of the farmer, William Eddy. Here she met Colonel Olcott.

In this year—says the latter—

" Madame Blavatsky and I met. I had been a student of practical psychology for nearly a quarter of a century. From boyhood no problem had interested me so much as the mystery of man, and I had been seeking for light upon it wherever it could be found. To understand the physical man I had read something of anatomy, physiology, and chemistry. To get an insight into the nature of mind and thought, I had read the various authorities of orthodox science, and practically investigated the heterodox branches of phrenology, physiognomy, mesmerism, and psychometry. . . . In the year above mentioned, I was investigating a most startling case of mediumship, that of William Eddy . . . in whose house were nightly appearing, and often talking, the *alleged* spirits of dead persons. . . .

" With my own eyes I saw, within the space of about three months, some five hundred of these apparitions, under circumstances which, to my mind, excluded the possibility of trickery or fraud. Madame Blavatsky and I met at this farmhouse, and the similarity of our tastes . . . led to an intimate acquaintance. She soon proved to me that, in comparison with the *chela* of an Indian *Mahatma*, the authorities I had been accustomed to look up to knew absolutely nothing. Little by little she opened out to me as much of the truth as my experience had fitted me to grasp. Step by step I was forced to relinquish illusory beliefs, cherished for twenty years. And as the light gradually dawned on my mind, my reverence for the unseen teachers who had instructed her grew apace. At the same time, a deep and insatiable yearning possessed me to seek their society, or, at least, to take up my residence in a land which their presence glorified and incorporate myself with a people whom their greatness ennobled.

"The time came when I was blessed with a visit from one of these *Mahatmas* in my own room at New York —a visit from him, not in the physical body, but in the 'double,' or *Mayavi-rupa* . . . from that moment I had a motive to live for, an end to strive after. That motive was to gain the Aryan wisdom ; that end to work for its dissemination."

One cannot wonder that such a meeting led to great things. Madame Blavatsky was said recently to have completed a course of occult study extending over a period of seven years, "in a Himalayan retreat " ; but the remarkable knowledge there imparted to her nevertheless unfitted her for the affairs of the mundane world. In Colonel Olcott she found an ideal partner, and the Theosophical Society was founded. Its objects were as follows :

(1) To form the nucleus of a Universal Human Brotherhood.

(2) To study Aryan literature, religion, and science.

(3) To vindicate the importance of such inquiry.

(4) To explore the mysteries of nature and the latent powers of man.

These views met with a ready acceptance in America, and branches of the Society were also formed successfully in England and elsewhere. Thereupon Madame Blavatsky repaired to India, in order to establish lodges among the natives. Here, many grave blunders were committed.

Unfamiliar with the peculiar social conditions of British India, she found English residents looking askance at her by reason of the fact that she openly

courted native society. Furthermore, her nationality
led the authorities to suspect that she was an agent
of the Russian Government! She discovered herself
subjected to a galling system of espionage.

Madame Blavatsky's indignation was very great
and very real. One can sympathize with this daughter
of the Russian ruling class—of the class wont to direct,
rather than to suffer, political surveillance. She made
public protest, thereby but intensifying the European
dislike for her methods. The sympathy of the natives
alienated that of the residents. In short, by reason
of her nationality, her temperament, and her American
views, she daily transgressed that code of good form
which, iron-bound, governs Anglo-Indian society.
Whilst no longer suspected of political motives, she
was voted "impossible," which is the sigil of social
leprosy.

Recently, American ideas have changed, and the *bon-
homie* of the United States citizen has lost something
of its catholicity. He has recognized the dangerous
kinship of the yellow races; and to-day American
society is as exclusive to the yellow as it has ever been
to the black. The inner significance of caste is as
keenly appreciated in New York as in Calcutta.

But, since 1879, thirty-five years have left their
mark upon history; and a nation may grow wise in
thirty-five years. It was not until 1880, when Madame
Blavatsky visited Simla, that she began to reconcile
her American training with her Indian environment.
One assumes that the wisdom of Tibet does not concern
itself with social conditions.

She now re-approached her task in the right spirit
and from the right direction. At last, the real woman
was recognized; but such a ban as that which, earlier,

had been put upon her, is not shortly broken down. European sympathy was not wholly withheld, yet the fighting spirit of the woman kept her eternally under arms. Capitulation was foreign to her nature; she must ever be duelling.

Real enemies she had in plenty, led by the press; but she was cursed with that failing common to all of her temperament, an inability to distinguish friend from foe. So she needs must wound one truly devoted to her, while bestowing the kiss of friendship upon another who carried a knife in his bosom.

" No . . . Columbus in chains for discovering a new world," says A. P. Sinnett, " or Galileo in prison for announcing the true principles of astronomy, is more remarkable for those who know all the bearings of the situation in India, as regards the Theosophical Society, than the sight of Madame Blavatsky, slandered and ridiculed by most of the Anglo-Indian papers, and spoken of as a charlatan by the commonplace crowd, in return for having freely offered them some of the wonderful fruits—as much as the rules of the great occult association permit her to offer—of the life-long struggle in which she has conquered her extraordinary knowledge."

III. INDIAN PHENOMENA

Some of the phenomenal feats recorded of Madame Blavatsky during her sojourn in Allahabad and elsewhere are worth recalling. Due recognition of our own ignorance is the first essential step toward wisdom, for only he who knows himself a fool can hope to become a wise man. Any consideration of such a career as this, or as those dealt with in earlier chapters, can be nothing but a feckless waste of time on the part of one who is already determined that his views are inexpansible. The marvels recorded of Madame are chiefly of interest to me because (unlike those of the Arabian romancers) they *may* have been performed ; I must confess that I have encountered no really acceptable evidence disproving their authenticity.

Her explanation, that the Masters were governed by certain natural laws just as lesser men are governed, and that some of the miracles demanded by sceptics were as much above the power of Koot Hoomi as they were above her own, I regard as reasonable. That the Adepts had no wish to attract candidates for initiation by an exhibition of wonders is also an acceptable statement, I think. I shall ask you to bear these points in mind ; for, as Mr. A. E. Waite has said, theosophy " is certainly worthy of study—and they are wise who suspend their judgment till the time for judgment arrives."

The mysterious rapping, which, apparently, she had power to control, was a phenomenon trivial enough in character, but far from trivial if produced as she claimed it to be produced. The " singing " of a kettle is not a sensational happening, but it demonstrates the existence of a force which has revolutionized the world !

Unlike the rapping which is heard at the spiritualistic séance, these raps could be produced at will, in any place, and at any time. She could produce them upon a table, a window-pane, a door, or even upon a person's skull.

" Another very satisfactory way of obtaining the raps—one frequently employed in the evening—was to set down a large glass clock-shade on the hearthrug, and get Madame Blavatsky, after removing all rings from her hands, and sitting well clear of the shade, so that no part of her dress touched it, to lay her hands on it. Putting a lamp on the ground opposite, and sitting down on the hearthrug, one could see the under-surface of the hands resting on the glass, and still, under these perfectly satisfactory conditions, the raps would come, clear and distinct, on the sonorous surface of the shade."

But even more satisfactory was her production of raps upon a table which she did not touch in any way and which no one else was touching. The latter experiment, we are told, was performed a number of times and with a number of tables which could not possibly have been prepared by the operator. I find myself in agreement with the writer who says :

" Her conversation and her book, *Isis Unveiled*, disclosed a view of things which we naturally desired to explore further ; and it was tantalizing to feel that she could, and yet could not, give us the final proofs we so much desired to have, that her occult training really had invested her with powers over material things of a kind which, if one could but feel sure they were actually in her possession, would utterly shatter the primary foundations of materialistic philosophy."

A picturesque demonstration of Madame's powers is related of her during her stay at Benares, in a house belonging to the Maharajah of Vizianagram. The party were seated in the central hall one evening after dinner, when suddenly three or four roses fell in their midst ! We perceive the possibility of trickery, of course, at once ; but in the absence of proof must also concede the possibility of the phenomenal.

Here I may refer to the " astral bell " which occasioned so much comment. This was a clear, silvern note, or succession of notes, which sounded in the air around and about the High Priestess of Theosophy. It was said to be a mode of communication between Madame and the " Brothers." Whilst the sound was sometimes produced under conditions which by no means excluded the possibility of deception, at other times the bell was heard under circumstances which, examine as closely as we may, defy explanation. Thus, in the *Occult World*, we read how Madame Blavatsky was, on one occasion, leaning on a balustrade, " and looking over the wide sweep of the Simla Valley ; she remained for a few minutes perfectly motionless and silent . . . and the night was far enough advanced for all commonplace sounds to have settled down, so that the stillness was perfect. Suddenly, in the air . . . there sounded the clear note of an occult bell."

I shall not deal here with the letters from the Mahatma Koot Hoomi phenomenally delivered to Mr. A. P. Sinnett. His path is strewn with split infinitives, but, saving this slaughter of the innocents, I have no particular fault to find with the correspondence of the Mahatma. Transcriptions may be found in Mr. Sinnett's book, to which I shall also refer inquirers for the account of the famous recovery of Mrs. Hume's lost brooch. Mr. Sinnett writes as a disciple of Madame Blavatsky, and I prefer to take my facts from a more hostile chronicler, for, strangely enough, her enemies have done more to show her as she claimed to be than have her friends.

IV. "A MODERN PRIESTESS OF ISIS"

In 1884 Madame Blavatsky left India and came to Europe. She lived for a time in the Rue Notre Dame des Champs, Paris, and amongst those whom she attracted to her at this time was a compatriot, M. V. S. Solovyoff—her harshest critic, and the man who seems to have been directly instrumental in breaking up the French Theosophical Society (the "Société Théosophique d'Orient et d'Occident").

I cannot hope to portray Madame as she was at this period so skilfully as M. Solovyoff has portrayed her. His articles originally appeared in the *Russky Vyestnik*, and were translated for and published by the Society for Psychical Research, under the title *A Modern Priestess of Isis*. Let us accompany him to his first audience at the Rue Notre Dame des Champs.

"The door opened," he says, "and she was before me; a rather tall woman, though she produced the impression of being short, on account of her unusual stoutness. Her great head seemed all the greater from her thick and very bright hair, touched with a scarcely perceptible grey, and very slightly frizzed— by nature and not by art, as I subsequently convinced myself.

"At the first moment her plain, old, earthy-coloured face struck me as repulsive; but she fixed on me the gaze of her great, rolling, pale blue eyes, and in these wonderful eyes, with their hidden power, all the rest was forgotten.

"I remarked, however, that she was very strangely dressed, in a sort of black sacque, and that all the fingers of her small, soft, and as it were boneless hands, with their slender points and long nails, were covered with great jewelled rings."

Following some conversation touching the Masters, Madame quitted the room for a few minutes, in order, she said, to tell Babula, her Hindu servant, to prepare her dinner. Upon her return, M. Solovyoff was treated to a manifestation of the astral bell, and it is interesting to compare his account with that of Mr. Sinnett:

" She made a sort of flourish with her hand, raised it upwards, and suddenly, I heard distinctly, quite distinctly, somewhere above our heads, near the ceiling, a very melodious sound like a little silver bell or an Æolian harp."

I am not aware that any explanation, covering all the facts, anent this bell device has ever been advanced. Even if a purely mechanical trick, it was a trick difficult to explain. And what does M. Solovyoff say ? He inquires : " Why was the sound of the silver bell not heard at once, but only after she had left the room and come back again ? "

With all deference I submit that a conjurer so clever as he would have us believe Madame to have been was the last person in the world to have forgotten to wind up her apparatus !

On the same occasion, M. Solovyoff made the acquaintance of Mohini, a " *chela* " of the Mahatma (or Master) Koot Hoomi.

" He seemed to be not more than from twenty-five to twenty-seven years of age. His figure, which was narrow-shouldered and not tall, was clad in a black cashmere cassock ; his thick, blue-black wavy hair fell to his shoulders. The upper part of his bronzed face was strikingly handsome—a wise forehead, not very high, straight eyebrows, not too thick, and most magnificent velvety eyes, with a deep and gentle expression. . . . It was only his nose, straight but too broad, and his thick, dark blue lips, projecting through a not over-abundant growth of moustache and beard, which prevented his being perfectly beautiful. In any case his appearance might be considered very attractive, and several female hearts in Asia and Europe could tell tales of the beauty of this young apostle of the newest theosophy."

M. Solovyoff returned to his rooms with a somewhat confused impression. His various ideas refused to become reconciled. "As for her silver bell," he says, "that looked like a trick. . . ." Yet two days later he enrolled himself in the theosophical ranks and was initiated there and then. The initiation over, he shortly departed, experiencing "a longing to get out at once into a purer atmosphere."

These being his sentiments, I should like to ask, if the question be permissible, with what object M. Solovyoff joined the organization.

The Paris lodge would seem to have met with but little success. Charles Richet came to inquire, as did Camille Flammarion, but neither would appear to have been deeply impressed. Colonel Olcott joined Madame Blavatsky in France, and M. Solovyoff has given us the following sketch of him, fine in its lines as a Toledan blade, double-edged, too, and cruelly sharp as any scimitar ever swung within the Alcazar.

"And I saw the 'colonel,'[1] Madame Blavatsky's trusty companion and fellow-labourer, the president of

[1] Despite the inverted commas, Colonel Olcott actually served as an officer in the American army, and was highly enough esteemed to have borne an autograph letter of introduction from the President when he sailed for India in 1878.

the Theosophical Society. His appearance produced on me at once a very favourable impression. He was a man of fully fifty years of age, of medium height, robust and broad, but not fat ; from his energy and vivacity of movement he looked anything but an old man, and showed every sign of great strength and sound health. His face was handsome and pleasant, and suited his bald head, and was framed in a full and perfectly silver beard. He wore spectacles, somewhat concealing thereby the one defect of his appearance, which none the less was a real ' spoonful of tar in a barrel of honey ! ' The fact is that one of his eyes was extremely disobedient, and from time to time used to turn in all directions, sometimes with startling and most disagreeable rapidity. As long as the disobedient eye remained still, you had before you a handsome, agreeable and kindly, but not particularly clever man, who won you by his appearance and inspired you with confidence. Then suddenly something twitched, the eye got loose and began to stray suspiciously and knavishly, and confidence vanished in a moment."

Although I hold no instructions on behalf of Colonel Olcott, and am innocent of any desire unjustly to pillory M. Solovyoff, I feel constrained to mention that I have never before met with a case of paralysis of the *motor oculi* adduced as evidence of moral turpitude !

V. THE MAHATMA MORYA

During the second half of this eventful summer, Madame Blavatsky having gone to London, we find M. Solovyoff " flooded with . . . rarities, curiosities, and unexpected finds " in mystic literature, from the bookshops of the Quartier Latin and the stalls on the Quai-de-Louvre.

He read *Isis Unveiled*, and considered it to be a huge sack, into which the writings of Éliphas Lévi, Saint-Ives, Franck, and others had been thrown haphazard. Then, apparently as a relief from overwork, " on a hot August day, the 24th, new style," he left Paris to join Madame in Elberfeld, whence she had proceeded from London.

At Brussels he broke his journey, and met Miss A., a proselyte of the new theosophy. From this hour to that of their arrival at Elberfeld, they were subjected to certain manifestations which at the time neither seem to have doubted to proceed from some source controlled by Madame. M. Solovyoff's sleep was disturbed, and at about eight o'clock on the following morning he received a note from Miss A. saying that she, too, had passed a sleepless night ; " a sort of invisible struggle had been going on about her . . . and *all* her keys were lost."

" Send for a locksmith," suggested M. Solovyoff.

" I have sent."

In due course the locksmith appeared, and opened the lady's portmanteau. " In the portmanteau was a bunch of keys, and on the bunch the key of the port-manteau itself ! "

Having decided to catch the one o'clock train, M. Solovyoff " suddenly began to feel an unusual weakness, and a desire to sleep. . . . I begged Miss A. to excuse me," he writes, " went to my own room, and threw myself on the bed. However, I did not fall asleep, but lay with my eyes closed—and there before me, one after the other, passed, quite clear and distinct, various landscapes which I did not know.

This was so new to me, and so beautiful, that I lay without stirring, for fear of interrupting and spoiling the vision. At last all became misty, little by little, then grew confused, and I saw no more."

He opened his eyes. The sensation of weakness, together with the desire for sleep, had passed ; and, returning to Miss A., he described in detail, with all the accompanying circumstances, his vision or series of visions.

They proceeded to the station and took their seats in a *coupé* of the train. The journey had but just commenced when the lady, looking out of the window, exclaimed :

" See ! Here is one of your landscapes ! "

" The effect," says the writer, " was almost painful. There could be no doubt about it, just as I could not doubt that this was the first time I had ever travelled by this line or been in this region. Until it grew dark, I continued to gaze in reality upon all that I had seen . . . as I lay on the bed with my eyes closed."

But yet another phenomenon was in store for the sceptic. At " the house of the merchant Gebhard," Elberfeld, M. Solovyoff and his companion visited Madame Blavatsky, and found her " all swollen with dropsy, and almost without movement, in an enormous arm-chair," surrounded by Olcott, the *chela* Mohini, and some nine or ten others. In the course of the evening M. Solovyoff's attention was directed to a recess, or portion of the large drawing-room, before which hung heavy draperies.

The curtains being suddenly drawn back, " two wonderful figures, illuminated with a brilliant, bluish light, concentrated and strengthened by mirrors," arose before them. At the first moment M. Solovyoff thought that he looked upon living men, but in reality these were two great draped portraits of the Mahatmas Morya and Koot Hoomi, painted in oils by Schmiechen, an artist related to the Gebhard family.

" Mahatma Koot Hoomi, clad in a graceful sort of robe, trimmed with fur, had a tender, almost feminine face, and gazed sweetly with a pair of charming light eyes.

" But as soon as one looked at the ' Master,' Koot Hoomi, for all his tender beauty, was at once forgotten. The fiery black eyes of the tall Morya fixed themselves sternly and piercingly upon one, and it was impossible to tear oneself away from them. The ' Master ' was represented . . . crowned with a white turban and in a white garment. All the power of the reflectors was turned upon this sombrely beautiful face, and the whiteness of the turban and dress completed the brilliance and lifelikeness of the effect. . . . One had to force oneself to remember that it was not a living man. I could not turn my eyes away."

Reaching his room at the Hotel Victoria, M. Solovyoff locked the door, undressed, and retired to bed.

" Suddenly," he says, " I woke up, or, what is more probable, I dreamt, I imagined that I was awoke by a warm breath. I found myself in the same room, and before me, in the half-darkness, there stood a tall human figure in white. I *felt* a voice, without knowing how or in what language, bidding me light the candle. I was not in the least alarmed, and was not surprised. I lighted the candle, and it appeared to me that it was two o'clock by my watch. The vision did not vanish. There was a living man before me, and this man was clearly none other than the original of the wonderful portrait—an *exact repetition* of it. He placed himself in a chair beside me, and told me in *an unknown but intelligible language* various matters of interest to myself. Among other things he told me that in order to see him in his astral body I had had to go through much preparation, and that the last lesson had been given me that morning, when I saw with closed eyes the landscapes through which I was to pass on the way to Elberfeld ; and that I possessed a great and growing magnetic force. I asked how I was to employ it ; but he vanished in silence. I thought that I sprang after him ; but the door was closed. The idea came upon me that it was an hallucination, and that I was going out of my mind. But there was Mahatma Morya back again in his place, without movement, with his gaze fixed upon me, the same, exactly the same, as he was imprinted on my brain. He began to shake his head, smiled, and said, still in the voiceless, imaginary language of dreams, ' Be assured that I am not an hallucination and that your reason is not deserting you. . . .'

"He vanished ; I looked at my watch, and saw that it was about three o'clock ; I put out the candle, and went to sleep at once.

"I woke at ten o'clock and remembered everything quite clearly. The door was locked ; it was impossible to tell from the candle if it had been lighted during the night, and if it had been long burning, as I had lighted it on my first arrival before the visit to Madame Blavatsky."

I have only to add that M. Solovyoff regarded this vision, in some way, as a new proof of the falsity of Madame's claims ! Frankly, I cannot see his point of view. The phenomenon of his seeing a panorama of Belgian scenery *prior* to visiting Belgium was distinctly *supersensual*, and some of the circumstances attendant upon the vision of Morya mark it as wholly different from any normal dream.

Let me say at once that the former experience (even if we disregard the latter) cannot be explained by any generally accepted natural law. Yet we find a man fresh from such phenomena writing:

" Then *she* was there, this old, sick woman, suffering tortures from her deep-seated maladies, looking death full in the face, and then looking full in the face at me, as a man looks whose conscience is clear, who feels his own innocence and fears no reproach ! "

What reproach had she to fear from M. Solovyoff ? If she employed trickery, then some of it was of a sort inimitable by any professional conjurer in Europe. If M. Solovyoff's experience proved nothing beyond the existence of an unsuspected law of nature, then was he indebted to Madame Blavatsky ; and an inquiring age would be eternally indebted to M. Solovyoff had he offered us a suitable explanation. But he does not even attempt the task ; he says :

" There must have proceeded from this terrible and unhappy woman some sort of magnetic attraction, not to be translated into words, which so many calm, healthy, and judicious people experienced in their own persons. I was so sure of myself ; and lo, she was making me waver ! "

VI. " ISIS UNVEILED "

Shortly afterwards came Mr. F. Myers, of the London Society for Psychical Research, and the tragic downfall of Madame Blavatsky drew near. Those who are curious respecting the Report of the Committee on Theosophical Phenomena may profitably consult Vol. III. of the *Proceedings of the Society for Psychical Research.* If I have formed any opinion respecting the Report I shall not advance it here. Mr. Hodgson's conclusion, that Madame Blavatsky was a Russian spy, does not concern us. Suffice it that she was found guilty of fraud, whilst Colonel Olcott was acquitted.

M. Solovyoff's account of the exposure of the astral-bell device is not entirely satisfactory ; and Madame's " confession " is the most tragic document in the *dossier* Blavatsky. The voluminous correspondence it will be impossible to deal with here, but a letter from M. Solovyoff, dated December 22, 1884, has struck me as curious. In it he says :

" . . . I dined in the green dining-room . . . with V——. I ate with a good appetite. I drank very little, as always—in a word, I was quite myself. When dinner was over I went up to my room to have a cigar. I opened the door, lit a match, lighted the candle, and there was Helena Petrovna " (Madame Blavatsky) " standing before me in her black sacque. She greeted me, smiled, said, ' Here I am,' and vanished ! What does this mean ? . . . hallucination or not ? How am I to tell ? That it is enough to make one go out of one's mind is certain . . ."

But, in truth, the history of this amazing woman is full of such occurrences, and I must abandon any

MADAME H. P. BLAVATSKY

further reference to this phase of the subject if we are to glance, even briefly, at the phenomenal *Isis Unveiled.*

According to the theosophists, Madame Blavatsky " set to work on *Isis* without knowing anything about the magnitude of the task she was undertaking. She began writing to dictation—the passages thus written not now standing first in the completed volumes—in compliance with the desire of her occult friends. . . . But on and on it grew . . . and, fairly launched on her task, she in turn contributed a good deal from her own natural brain."

The Brothers were her unseen collaborators, not only controlling the brain of the writer, but " precipitating " actual manuscript whilst she slept. " In the morning she would sometimes get up and find as much as thirty slips added to the manuscript she had left on her table overnight." No one but a professional penman, perhaps, can be expected fully to appreciate this delightful phenomenon.

In this way, then, Madame's apologists explain the confusion of arrangement and absence of any continuous style which are the outstanding and irritating features of this really remarkable work. The following paragraph, from *The Occult World*, is curious :

" The book (*Isis*) was written—as regards its physical production—at New York, where Madame Blavatsky was utterly unprovided with books of reference. It teems, however, with references to books of all sorts, including many of a very unusual character, and with quotations the exactitude of which may easily be verified at the great European libraries, as foot-notes supply the numbers of the pages from which the passages taken are quoted."

But Mr. William Emmette Coleman says :

" In *Isis Unveiled*, published in 1877, I discovered some 2,000 passages copied from other books without proper credit. By careful analysis I found that in compiling *Isis* about 100 books were used. About 1,400 books are quoted from and referred to in this work; but, from the 100 books which its author possessed, she copied everything in *Isis* taken from and relating to the other 1,300."

Of the *Secret Doctrine*—ostensibly based upon the *Book of Dzyan*, the oldest book in the world, and written in a language unknown to philology—the same critic says that it was entirely the work of Madame, being largely plagiarized from Wilson's *Vishnu Purana* and other modern sources. The *Voice of the Silence*, 1899, he condemns upon similar grounds.

It would be impossible to attempt to summarize the teachings of *Isis Unveiled*; but the following passage has been selected by Mr. A. P. Sinnett as illuminating the final purpose of occult philosophy:

" That which survives as an individuality, after the death of the body, is the actual soul, which Plato, in the *Timæus* and *Gorgias*, calls the mortal soul; for, according to the hermetic doctrine, it throws off the more material particles at every progressive change into a higher sphere . . . the divine, the highest immortal spirit, can be neither punished nor rewarded. To maintain such a doctrine would be at the same time absurd and blasphemous; for it is not merely a flame lit at the central and unextinguishable fountain of light, but actually a portion of it and of identical essence. It assures immortality to the individual astral being in proportion to the willingness of the latter to receive it. So long as the double man—*i.e.*

the man of flesh and spirit—keeps within the limits
of the law of spiritual continuity; so long as the
divine spark lingers in him, however faintly, he is on
the road to an immortality in the future state.   But
those who resign themselves to a materialistic existence,
shutting out the divine radiance shed by their spirit,
at the beginning of their earthly pilgrimage, and
stifling the warning voice of that faithful sentry the
conscience, which serves as a focus for the light in
the soul—such beings as these, having left behind
conscience and spirit, and crossed the boundaries of
matter, will, of necessity, have to follow its laws."

VII.   IMPRESSIONS

To follow in detail the travels of Madame Blavatsky,
Colonel Olcott, and Mohini the *chela*, would be impossible within the limits of the present account; furthermore, it would be profitless, since it could result in
little else than a chronicle of the occasional successes
and frequent failures of this tragic old woman, in her
giant endeavour to close the Book of Creeds with the
seal of theosophy.

We have glanced, if hastily, at her tenets; we have
witnessed, with M. Solovyoff and others, cases of
phenomena performed by her; witnesses for the pro-
secution and witnesses for the defence have been
heard.   Yet I cannot disguise from myself that the
portrait remains incomplete.   I had hoped to round it
off with the aid of Colonel Olcott's *Old Diary Leaves*,
but I was disappointed.   One casts one's net into the

deep sea of *Old Diary Leaves*, and, as the Arabian fishermen brought up the *ginn*, brings up Colonel Olcott. This may be as it should be ; and I concede with pleasure that my perusal of the lengthy work has increased my knowledge—of Colonel Olcott.

But Madame Blavatsky, although her activities were so recent, remains a more elusive personality than Apollonius of Tyana himself. A rather illuminating sketch of her appeared some time ago in *The Vahan*, over the signature E. J. Dunn. Some of the writer's impressions struck me as particularly clear-cut, showing us Madame as she was in 1889.

Mr. Dunn states that he had thrown aside the report of the Society for Psychical Research as a stupid and inane production. The press was full of Blavatsky stories, and it seemed " that the eyes of the whole world were upon her." He determined to see her ; but Fate willed that he should first hear her.

" Well do I remember," he says, " walking up Lansdowne Road,[1] wondering which house it was, when—hark ! what was that I heard ? Through an open window of an upper room, I could hear a voice talking in stentorian tones at express speed, and I knew that only Madame Blavatsky could possess a voice like it. There was no need to look for the number of the house. That was Madame Blavatsky and no other ! But there was something about the voice which made me pause ; I had not reckoned on any-thing quite so sensational. I walked up and down the street, passed and repassed the house, gradually mustering up courage, for, barely out of my teens, born and bred in a secluded country district, here I was alone in the great city of London, within a stone's

[1] Madame Blavatsky lived for a time at No. 17, Lansdowne Road.

throw of this world-wide celebrity, philosopher, magician—who possessed a voice like that!"

But having come thus far, he mastered hesitancy,
handed in his card, and was shown upstairs.

He found Madame Blavatsky seated in an arm-chair
with a circle of inquiring people around her—among
others, the two Keightleys, G. R. S. Mead, Walter Old,
and Countess Wachtmeister. Before he quitted the
house that day, Mr. Dunn assures us, every question
or problem which he had had in his mind, consciously
or subconsciously, was dealt with and answered by
"H. P. B." without his asking a single question
personally.

"First one person asked one of my questions, and
then another. One individual who sat just behind me
persisted in asking a string of questions about which
I had been previously thinking, until I could stand it
no longer, and right-about-faced, to see whether this
thought-reader was man, god, or devil. I thought he
looked rather a stupid kind of man, and put him down
as a medium, resigning myself to having my brains
still more completely riddled, while reflecting that one
really must not be surprised at anything happening
in the atmosphere surrounding this miracle-worker,
H. P. B.

"According to her, every one who asked a silly
question or failed to grasp her explanation readily
was a 'flapdoodle.' The afternoon and evening were
mostly taken up with questions by the circle of neophytes and visitors, and answers by H. P. B."

These questions and answers ranged from problems
of abstruse metaphysics and occultism, to those of
practical everyday life, and presented a most hetero-
geneous display of thought. Madame's answers were

ready, witty, and unequivocal. On the subject of marriage she let loose the vials of her wrath upon the multitudinous weaknesses of woman. When one of the ladies ventured upon a mild expostulation, the reply was: "My dear, I am a woman, and so I know."

With a card-table before her, Madame Blavatsky would call for chalk and draw diagrams upon the table to illustrate her tenets. One question (on the reversed pentagram) drew forth a lengthy discourse on the various forces correlated to each of the five lines, and on the difference, when reversed, for Black Magic.

"I attained the object of my visit. No one could speak like H. P. B. without being true to the core. She had the courage to face, practically single-handed, the obloquy of the world, and this dauntless courage came out in the treatment of every subject which was discussed. Eyes that could look one through and through, steady as a rock, penetrating as the ether, intelligence incarnate, portrayed a reliable and heroic soul behind them. The contrast between this giant soul and the deceptions and pusillanimity attributed to her, was not worth a moment's hesitation."

Whilst Madame would speak at one moment "with a vehemence like that of a violent thunderstorm," yet, if she found that unwillingly she had injured any one's susceptibilities, she would instantly exhibit "the tenderness of a mother."

I am indebted to Mr. Dunn for his useful contribution to the history of a strange character; but in my quest of Madame Blavatsky's finished written portrait, I find myself always thrown back upon M. Solovyoff, throughout the progress of whose internecine warring I meet with a lovable woman and another than she whom he so skilfully has limned as a *Modern Priestess of Isis*. No finer tribute has been paid to the founder of the Theosophical Society than this fierce onslaught which, posthumously, destroyed her.

Madame Helena Petrovna Blavatsky died in London, in 1891, and her ashes are preserved in three urns.

SORCERY AND THE LAW

I. THE BLACK SABBATH

THE annals of sorcery contain some dark pages, but none so black as those that deal with the wholesale torturings, hangings, and burnings whereby it was proposed to stamp out witchcraft. To-day it is difficult, if not impossible, to appreciate the panic which at one period of European history prevailed throughout society; to understand the fear of bewitchment which ruled men's hearts, from king to peasant.

When we remember that space was supposed to be peopled with demons, numbering, according to Wierus, 7,405,925, we perceive upon what this fear was founded; for the whole legion was at command of the witch! Indeed, in those days of universal witchcraft, one was fortunate who avoided possession. St. Gregory of Nice relates a story of a nun who forgot to say her *benedicite* before she sat down to supper, and who in consequence swallowed a demon concealed amongst the leaves of a lettuce.

Satan, of course, was lord of the unclean host, and he frequently manifested himself in person. For instance, in the reign of Philippe le Bel he appeared to a monk in the shape of a dark man riding a tall black horse, then as a friar, next as an ass, and finally as a coach-wheel. But he and his demons could also assume the forms of handsome youths, and instances are recorded of children born of unions between such demons and beautiful women of whom they had become enamoured. These demoniacal offspring were readily recognizable, however, by their ceaseless howling, by their requiring five nurses to suckle them, and by their never growing fat.

Periodically, Satan summoned a meeting of demons, wizards, and witches. It was termed the Sabbath, taking place (according to some accounts) immediately after Friday midnight. These Sabbaths were held, of course, in various districts, but once every year a grand Sabbath was held on the Brocken, attended by all the fiends of Christendom. Accounts of these Sabbaths are for the most part based upon the confessions of convicted witches. They correspond curiously.

According to Pope Gregory IX, Satan was adored by the witches under the name of *Asmodeus* :

"The devil appears to them in different shapes—sometimes as a goose or a duck, and at others in the figure of a pale, black-eyed youth, with a melancholy aspect, whose embrace fills their hearts with eternal hatred against the holy Church . . . this devil presides at their Sabbaths, when they all kiss him and dance around him. He then envelops them in total darkness, and they all, male and female, give themselves up to the grossest and most disgusting debauchery."

The idea that Satan presided in the form of a man having the head of a goat is frequently met with. Between the horns a mysterious, lambent light shone incessantly. His body diffused a ruddy glow, and a sulphurous odour intoxicated the participants in the unholy rites. Attendant imps surrounded him and weird winged creatures flew about. In the foreground was the seething cauldron in which was distilling the hell-brew for the composition of poisonous potions.

De Lancre, however, speaks of the devil having five horns, from the centre one of which a flame proceeds, serving as a means of obtaining light for the fires and candles used during the proceedings. He also says that on each occasion the devil appointed a favourite witch Queen of the Sabbath, crowned her, and placed her on a throne at his right hand, whilst a second favourite occupied a seat on his left. A similar ceremony is mentioned in Michelet's *La Sorcière.* Boguet [1] says that " often Satan assists in the musical part of the programme, by playing a flute."

The following English account of the Sabbath is taken from *A Pleasant Treatise of Witches*, etc., published at London in 1673 :

" They (Witches) are likewise reported to have each of them a Spirit or Imp attending on and assigned to them, which never leave those to whom they are subject, but assist and render them all the service they command. These give the Witches notice to be ready at all Solemn appointments, and meetings, which are ordinarily on Tuesday or Wednesday night, and then they strive to separate themselves from the company of all other Creatures, not to be seen by any ; and night being come, they strip themselves naked, and anoint themselves with their Oyntments. Then are they carryed out of the house, either by the Window, Door, or Chimney, mounted on their Imps in form of a Goat, Sheep or a Dragon, till they arrive at their meeting place, whither all the other Witches and

---

[1] Henry Boguet. He wrote *Discours des Sorciers*, 1608.

Wizards, each one upon his Imps, are also brought. Thus brought to the designed place, which is sometimes many hundred miles from their dwellings, they find a great number of others arrived there by the same means ; who, before Lucifer takes his place in his Throne as King, do make their accustomed homage, Adoring and Proclaiming him their Lord, and rendering him all Honour.

" This solemnity being finished, they sit at table where no delicate meats are wanting to gratifie their Appetites, all dainties being thither brought in the twinkling of an eye, by those spirits that attend the Assembly. This done at the sound of many pleasant Instruments (for we must expect no Grace in the company of Devils), the table is taken away, and the pleasant consort invites them to a *Ball* ; but the dance is strange, and wonderful, as well as diabolical, for twining themselves back to back, they take one another by the arms and raise each other from the ground, then shake their heads to and fro like Anticks, and turn themselves as if they were mad. Then at last, after this Banquet, Musick and Ball, the lights are put out, and their sleeping Venus awakes.

" The incubus's (*Incubi*) in the shape of proper men," continues the *Treatise*, entertain the witches, " and the succubus's (*Succubi*) serve . . . for the Wizards.

" At last, before *Aurora* brings back the day, each one mounts on his spirit, and so returns to his respective dwelling place, with that lightness and quickness, that in little space they find themselves to be carried many hundred miles ; but are charged by their spirit in the way, not to call in any wise on the name of God, or to bless themselves with the sign of the Cross, upon pain of falling, with peril of their lives, and being grievously punished by their Demon.

" Sometimes at their solemn assemblies, the Devil commands, that each tell what wickednes he hath committed, and according to the heinousness and detestableness of it, he is honoured and respected with a general applause. Those on the contrary, that have done no evil, are beaten and punished ; at last when the assembly is ready to break up, and the Devil to dispatch them, he publisheth this law with a loud voice, *Revenge yourselves or also you shall dye*, then each one kissing the . . . Devil returns upon their aiery Vehicles to their habitations."

Many of the available particulars relating to the Sabbath are quite unprintable, and the folding plate of the Sabbath in Pierre De Lancre's *Tableau de l'Incontance des Mauvais Anges*, etc., 1613—is also too realistic for reproduction !

Reginald Scott, in his *Discoverie of Witchcraft*, gives the following recipes for preparing the ointment with which the witches anointed themselves in order to be transported to the Sabbath. (For an account of this in fiction, see Algernon Blackwood's story *Ancient Sorceries*.)

I. " The fat of yoong children, and seeth it with water in a brasen vessell, reserving the thickest of that which remaineth boiled in the bottome, which they laye up and keep, untill occasion serveth to use it. They put hereunto *Eleoselinum, Aconitum, Frondes populeas*, and Soote."

II. " *Sium, acarum vulgare, pentaphyllon*, the blood of a flitter mouse, *solanum somniferum* and *oleum*. They stampe all these together, and then they rubbe all parts of their bodies exceedinglie, till they looke

THE BLACK SABBATH

FROM OUFLE'S *IMAGINATIONS EXTRAVAGANTES*

red, and be verie hot, so as the pores may be opened, and their flesh soluble and loose. They joine herewithall either fat, or oil in stead thereof, that the force of the ointment maie the rather pearse inwardly, and so be more effectuall. By this means in a moonlight night they seeme to be carried in the aire."[1]

One pictures the scene only with the utmost difficulty —those shapes gliding down from the night, witches young, witches old, hideous and comely, their bodies aglisten with the unholy anointing, demon lovers and unsexed mistresses hastening to the tryst. The woods are peopled with grey things, the branches burdened with winged creatures arisen from the pit ; the darkness is a curtain broidered with luminous eyes—cat-eyes, ghoul-eyes—eyes aflame with the fire of hell. Awful chants rise and fall, gleaming shapes leap out into the light cast by the cauldron, and are lost again in the gloom. Unholiness sighs and pants and laughs in lost abandon about the awful, majestic figure of the fallen Angel.

This, then, was the Black Sabbath, the nightmare that haunted the Middle Ages ; this was the annual gathering of those against whom Charlemagne directed his edicts ; but if it was in the time of Charlemagne that the crime of sorcery began to assume importance, it was not until 1484, when Pope Innocent VIII issued his bull *Summis desiderantes affectibus*, that the real reign of terror began. From the issue of this bull up to the year 1782—when a girl witch was put to death at Glarus in Switzerland—it is computed that 300,000 women, accused of witchcraft, perished at the hands of the law !

[1] According to Mr. C. W. Leadbeater, certain ointments rubbed over the body will very greatly assist the astral entity to leave the physical body in full consciousness.

II. SORCERY IN FRANCE

Whilst England was for long preserved from the horrors of the witch-trial, France very early became witch-ridden. At the commencement of the fifth century, the Franks, under Pharamond, crossed the Rhine and settled in Gaul. With them they brought their superstitions, which admitted of the existence of sorcerers, and of the almost universal power of demons.

In the Salic laws, which Siegbert attributes to Pharamond, and which he supposes to have been promulgated in A.D. 424, we find the following dispositions :

" Whosoever shall call another a *sorcerer*, or accuse him of having carried the cauldron at the Sabbath, where sorcerers assemble, shall, if unable to bring proof, be condemned to a fine of two thousand five hundred deniers, or, sixty-two sous and a half.

" If any one shall call a free woman a sorceress or prostitute, without being able to support the accusation by proof, he shall be condemned to a fine of seven thousand five hundred deniers, or, one hundred and eighty-seven sous and a half.

" If a sorceress has devoured (?) a man, and she is convicted, she shall be condemned to pay eight thousand deniers, or, two hundred sous." [1]

" Truly, the laws were not made in order to dissipate superstition," says Jules Garinet ; and in those dark days any unusual phenomena were regarded either as miracles or as the work of the devil. Under the reign of Merovée, Attila, King of the Huns, appeared in

---

[1] The sou above mentioned was a gold coin, weighing eighty-five grains plus a third of a grain. It would be worth about eight or nine francs (7s. to 7s. 6d.). The denier was of silver, and forty deniers made a sou.

France like a torrent, ravaging and laying waste the country through which he passed. The people of Paris gave themselves up to despair when they learned of the approach of the barbarian, in whose train was an army of five hundred thousand men; but St. Geneviève endeavoured to calm the terror-stricken citizens, and predicted in the name of Heaven that Attila would not besiege Paris. Many believed in her prophetic utterance, and were reassured; but others accused her of being in league with the enemy, or with the devil, who had revealed the future to her.

Childeric succeeded to Merovée, but the dissoluteness of his habits and his passion for seducing all women caused him to be driven from the throne. He took refuge in Thuringe, where he won the heart of the Queen Bazine, who left her husband in order to wed the King of France.

Some historians describe this princess as a great sorceress. If we are to believe Aimoin and Trédégaire, on the evening of the marriage Bazine requested her new husband, Childeric, to remain the whole night in absolute continence, to get up from bed, to go to the gateway of his palace, and to return and tell her what he had seen. Childeric regarded this advice with respect, since it appeared full of mystery, and, in accordance with his wife's request, went out. Hardly had he reached the gateway ere he saw enormous animals walking about the courtyard—leopards, unicorns, and lions. Astonished at this spectacle, he returned as quickly as possible to his Queen, and related to her what he had seen. Then, addressing him in a mysterious voice, as of an Oracle, she told him not to be afraid, but to go a second time, and even a third. Childeric obeyed. On the second visit to the courtyard he saw wolves and bears ; and upon the third occasion dogs and other small animals fighting and tearing each other to pieces.

It was but natural that the King should ask of Bazine the explanation of these extraordinary visions.

" You shall know," said the Queen ; " but you must pass the rest of the night quietly, and, at the break of day, you shall learn that which you wish to learn."

Childeric promised to do as the Queen had requested, and kept his promise. Bazine also was as good as her word, and she now revealed to the King the meaning of the enigma :

" Have no fear, and listen attentively to what I am about to say. The wonderful things you have seen are but a vision of the future ; they represent the morals and the character of all our posterity. The lions and the unicorns denote the son who will be born of us (Clovis I) ; the wolves and the bears are his children, vigorous princes seeking their prey ; whilst the dogs, animals blindly given up to their passions, are symbolic of the last Kings of your race. The little animals that you saw amongst the dogs are the people, impatient of servitude, risen against their Kings, given over to the passions of the great, unfortunate victims first of the one and then of the other."

Bazine became mother of Clovis I, the first Christian King of France, and, according to some, " the first who was really (*véritablement*) King."

Pierre-le-Vénérable, who, born in 1092, became Abbé de Cluni, and who died beatified about the year 1156, wrote two books of miracles with which he was acquainted, in which he records some remarkable events. The facts which he relates took place

in the eleventh and twelfth centuries, under the Kings
Robert, Henri I, Philippe I, Louis VI, and Louis VII.
As several of his tracts deal with sorcery, I may give
a few examples :

" The devil took up a position at the monastery of
Cluni, and, in the guise of an abbé, advised an Italian
monk to flee.   Two other devils, disguised as monks,
accompanied the false abbé ; but the Italian would
consent to none of their wishes.   The dinner-hour
having arrived, the monk repaired to the refectory
with the three false ecclesiastics.   The repast eaten,
the prior, according to custom, gave the signal that
dinner was over.   The demon who had passed himself
off as an abbé no sooner heard the noise, than, impelled
by a superior force, he ran from the brother to whom
he had been speaking, and, springing, precipitated
himself violently into the latrines . . . in view of
the brother of whom we have just spoken.   Thus did
the spirit of darkness escape from this monastery
by a route worthy of him." [1]

Near Lisieux, in Poitou, a priest, who had lived an
evil life, in order to hide his iniquity received the
sacrament several times whilst passing his days in
performing acts of lewdness.   But the end came.   His
hypocrisy became known, and he was remonstrated
with by the monks of Bonneval.   The prior visited
him, and stayed the night in his cell.   Suddenly, in
the middle of the night, the priest cried out loudly
for help :

" Two enormous lions," he screamed, " are throwing
themselves upon me ; their jaws are opened to devour
me."

In saying these words his whole body trembled.   The

[1] Pierre-le-Vénérable, *Des Miracles*, Book I., Chaps. xii. and xiii.

prior endeavoured to reassure him, and commenced to
pray.

"Good, good," said the curé; "the lions have fled."
He now spoke more quietly.

An hour afterwards, however, the priest once more
was thrown into convulsions.

"I see fire descending from heaven which is about
to burn me like straw," he cried. "I pray you offer
your supplications to God for me"; and the prior
repeated his prayers.

"It is well," said the curé, "the fire is extinguished;
but do not leave me."

The prior seated himself close to the bed of the
other, and several hours passed in quietness. Suddenly
the unfortunate priest exclaimed:

"I am damned for eternity. The devil is throwing
me into a boiling cauldron; I see an ocean of ice in
which I shall freeze. Pray to God no more for me. It
is useless!"

Thereupon terror seized all who inhabited the
monastery, which was deserted immediately upon the
death of this unhappy man.

III. FRENCH SORCERERS AND SORCERESSES

It was in the tenth or eleventh century that the
wondrous Mélusine, appeared. I have already referred to Mélusine whom the old French romance by
John of Arras has immortalized. According to certain theologians, she was a sorceress, or a female
demon of the sea. (We are reminded of "Jullanar of
the Sea," in *The Thousand and One Nights*.) Others
have it that she was descended from a King of Albania
and a fairy. Paracelsus classes her as a nymph, but

most writers regard her as a powerful Elemental, who
wedded a seigneur of the House of Lusignan, and two
great Houses of Poitou and Dauphiny have carried on
their arms Mélusine represented as a siren. M. de
Saint-Albin has given, in his *Contes Noirs* (tome I,
p. 63) the history of Mélusine, according to the
popular opinion in certain cantons of Poitou. He
makes of her a sylphid or a fairy. After having
recorded her adventures, he concludes :

" Since she disappeared, every time that death
menaces one of her descendants, Mélusine shows herself in mourning on the Great Tower of the Château
of Lusignan, which she built. Her apparition also
announces the death of our Kings. . . ."

Some historians say that Mélusine was a woman
as adroit as she was beautiful, who claimed to possess
the power of transformation. She would have been
readily believed in an era when the changing of men
and women into wolves and other animals was not
regarded as phenomenal.

No notice of French sorcery, however brief, would be
complete without a reference to the French sorcerer
par excellence, Gilles de Rais, Baron de Laval and a
Marshal of France—the traditional " Blue Beard "—
who was burnt alive at Nantes in October 1440, for
the murder of some two hundred children, whose
throats were cut by this monster in order to obtain
their blood for use in magical rites and for the
evocation of the devil.[1]

It was proven that in a magnificent chapel which he
had erected, and which was served by priests whom

[1] A despatch from Havana, December 1913, contained particulars
of voodoo orgies in Cuba, a white girl having been sacrificed and the
blood drawn from her body by negro sorcerers.

he had seduced to his abominable opinions, the most
ghastly scenes of butchery took place, whilst these
wretched Churchmen sang hymns and offered up
prayers for the repose of the souls of the innocent
children immolated before their eyes.

A French author states that, although Laval was
condemned, his accomplices were saved by the Inquisition lest discredit might fall upon the clergy in general.
I have been unable to confirm this ; but let us pass on.

In the year 1472, the ferocious and pious Louis XI
caused his brother Charles, Duc de Guyenne, to be
imprisoned. The circumstances of this crime are
curious, and come strictly within the province of
sorcery. The Duc de Guyenne, a man of naturally
weak character, at the instigation of d'Ode Daidie,
Seigneur de Lescun, joined the league formed against
Louis XI. At the Court of the Duc was an abbé of
Saint-Jean d'Angely, a man, we are told, capable of
committing the worst of crimes, named Faure de
Versois, who readily entered into the schemes of the
French Nero. The monk presented to the Duc a
poisoned fish ; and the Comtesse de Monsoireau, the
mistress of this Prince, accepted half, but died almost
immediately after eating it.

It appears that nobody suspected Faure de Versois
at the moment, for he continued in favour with the
Duc—and was even named executor of the will of
the Comtesse de Monsoireau. The poisoner carried
on a correspondence with the King, to whom he wrote
saying that de Guyenne was approaching his end,
which was no more than true.

But now the villainous abbé of Saint-Jean was
suddenly arrested, and taken by sea to Brittany.
The Duc de Bretagne conducted him to the Boufflay

de Nantes, and the trial of the poisoner was commenced by the Bishop of Angers. Louis XI obtaining possession of the fragments of fish, which alone constituted the evidence of the poisoning, he burnt them.

The abbé, however, put to the question at Nantes, made a full confession, and a new accusation followed the judgment. The gaoler came, trembling, to the judges and told them that the abbé was a sorcerer, and that the prison must be emptied, as it had become impossible *to live there any longer, because of the fearful figures that were seen, and the howlings and lamentations that were heard.*[1]

When judgment was about to be pronounced a tremendous storm arose, so that the awesome noise of the thunder must have penetrated even to the abbé's dungeon. He was found lying on the ground, with tongue out, and his face black, swollen, and hideous ; and it was given out that the devil had strangled the sorcerer (but the friends of the Duc de Guyenne, we read, were very well able themselves to perform the office of the devil in this affair of intrigue).

The Duc de Bourgogne published, on the death of his ally, the Duc de Guyenne, a bloody manifesto against Louis XI. He accused the latter of having been the cause of the murder of his own brother by means of poisons, witchcraft, sorcery, and diabolical invocations. According to Argentré, an almost contemporary writer, who charges Louis XI with these crimes, we have the confession straight from the mouth of the fratricide. One day, whilst in the chapel of Notre Dame de Cléry, he is said to have addressed this prayer to the Virgin :

" Ah ! good Lady, my little mistress, my great

---

[1] *Histoire de la Bretagne*, Book XII., Chap. 423.

friend, in whom I always find comfort, I pray that thou wilt supplicate God for me, and be my advocate, that He will pardon me for the death of my brother, whom I caused to be poisoned by the hand of that bad abbé of Saint-Jean. Obtain my pardon, good Lady, and I know what I will give thee!"

In the year 1571, the notorious sorcerer, Trois Échelles, was executed in the Place de Grève. He confessed before the King, Charles IX, and in the presence of Ambroise Paré, the Maréchaux Montmorency and Ritz, the Seigneur de Lansac, and Mirzille, chief physician to the King, that he performed marvels by the aid of a spirit to whom he was bound, and that this spirit had tormented him for three years. He beseeched the King to pardon him, promising to reveal his accomplices; and that he might recognize them, he looked to see if they bore the devil's mark.

He conversed at length upon the Sabbath, the sacrifices which were offered, and on the lewd practices of women and devils. He spoke also of the composition of powders and ointments. Admiral de Coligny, who also was present, recollected that by means of these powders a valet had caused the death of two gentlemen by sprinkling their beds where they slept. He added that after their death they were found black and swollen.

The next case to which I beg leave to draw your attention is that of Loyse, daughter of Claude Maillat, of the village of Courières, aged eight years, who, on Saturday, June 15, 1598, was rendered impotent in all her limbs to such an extent that she was compelled to walk on all-fours, whilst her mouth was twisted in a most extraordinary manner. This continued until the 19th of July following, and her father and mother, convinced that she was possessed, took her to the Church of the Holy Saviour, where were discovered five demons whose names were given as *Loup*, *Chat*, *Chien*, *Joly*, and *Griffon*.

When the priest demanded of the girl who had been the cause of her troubles, she replied that it was a certain Françoise Secretain, at the same time pointing with her finger to one who assisted at the exorcism.

But the demons, according to Henri Boguet, would not leave her body. She was therefore taken back to the house of her parents, whom she begged to pray for her, saying that if they would do this she would very soon be delivered from the evil spirits. The hour of midnight was approaching when Loyse told her parents that two of the demons were dead, and that if they would continue to pray the others would meet with the same fate. Accordingly her parents remained all night in prayer, praying with an invincible ardour; and in the morning, at break of day, Loyse found herself suffering worse than ever. Nevertheless, throwing herself finally upon the floor, the demons left her body by the mouth in the form of large pellets—as big as one's fist, and red as fire, except that *Chat* was black. Those which she had pronounced as dead left last of all, but with less violence.

All these demons then jumped three or four times around the fire, and disappeared; from which time onwards Loyse steadily recovered.

Françoise Secretain confessed in the first place to having caused five demons to enter the body of Loyse Maillat, and that she had for some time been in the service of the devil, who appeared to her in the shape of a black man; that the devil had approached her amorously in the forms of a cat, a dog, and a fowl,

adding that the embrace of the Evil One was very cold ;
that she had attended the Sabbath on an infinite
number of occasions, and the assembly of sorcerers
below the village of Courières, in a place called Combes,
near the water ; that she had journeyed thither astride
a white staff ; that she, and others, had caused the
death of one Loys Monneret, by means of a piece of
bread which had been given him to eat, and which they
had sprinkled with a powder provided by the devil ;
that she had caused the death of several cows, by
touching them with her hand, or rather with a wand,
at the same time uttering an incantation.

" The glory of God," says our author, " was made
manifest in the imprisonment of Françoise."

The Italians who had come to the Court of France
in the train of the Queen, Marie de Médicis, had a
profound belief in the powers of magic. The famous
Maréchal d'Ancre, Concini Concini, was killed by a
pistol-shot on the drawbridge of the Louvre by Vitry,
Captain of the Bodyguard, on April 24, 1617. The
Parlement proceeded against the memory of the
deceased soldier ; and his wife, Léonora Galigai, was
included in the accusation—one of sorcery directed
against Marie de Médicis.

When the president, Courtin, demanded of her in
what manner she had caused the enchantment of the
Queen, she proudly replied :

" My witchcraft has been the power that a strong
will should have over a weak will."

At the *procès* were produced *agnus deis* (wax seals)
which were said to be talismans, and a letter that
Léonora had ordered to be written to the sorceress
Isabella. In the room of the Maréchale were found
three books of characters, five rolls of velvet for the

purposes of invoking the spirits of the great, and amulets to be suspended from the neck.

It was proved also that the Maréchal and his wife made use of wax images, which they kept in coffins, that they consulted magicians, astrologers, and sorcerers, notably one Cosmo Rugieri, an Italian, and the same who was put to the question on the occasion of the death of Charles IX. It was also established beyond doubt that they (the Maréchal and his wife) had brought sorcerers, notably from Nancy, in order to sacrifice a cock, and that one of them had burned incense in the garden, and blessed the earth; that Galigai ate nothing on these occasions but cocks' combs and the kidneys of a ram she had caused to be consecrated previously.

Léonora Concini was convicted of having been exorcised by Mathieu de Montmay, a charlatan who passed for a magician, in the Chapel of the Epiphany, a church of the Augustines. The monks of the convent were summoned, and the Maréchale d'Ancre confessed that she was exorcised at night, in their church, in order that her reputation might not suffer, as on occasions she was possessed. Upon this confession she was condemned to be beheaded, and her body to be burnt after death. The execution took place on July 8, 1617.

This affair serves to demonstrate the fearful beliefs which prevailed even in the houses of the principal officers of the Crown; consequently it is no matter for wonder that the lower classes saw sorcery in every ailment and witchcraft in every mishap.

In 1628, Desbordes, a valet-de-chambre of the Duc de Lorraine, Charles IV, was accused of having hastened the death of the Princess Christine, mother of the Duc, and of having caused divers maladies which the physicians attributed to sorcery. Charles IV had conceived grave suspicions against Desbordes, since the occasion of a hunting-party, when the valet-de-chambre had served, without other preparation than that of opening a small bottle, a grand banquet to the Duc and his companions; and, to crown the marvel, had commanded three unfortunate thieves, who were dead, and whose corpses still hung from the gibbet, to come and render homage and then to return to the gallows! Also, it was said of him that upon another occasion he commanded persons represented upon the tapestry to detach themselves from it and to come out into the middle of the room. One is almost tempted to sympathize with the suspicions of the Duc.

Charles IV desired that proceedings should be taken against Desbordes; and, accordingly, the valet was arrested and put to the question, being charged with having invoked the aid of sorcery. He made a partial confession and was condemned to be burnt at the stake.

This epoch, too, was notable for strange visions. Thus, the soldiers of the garrison of Lusignan declared that they saw two fiery horsemen fighting a single combat, about whom hovered a multitude of birds of sinister aspect, preceded by two torches and followed by the figure of a man making a noise like an owl!

IV. WITCH-FINDERS

With the increase of the sorcery epidemic uprose a class of persons whose business was the seeking out and burning of witches and sorcerers. Sprenger, in Germany, has the dubious honour of being the most active of these. He has laid down a regular form of trial, together with a course of examination by which his colleagues in other countries might discover the brand of Lucifer.

This individual alone made himself responsible for some 500 victims annually! Within three months, 900 perished in Würzburg, 600 in Bamberg, and 500 in Geneva. One judge of Lorraine boasted that he had personally condemned 900; and the Archbishop of Trèves, ascribing the cold spring of 1586 to witch-craft, burned 118 women at one time.

Pricking was the favourite mode employed by the witch-finder to learn if the suspected person were one of Satan's own, and the discharge of fourteen alleged witches by the Parlement of Paris, in 1589, appears to be the only notable instance of mercy throughout the whole black record. On this occasion, four com-missioners—Pierre Pigray, the King's surgeon, and Messrs. Leroi, Renard, and Falaiseau, the King's physicians—were appointed to examine these witches in quest of the devil's mark.

Pierre Pigray relates that the examination took place in the presence of two Court Counsellors. The witches were all stripped naked, and the physicians examined their bodies with great care, pricking them in all the marks they could find to learn if these were insensible to pain—a certain proof of guilt.

The poor women, however, were very sensible of the pricking, screaming when the pins were driven into them. " Many of them were quite indifferent about life, and one or two desired death as a relief from their sufferings." They were released, however.

A French theological Professor, who wrote in 1720, notes the following symptoms as being infallible signs of a person having been bewitched:

1. The vomiting of needles, nails, and pieces of glass.

2. Continual burning and lancinating pains, especially in the region of the heart, inability to retain food, and a sensation as if balls were rising and falling in the throat.

3. Suddenly falling ill of a grievous complaint, and wasting away without any apparent cause.

4. Medicines prescribed having the opposite effect from their known virtues and intensifying rather than modifying the disease.

To such an absurd extent were the proceedings against witches carried on the Continent, that it is related how, on one occasion, a sow and a litter of pigs were prosecuted. The whole family was found guilty and condemned to death ; but the infant porkers were reprieved on account of their youth !

The following is transcribed from an old chap-book which had a wide circulation in the seventeenth century :

" To help a Person under an ill Tongue, and make the Witch appear, or the Effect cease.

" Cut off some of the Party's Hair, just at the Nape of the Neck, clip it small and burn it to Powder, put the Powder in Sal-Armoniack, write the Party's Name you suspect backwards, and put the Paper, dipt in *Aqua Vitæ,* into the other two, then set it over a gentle Fire ; let the Party afflicted sit by it, and diligently watch it that it run not over to catch flame, speaking no Word, whatsoever Noise is heard, but take Notice of what Voice or Roaring is heard in the Chimney, or any part of the Room, and then write how often you hear it, and fix before each writing this Character, ☽ —and if the Party who afflicts you appear not Visible, though you may know the Voice, repeat it again, and if she appear in no visible shape, it may make her charm impotent, and give relief to the Afflicted Party."

Famous among witch-finders was James VI of Scotland; and, if his work on demonology has not rendered him immortal, by reason of his dealings with those suspected of witchcraft at least he is for ever execrable. The torturing of the young and handsome Gellie Duncan, and the infamous torments to which her reputed accomplice, Cunningham (Dr. Fian), was submitted, are but some of the items to the debit of James VI of Scotland.

Dr. Fian was far removed from a saintly character, but when his examination by James was concluded (restoratives having been administered again and again in order to render the victim conscious of re-newed tortures) he was less a man than a bleeding mass, for even the bones of his legs had been crushed to pulp in the boot; his nails had been withdrawn by pincers and needles thrust into his eyes to the sockets.

Euphemia Macalzean (another alleged accomplice of poor Gellie Duncan) was doomed " to be burned in ashes, *quick* [1] to the death." This inhuman sentence was carried out on June 25, 1591.

In 1597 James published in Edinburgh his treatise on demonology. In the introduction he says:

" The fearful abounding at this time and in this country of these detestable slaves of the devil, the witches or enchanters, hath moved me, beloved reader, to dispatch in post this following treatise of mine, not in any wise, as I protest, to serve for a show of mine own learning and ingene, [2] but only (moved of conscience) to press thereby . . . that the instrument . . . merits most severely to be punished, against

[1] *Quick* = alive.   [2] Ingenuity.

the damnable opinions of two, principally in our age ; whereof the one called Scot, an Englishman, is not ashamed in public print to deny that there can be such things as witchcraft. . . ."

Other parts of his work James thoughtfully cast in the form of dialogue, to render it, in his own words, " more pleasant and facile " !

England and Scotland, then, soon competed with the Continental countries in the burning of witches, and Zachary Grey, the editor of *Hudibras*, says that he himself perused a list of three thousand victims executed during the session of the Long Parliament alone. 1634 is notorious for the trial of the " Lancashire Witches," but it remained for Manningtree, Essex, about the year 1644, to present to the world a master witch-finder, in the vulgar person of Matthew Hopkins. Assuming the title of " Witch - finder General," Hopkins toured the counties of Norfolk, Essex, Hants, and Sussex, in quest of witches. In one year he brought no fewer than sixty to the stake.

The method of detection upon which he pinned his faith was that of " swimming "—so highly recommended by James VI of Scotland. The right thumb of the suspected person was tied to the toe of the left foot, and *vice versa*. She was then wrapped in a blanket and placed on her back in a pond. If she floated— which we are told was generally the case when placed carefully upon the water—she was guilty, and was burned forthwith ; if she sank, she was innocent !

Hopkins travelled like a gentleman, attended by his two assistants, always putting up at the principal inn of the town—at the cost of the authorities. He charged 20s. per visit, with expenses, and 20s. per head for each witch convicted.

THE FRONTISPIECE OF MATTHEW HOPKINS' "DISCOVERY OF WITCHES,"
1644

He had carried on his outrageous trade for three years when the Rev. Mr. Gaul, of Houghton, published a pamphlet directed against the cruel rogue. In it he describes another method employed by Hopkins to detect a witch. He relates that the Witch-finder General used to place the suspected woman in the middle of a room, cross-legged upon a stool. Hopkins then caused her to be watched by his assistants for four-and-twenty hours, during which time she was kept without food or drink.

The interesting theory was that one of her imps would come during that time to suck her blood. As the imp might come in the form of a fly, of a wasp, or of any other insect, and as doors and windows were thoughtfully left open, visitations by imps were common under the circumstances. It was the duty of the watchers to kill any insect which appeared ; if a fly escaped, it was her imp—the woman was guilty, she was sentenced to the stake, and Matthew Hopkins collected his modest fee of 20s. from the local authorities.

Of Matthew Hopkins Butler says in *Hudibras* :

> Hath not this present Parliament
> A lieger to the devil sent,
> Fully empowered to treat about
> Finding revolted witches out ?
> And has he not within a year
> Hang'd threescore of them in one shire ?
> Some only for not being drown'd,
> And some for sitting above ground
> Whole days and nights upon their breeches,
> And feeling pain, were hang'd for witches ;
> And some for putting knavish tricks
> Upon green geese or turkey chicks ;
> Or pigs that suddenly deceased
> Of griefs unnatural, as he guessed ;
> Who proved himself at length a witch,
> And made a rod for his own breech.

One rejoices to learn that Matthew Hopkins was
" swum," according to his own recipe, in a Suffolk
village-pond, and either drowned or subsequently
executed.

In Scotland, at this period, witch-finders flourished
under the generic title of " common prickers," receiving,
like the talented Hopkins, a fee for each conviction.
John Kincaid, the common pricker of Dalkeith, in
1646, was caused by the magistrates to exercise his
craft upon the person of one Janet Peaston.

" He found two marks of the devil's making," says
Pitcairn, in *Records of Justiciary*, " for she could
not feel the pin when it was put into either of the
said marks . . . they were pins of three inches in
length " !

Hundreds of innocent persons had suffered at the
hands of the common prickers ere, in 1678, the Privy
Council of Scotland sat to consider the appeal of an
honest woman who had been indecently exposed by
one of them, and expressed the opinion that " common
prickers were *common cheats*." [1]

V. THE STAKE

Many persons were averse from witches being
hanged, contending that burning was the better form
of death because, the body of a witch being burnt, her
blood was prevented thereby from " becoming here-
ditary to her Progeny in the same evill, which by
hanging is not."

[1] A " bewitching " in the village of Higher Bockhampton (Thomas
Hardy's "Upper Melstock") in December 1913, brought to light a
practising witch-finder in that place.

On March 4, 1647, at Worcester, four witches, Cock, Landish, Rebecca West, and Rose Hallybread, were sentenced to be burnt at the stake together. The following is taken from a rare tract published the same year:

"When being come to the Place of Execution, they made a strange and lamentable Yeling and Howling, after which they Confessed the Crimes for which they Suffered, and also declared how they had killed abundance of Cattle for several years past, and that it was extream Pride, Malice, and Revenge, that caused them to enter into such a cursed and Hellish League with the Devil, who told them to the Last, that he would secure them from Public Punishment, but now, too late, they found him a Lyer, as he was from the beginning of the World. Cock and Landish seemed penitent, desiring all young Women to take Warning by their Devilish Lives, and Shameful Deaths, assuring the Spectators, that as Satan in the first Infancy of the World, prevail'd on the Woman to bring his Hellish attempts to pass, so he still strives with that Sex as the weaker Vessels, to Work their Destructions; they both said the Lord's Prayer very distinctly, but Rebecca West and Rose Hallybread dyed very Stuborn and Refractory, without any remorse, or seeming Terror of Conscience for their abominable Witchcraft."

Pitcairn in his *Criminal Trials in Scotland* writes:

"Among the circumstances which peculiarly characterize the earlier Criminal proceedings of Scotland, as well as those of England, France, and Germany, etc., none are more prominent than the unmitigated vigour with which the profession as well as the practice of Witchcraft, Sorcery, and Necromancy, were punished.

The hecatombs of innocent victims, whose lives were sacrificed to satisfy the gloomy superstitions of Nations termed Christian and civilized, but who in reality were only emerging from a state of semi-barbarism, sufficiently attest the Justice of this observation . . . matters were no better in England, where the most shocking atrocities were perpetrated during the reigns of Charles I and Charles II, and also under the Puritans of Oliver Cromwell's time."

He also says :

" Perhaps there cannot be adduced a more touching qroof of the nefarious wickedness which must have been perpetrated in Scotland during the reign of James VI, than the following memorandum, which is preserved by Thomas, Earl of Haddington . . . in his Minutes of Privy Council Proceedings. He relates, under date December 8, 1608 : [1] ' The Earl of Mar declareth to the Council, that some women were taken in Broughton as Witches ; and being put to an Assize, and convicted, albeit they persevered in their denial to the end, they were burnt alive after such a cruel manner, that some of them died in despair, renouncing their baptism and blaspheming ; and others half-burnt brake out of the fire and were cast in alive in it again until they were burnt to death.' "

The following quaint remarks on witches are worth quoting. They are taken from Reginald Scot's *Discoverie of Witchcraft*, written against the popular superstitions of the time. Reginald Scot was a refreshing example of an enlightened mind in a superstitious age. His book, written in 1584, is brimful of humour and quaint good sense. James VI of Scot-

---

[1] I have rendered the relation in modern English, and not as Pitcairn quotes it in *Braid Scots*.

land ordered all copies of the work that could be found to be burnt by the common hangman, and we have already seen, from a portion of the Royal author's *Demonologie*, quoted, that he counted Scot a friend of Satan.

"The true idea of a *Witch*, an old weather-beaten *Crone*, having her Chin and her Knees meeting for Age, walking like a Bow leaning on a Staff, Hollow-Ey'd, Untooth'd, Furrow'd on her Face, having her Lips trembling with the Palsy, going mumbling in the Streets : One that hath forgotten her *Pater-Noster*, and yet hath a shrewd Tongue to call a *Drab* a *Drab*. If she hath learn'd of an old Wife in a Chimney End, *Pax, Max, Fax* for a Spell ; or can say Sir John Grantham's Curse for the Miller's Eels, All ye that have stolen the Miller's Eels, *laudate Dominum de Cœlis* : And all they that have consented thereto, *benedicamus Domino* : Why then beware, look about you my Neighbours. If any of you have a sheep sick of the Giddies, or a Hog of the Mumps, or a Horse of the Staggers, or a Knavish Boy of the School, or an idle Girl of the Wheel, or a young Drab of the Sullens, and hath not Fat enough for her Pottage, or Butter enough for her Bread, and she hath a little Help of the Epilepsy, or Cramp, to teach her to roll her Eyes, wry her Mouth, gnash her Teeth, startle with her Body, hold her Arms and Hands stiff, etc. And then when an *old Mother Nobs* hath by Chance call'd her *Idle young Housewife*, or bid the Devil scratch her ; then no doubt but Mother Nobs is the Witch, and the young Girl is *Owlblasted*. . . .

"They that have their Brains baited, and their Fancies distemper'd with the Imaginations and Apprehensions of Witches, Conjurors, and Fairies, and all

that Lymphatical *Chimæra*, I find to be marshall'd
in one of these five Ranks ; Children, Fools, Women,
Cowards, sick or black melancholick discompos'd
Wits."

VI. THE INCUBUS OF PAVIA

It is not remarkable that the confessions of these
poor tortured souls corresponded so closely ; the form
of interrogation was identical in each case, the answers
mere groaning " Nays " and all but inaudible " Yes."
But the views held by many people of considerable
intelligence at this time are less easy to explain.

The particular instance I have in mind is that of
Sinistrari of Ameno. Whilst searching for a certain
print in one of the shops of the Palais Royal I came
upon a copy of Sinistrari's book on *Demoniality*, translated from a seventeenth-century MS., and printed in
Paris. There is also a copy of this curious work in the
British Museum. As one peruses the reverend Father's
pages, much that has seemed incomprehensible in the
records of the sorcery laws becomes comprehensible ;
for it was men such as this who framed them.

I make no apology for the following long extract ;
I am confident that it will enlighten my reader as it
has enlightened me.

A most marvellous and well-nigh incomprehensible
fact (says Sinistrari) : the Incubi whom the Italians
call *Folletti*, the Spaniards *Duendes*, the French *Follets*,
do not obey the Exorcist, have no dread of exorcism, no
reverence for holy things, at the approach of which
they are not in the least overawed ; very different in
that respect from the Demons who vex those whom they
possess ; for, however obstinate those evil Spirits may

be, however restive to the injunctions of the Exorcist who bids them leave the body they possess, yet, at the mere utterance of the holy names—or of some verses of holy Writ, at the mere imposition of relics, especially of a piece of the wood of the Holy Cross, or the sight of the holy images, they roar at the mouth of the possessed person, they gnash, shake, quiver, and display fright and awe. But the Folletti show none of those signs, and leave off their vexations but after a long space of time. Of this I was an eye-witness, and shall relate a story which verily passes human belief; but *I take God to witness that I tell the precise truth*,[1] corroborated by the testimony of numerous persons.

About twenty-five years ago, when I was a lecturer on Sacred Theology in the convent of the Holy Cross, in Pavia, there was living in that city a married woman of unimpeachable morality, and who was most highly spoken of by all such as knew her, especially by the Friars; her name was Hieronyma, and she lived in the parish of St. Michael. One day, this woman had kneaded bread at home and given it out to bake. The oven-man brought her back her loaves when baked, and with them a large cake of a peculiar shape, and made of butter and Venetian paste, as is usual in that city. She declined to take it in, saying she had not made anything of the kind.

" But," said the man, " I had no other bread but yours to bake to-day, therefore this cake also must have come from your house; your memory is at fault."

The good lady allowed herself to be persuaded, and partook of the cake with her husband, her little girl three years old, and the house servant. The next night, whilst in bed with her husband, and both asleep,

---

[1] The italics are mine.

she suddenly woke up at the sound of a very slender voice, something like a shrill hissing, whispering in her ears, yet with great distinctness, and inquiring whether "the cake had been to her taste." The good lady, frightened, set about guarding herself with the sign of the cross and repeatedly calling the holy names.

"Be not afraid," said the voice, "I mean you no harm ; quite the reverse. I am prepared to do any-thing to please you ; I am captivated by your beauty, and desire nothing more than to enjoy your em-braces."

And she felt some one kissing her cheeks, so lightly, so softly, that she might have fancied being grazed by the finest down.

She resisted without giving any answer, merely repeating over and over again the names . . . and crossing herself ; the tempter kept on thus for nearly half an hour, when he withdrew.

The next morning the dame called on her confessor, a discreet and learned man, who confirmed her in her faith, exhorted her to maintain her energetic resistance and to provide herself with some holy relics. On the ensuing nights, like temptation with the same language and kisses, like constancy also on the part of the woman. Weary, however, of such painful and persistent molestation, taking the advice of her confessor and other grave men, she had herself exorcised by experi-enced exorcists, in order to ascertain whether perchance she was not possessed.

Having found in her no trace of the Evil Spirit, they blessed the house, the bedroom, the bed, and enjoined on the Incubus to discontinue his molestations. All to no purpose ; he kept on worse than ever, pretending to be love-sick, weeping and moaning in order to melt the heart of the lady, who, however, by the grace of God, remained unconquered.

The Incubus then went another way to work : he appeared in the shape of a lad or little man of great beauty, with golden locks, a flaxen beard that shone like gold, sea-green eyes calling to mind the flax-flower, and arrayed in a fancy Spanish dress. Besides, he appeared to her even when in company, whimpering, after the fashion of lovers, kissing his hand to her, and endeavouring by every means to obtain her embraces. She alone saw and heard him ; for everybody else, he was not to be seen.

The good lady kept persevering in her admirable constancy till, at last, after some months of courting, the Incubus, incensed at her disdain, had recourse to a new kind of persecution.

First, he took away from her a silver cross filled with holy relics, and a holy wax or papal lamb of the blessed Pontiff Pius V, which she always carried on her person ; then, leaving the locks untouched, he purloined her rings and other gold and silver jewellery from the casket wherein they were put away.

Next, he began to strike her cruelly, and after each beating bruises and marks were to be seen on her face, her arms, or other parts of her body, which lasted a day or two, then suddenly disappeared, the reverse of natural bruises, which decrease slowly and by degrees. Sometimes, while she was nursing her little girl, he would snatch the child away from her breast, and lay it upon the roof, or the edge of the gutter, or hide it ; but without ever harming it. Sometimes he would upset all the furniture, or smash to pieces saucepans, plates, and other earthenware which, in the twinkling of an eye, he restored to their former state.

One night that she was lying with her husband, the Incubus, appearing in his customary shape, vehemently urged his demand, which she resisted as usual. The Incubus withdrew in a rage, and shortly came back with a large load of those flagstones which the Genoese, and the inhabitants of Liguria in general, use for roofing their houses. With those stones he built around the bed a wall so high that it reached the tester, and that the couple could not leave their bed without using a ladder. This wall, however, was built up without lime ; when pulled down, the flags were laid by in a corner where, during two days, they were seen by many who came to look at them ; they then disappeared.

On St. Stephen's day, the husband had asked some military friends to dinner, and, to do honour to his guests, had provided a substantial repast. Whilst they were, as customary, washing their hands before taking their seats, the table prepared in the dining-room suddenly vanished ; all the dishes, saucepans, kettles, plates, and crockery in the kitchen vanished likewise, as well as the jugs, bottles, and glasses.

You may imagine the surprise, the stupor of the guests, eight in number ; amongst them was a Spanish captain of infantry, who, addressing the company, said to them :

" Do not be frightened, it is but a trick : the table is certainly still where it stood, and I shall soon find it by feeling for it."

Having thus spoken, he paced round the room with outstretched arms, endeavouring to lay hold of the table ; but when, after many circuitous perambulations, it was apparent that he laboured in vain and grasped at naught but thin air, he was laughed at by his friends ; and it being already high time for having dinner, each guest took up his cloak and set about to return home.

They had already reached the street-door with the husband, who, out of politeness, was attending them, when they heard a great noise in the dining-room ; they stood to ascertain the cause thereof, and presently the servant came up to announce that the kitchen was stocked with new vessels filled with food, and that the table was standing again in its former place. Having gone back to the dining-room, they were stupefied to see the table was laid, with cloths, napkins, salt-cellars, and trays that did not belong to the house, and with food which had not been cooked there.

On a large sideboard all were arranged in perfect order, crystal, silver and gold chalices, with all kinds of amphoras, decanters, and cups filled with foreign wines, from the Isle of Crete, Campania, the Canaries, the Rhine, etc. In the kitchen there was also an abundant variety of meats in saucepans and dishes that had never been seen there before.

At first some of the guests hesitated whether they should taste of that food ; however, encouraged by others, they sat down, and soon partook of the meal, which was found exquisite. Immediately afterwards, as they were sitting before a seasonable fire, everything vanished at once, the dishes and the leavings, and in their stead reappeared the cloth of the house and the victuals which had been previously cooked ; but, for a wonder, all the guests were satisfied, so that no one thought of supper after such a magnificent dinner, a clear proof that the substituted viands were real, and nowise fictitious.

This kind of persecution had been going on some months when the lady betook herself to the blessed Bernardine of Feltri, whose body is worshipped in the Church of St. James, a short distance from the walls of the city. She made a vow to him that she would wear, during a whole twelvemonth, a grey frock, tied round her waist with a piece of cord, and such as is worn by the Minor Brethren, the order to which had belonged the blessed Bernardine; this she vowed, in the hope of being, through his intercession, at last rid of the persecution of the Incubus.

And accordingly, on September 28, the vigil of the Dedication of the Archangel St. Michael, and the festival of the blessed Bernardine, she assumed the votive robe. The next morning, which was St. Michael's festival, the afflicted woman proceeded to the Church of St. Michael, her own parish, already mentioned; it was about ten o'clock, a time when a crowd of people were going to mass.

She had no sooner set foot on the threshold of the church than her clothes and ornaments fell off to the ground, and disappeared in a gust of wind, leaving her stark naked.

There happened fortunately to be among the crowd two cavaliers of mature age, who, seeing what had taken place, hastened to divest themselves of their cloaks, with which they concealed, as well as they could, the woman's nudity, and having put her into a vehicle, accompanied her home. The clothes were not restored by him before six months had elapsed.

I might relate many other most surprising tricks which that Incubus played on her, were it not wearisome. Suffice it to say that for a number of years he persevered in his temptation of her, but that, finding at last that he was losing his pains, he desisted from his vexatious importunities.

In the above case, as well as in others that may be heard or read of occasionally, the Incubus attempts no act against religion ; he merely assails chastity. In consequence (adds Sinistrari) consent is not a sin through ungodliness, but through incontinence.

VII. STORY OF THE NOBLE MAIDEN AND OF THE DEACON AUSTIN

One so rarely happens upon a lighter side to this dark subject, that I am loath to dismiss Sinistrari of Ameno without another short extract. I shall therefore transcribe paragraphs 71 and 72 from his valuable work :

To illustrate this subject (he says), I give two stories, the first of which I have from a Confessor of Nuns, a man of weight, and most worthy of credit ; the second I was eye-witness to.

In a certain monastery of holy nuns there lived, as a boarder, a young maiden of noble birth, who was tempted by an Incubus that appeared to her by day and by night, and with the most earnest entreaties, the manners of a most passionate lover, incessantly incited her to sin ; but she, supported by the grace of God and the frequent use of the sacraments, stoutly resisted the temptation. But, all her devotions, fasts, and vows notwithstanding, despite the exorcisms, the blessings, the injunctions showered by exorcists on the Incubus that he should desist from molesting her ; in spite of the crowd of relics and other holy objects

collected in the maiden's room, of the lighted candles
kept burning there all night, the Incubus none the less
persisted in appearing to her as usual, in the shape
of a very handsome young man.

At last, among other learned men, whose advice
had been taken on the subject, was a very erudite
Theologian, who, observing that the maiden was of a
thoroughly phlegmatic temperament, surmised that
the Incubus was an aqueous Demon (there are in fact,
as is testified by Guaccius, igneous, aerial, phlegmatic,
earthly, subterranean Demons, who avoid the light of
day), and prescribed an uninterrupted fumigation in
the room.

A new vessel, made of glass-like earth, was accordingly brought in, and filled with sweet cane, cubeb
seed, roots of both aristolochies, great and small cardamom, ginger, long-pepper, caryophylleæ, cinnamon,
cloves, mace, nutmegs, calamite, storax, benzoin,
aloes-wood and roots, one ounce of triasandalis, and
three pounds of half brandy and water; the vessel
was then set on hot ashes in order to distil the fumi-
gating vapour, and the cell was kept closed.

As soon as the fumigation was done, the Incubus
came, but never dared enter the cell; only, if the
maiden left it for a walk in the garden or the cloister,
he appeared to her, though invisible to others, and,
throwing his arms round her neck, stole or rather
snatched kisses from her, to her intense disgust.

At last, after a new consultation, the Theologian
prescribed that she should carry about her person
pills made of the most exquisite perfumes, such as
musk, amber, chive, Peruvian balsam, etc. Thus
provided, she went for a walk in the garden, where
the Incubus suddenly appeared to her with a threaten-

ing face, and in a rage. He did not approach her,
however, but, after biting his finger as if meditating
revenge, disappeared and was never more seen by her.

Here is the other story (according to Sinistrari). In
the great Carthusian Friary of Pavia there lived a
Deacon, Austin by name, who was subjected by a
certain Demon to excessive, unheard-of, and scarcely
credible vexations ; although many exorcists had
made repeated endeavours to secure his riddance, all
spiritual remedies had proved unavailing. I was consulted by the Vicar of the convent, who had the cure
of the poor clerk. Seeing the inefficacy of all customary exorcisms, and remembering the above-related
instance, I advised a fumigation like unto the one that
has been detailed, and prescribed that the Deacon
should carry about his person fragrant pills of the same
kind ; moreover, as he was in the habit of using tobacco,
and was very fond of brandy, I advised tobacco and
brandy perfumed with musk.

The Demon appeared to him by day and by night,
under various shapes, as a skeleton, a pig, an ass, an
angel, a bird ; with the figure of one or other of the
Friars, once even with that of his own Abbot or Prior,
exhorting him to keep his conscience clean, to trust
in God, to confess frequently ; he persuaded him to
let him hear his sacramental confession, recited with
him the psalms *Exsurgat Deus* and *Qui habitat*, and
the Gospel according to St. John : and when they came
to the words *Verbum carno factum est*, he bent his knee,
and taking hold of a stole which was in the cell, and of
the Holy-water sprinkler, he blessed the cell and the
bed, and, as if he had really been the Prior, enjoined
on the Demon not to venture in future to molest his

subordinate ; he then disappeared, thus betraying what he was, for otherwise the young Deacon had taken him for his Prior.

Now, notwithstanding the fumigations and perfumes I had prescribed, the Demon did not desist from his wonted apparitions ; more than that, assuming the features of his victim, he went to the Vicar's room, and asked for some tobacco and brandy perfumed with musk, of which, said he, he was extremely fond. Having received both, he disappeared in the twinkling of an eye, thus showing the Vicar that he had been played with by the Demon ; and this was amply confirmed by the Deacon, who affirmed upon oath that he had not gone that day to the Vicar's cell.

All that having been related to me, I inferred that, far from being aqueous like the Incubus who was in love with the maiden above spoken of, this Demon was igneous, or, at the very least, aerial, since he delighted in hot substances such as vapours, perfumes, tobacco, and brandy. Force was added to my surmises by the temperament of the young Deacon, which was choleric and sanguine, choler predominating however ; for these Demons never approach but those whose temperament tallies with their own—another confirmation of my sentiment regarding their corporeity. I therefore advised the Vicar to let his penitent take herbs that are cold by nature, such as water-lily, liver-wort, spurge, mandrake, house-leek, plantain, henbane, and others similar, make two little bundles of them and hang them up, one at his window, the other at the door of his cell, taking care to strow some also on the floor and on the bed.

Marvellous to say, the Demon appeared again, but remained outside the room, which he would not enter ;

and, on the Deacon inquiring of him his motives for such unwonted reserve, he burst out into invectives against me for giving such advice, disappeared, and never came again.

VIII. WITCH TRIALS

In an age of such beliefs, what chance had a suspect to prove her innocence ?   I shall give examples, now, of some of the *evidence* upon which unfortunate women were convicted in England.   The dreadful Salem Cases (1691–2) I cannot hope to touch upon in the space at my disposal.   " In all the trials of this kind," says Lowell in his *History of the Salem Delusion*, " there is nothing so pathetic as the picture of Jonathan Cary holding up the weary arms of his wife during her trial, and wiping away the sweat from her brow and the tears from her face."

The first example of evidence which I shall quote I take from Hutchinson's *Historical Essay concerning Witchcraft*—written in 1720.   The defendant in this case was acquitted.

" *Elizabeth Horner* was tried before the Lord Chief Justice *Holt* at *Exeter* (in 1696).   Three children of *William Bovet* were thought to have been bewitched by her, whereof one was dead.   It was deposed that another had her legs twisted, and yet from her Hands and Knees she would spring five Foot high.   The Children vomited Pins, and were bitten (if the Depositions were true) and pricked and pinched, the Marks appearing.   The Children said *Bess Horner's* Head would come off from her Body, and go into their Bellies.   The Mother of the Children deposed, that one

of them walked up a smooth plaistered Wall, till her
Feet were nine Foot high, her Head standing off from
it.   This, she said, she did five or six times, and laughed
and said *Bess Horner* held her up.   This poor Woman
had something like a Nipple on her Shoulder, which
the Children said was sucked by a Toad.   Many other
odd things were deposed, but the Jury brought her in
Not Guilty."

The defendants in the following case were not so
fortunate.   I transcribe some of the evidence from a
report of the trial published in 1682.   A certain amount
of interest is attached to this trial, as it took place
before Sir Matthew Hale, admittedly a virtuous and
learned judge, and Sir Thomas Browne, of *Vulgar Errors*
fame, was called to give expert evidence.   Indeed,
Hutchinson in his essay on witchcraft asserts that
Browne's evidence turned the scale against the unfortunate prisoners.   I have selected some of the most
interesting points that transpired during the trial,
from a mass of tedious and irrelevant matter.

" At the Assizes held at Bury St. Edmonds for the
County of Suffolk the tenth day of March, in the Sixteenth Year of the Reign of our Sovereign Lord King
Charles II before Matthew Hale, Knight . . . Rose
Cullender and Amy Duny, Widows both of Leystoff
(*i.e.* Lowestoft) were severally indicted for bewitching
Elizabeth and Ann Durent, Jane Bocking, Susan Chand-
ler, William Durent, Elizabeth and Deborah Pacey :
And the said Cullender and Duny, being arraigned
upon the said Indictments, pleaded Not Guilty : And
afterwards, upon a long evidence were found Guilty,
and thereupon had Judgment to dye for the same."

Thus stands the grim official record.

The account of the trial opens by stating that three

of the " bewitched " persons, coming to the hall upon
the morning of the trial, " fell into strange and violent
fits, screeking out in a most sad manner, so that they
could not in any wise give any Instructions in the
Court who were the Cause of their Distemper. And
although they did after some certain space recover . . .
yet they were every one of them struck Dumb, so that
none of them could speak . . . until the Conviction of
the supposed Witches."

The first witness called was the mother of William
Durent (an infant). She deposed that she had requested old Amy Duny to look to her child whilst she
was from home. During her absence the old lady, in
order to keep the child quiet, gave him the breast. On
the mother's return, she remonstrated with Duny for
having done so. Duny then used threatening speeches
to her, telling her " that she had as good to have done
otherwise than to have found fault with her, and so
departed out of the House."

That very night, continued the mother, " her son
fell into strange fits of swooning," which continued
for several weeks. A certain Dr. Jacob of Yarmouth,
of local repute as a healer of bewitched children, was
consulted. His advice was " to hang up the Child's
Blanket in the Chimney corner all day, and at night
when she put the Child to Bed, to put it into the said
blanket, and if she found anything in it, she should
not be afraid, but to throw it into the Fire."

This was done accordingly, and at night there fell
out of the blanket " a great Toad which ran up and
down the hearth." This, when caught and thrown
into the Fire, " made a great and horrible noise, and
after a space there was a flashing in the Fire like
Gun-powder," and the Toad disappeared.

On the following day Amy Duny was observed to be in a lamentable condition, " having her face all scorched with fire." On being asked by the deponent " how she came in that sad condition, the said Amy replied, she might thank her for it . . . but that she should live to see some of her Children dead, and she upon crutches. And this Deponent further saith that after the burning of the said Toad, her child recovered, and was well again."

Shortly afterward her daughter, Elizabeth, aged ten, was taken in like manner, " and in her fits complained much of Amy Duny and said that she did appear to her, and Afflict her." The child died in a few days and the mother herself was shortly " taken with a Lameness in both her Leggs " and had to use crutches as the witch had prophesied. It is related that at the conclusion of the trial, when a verdict of Guilty was returned, her lameness vanished and she returned home without her crutches.

Some very curious evidence was given with regard to the alleged bewitching by Amy Duny and Rose Cullender of the two children of Samuel Pacey, a fishmonger of Lowestoft—Deborah and Elizabeth.

It appears that the old woman, on having been refused when desiring to purchase herrings of the parents of the children, threatened them, and soon afterwards the children became " grievously afflicted." The father deposed that " their fits were various, sometimes they would be lame on one side of their Bodies, sometimes on the other . . . once they were wholly deprived of their Speech for Eight days together. . . . Upon the recovery of their Speech they would Cough extreamly, and bring up much Flegme, and with the same crooked Pins, and one time a two-penny Nail, with a very broad head, which Pins (amounting to Forty or more) together with the Two-penny Nail, were produced in Court.

" The said Children after their fits were past would tell how that Amy Duny and Rose Cullender would appear before them, threatening that if they related either what they saw or heard, that they would torment them ten times more than ever they did before." Another witness stated that " the children (only) would see things run up and down the House in the appearance of Mice ; and one of them suddenly snapt one with the Tongs, and threw it into the fire, and it screeched like a Rat. At another time, the younger Child being out of her Fitts went out of Doors to take a little Fresh Air and presently a little thing like a Bee flew upon her Face." The witness continued, " The Child fell into her swooning Fitt, and at last with much pain straining herself, she vomited up a Twopenny Nail with a broad head, . . . and being demanded by this Deponent how she came by the Nail ? She Answered, That the Bee brought this Nail and forced it into her Mouth.

" And at other times, the Elder Child declared upon this Deponent, that during the time of her Fitts, she saw Flies come unto her, and bring with them in their Mouths crooked Pins ; and after the Child had thus declared the same, she fell again into Violent Fits, and afterwards raised several pins."

Upon yet another occasion, " being recovered out of her Fitts, the Younger daughter declared that Amy Duny had been with her, and that she tempted her to Drown herself, and to cut her Throat, or otherwise to Destroy herself."

Much similar evidence was given regarding the cases

of these children which apparently did not satisfy some of the " divers Known persons " learned in the law, in court, viz., Mr. Sergeant Keeling, Mr. Sergeant Earl, and Mr. Sergeant Barnard.

" Mr. Sergeant Keeling seemed much unsatisfied with it," proceeds the account, " and thought it not sufficient to Convict the Prisoners."   " There was also Dr. Brown of Norwich, a Person of great Knowledge ; who after this Evidence given, and upon view of the three persons in Court, was desired to give his Opinion, what he did conceive of them ; and he was clearly of Opinion that the persons were Bewitched ; and said That in Denmark there had been lately a great Discovery of Witches, who used the very same way of Afflicting Persons, by conveying Pins into them, and crooked, as these pins were, with Needles and Nails. And his Opinion was, That the Devil in such cases did work upon the Bodies of Men and Women, upon a Natural Foundation (that is) to stir up, and excite such humours super-abounding in their Bodies to a great excess, whereby he did in an extraordinary manner Afflict them with such Distempers as their Bodies were most subject to, as particularly appeared in these Children ; for he conceived that these swooning Fits were Natural . . . only heightened to a great excess by the subtilty of the Devil, Co-operating with the Malice of these which we term Witches, at whose Instance he doth these Villanies."

It becomes painful to continue recording the puerile evidence upon which these poor old women were condemned ; the deposition of one more complainant must therefore suffice :

" Robert Sheringham deposeth against Rose Cullender, That about two years since, passing along the

Street with his Cart and Horses, the Axletree of his
Cart touched her House, and broke down some part
of it, at which she was very much displeased, threatening him that his Horses should suffer for it ; and so it
happen'd, for all those Horses, being four in Number,
died within a short time after ; since that time he hath
had great Losses by the suddain dying of his other
Cattle ; as soon as his Sows pigged, the Pigs would
leap and caper, and immediately fall down and dye.
Also not long after he was taken with a Lameness in
his Limbs that he could neither go nor stand for some
days. After all this, he was very much vexed with
great Number of Lice of an extraordinary bigness, and
although he many times shifted himself, yet he was
not anything the better, but would swarm again with
them ; so that in the Conclusion he was forced to burn
all his Clothes, being two suits of Apparel, and then was
clean from them."

The Judge summed up briefly, leaving the matter
entirely in the hands of the jury, remarking :

" That there were such Creatures as Witches he
made no doubt at all ; for *First*, the Scriptures had
affirmed so much. *Secondly*, the wisdom of all Nations
had provided Laws against such Persons, which is an
Argument of their confidence of such a Crime."

In less than half an hour the jury returned, and
found both the accused guilty upon every count in the
indictment, thirteen in all.

The following day they were brought up for judgment,
and the narration concludes :

" The Judge and all the Court were fully satisfied
with the Verdict, and thereupon gave Judgment
against the Witches that they should be Hanged.

" They were much urged to confess, but would not,

no Reprieve was granted, And they were executed on Monday the Seventeenth of March following, but they Confessed nothing."

The chronicler remarks that " within less than half an hour after the Witches were Convicted," the children were all restored to perfect health again.

In Britain, then, as elsewhere, the Black Art died hard. The last witch executed in Scotland was an old woman—I have been unable to ascertain her name —who was burnt at Dornoch in 1722. It is related of her that " having been brought out for execution, the weather proving very severe, she sat composedly warming herself by the fire, while the other instruments of death were made ready."

Scotland thus has the honour, by six years, of having executed the last witch ; for Mrs. Hicks and her daughter, aged *nine*, were the last sufferers in England. They were hanged at Huntingdon in 1716 for selling their souls to the devil, and raising a storm by pulling off their stockings and making a lather of soap !

CONCLUSION

SORCERY AND SCIENCE

TOWARD the conclusion of his address to the British Association at Birmingham, September 10, 1913, Sir Oliver Lodge said:

"' Either we are immortal beings or we are not. We may not know our destiny, but we must have a destiny of some sort. Science may not be able to reveal human destiny, but it certainly should not obscure it. I am one of those who think that the methods of science are not so limited in their scope as has been thought; that they can be applied much more widely, and that the psychic region can be studied and brought under law, too. Allow us, anyhow, to make the attempt. Give us a fair field. Let those who prefer the materialistic hypothesis by all means develop their thesis as far as they can; but let us try what we can do in the psychical region, and see which wins."

He expressed a conviction that occurrences now regarded as occult could be examined and reduced to order by the methods of science, carefully and persistently applied.

" The evidence, to my mind, goes to prove," he continued, " that disincarnate intelligence, under certain conditions, may interact with us on the material side, thus indirectly coming within our scientific ken; and that gradually we may hope to attain some understanding of the nature of a larger, perhaps ethereal, existence, and of the conditions regulating intercourse across the chasm. A body of responsible investigators has even now landed on the treacherous but promising shores of a new continent."

Thus, on the one hand, we have a quest of occult truth proceeding in the direction of a new continent, whilst the theosophists are looking for light toward a very old continent, *i.e.* Atlantis !

I am certainly disposed to believe that many so-called discoveries of modern occultism would more properly be called re-discoveries. Those advanced writers who have laid down certain dogmas, who have split man into his component parts, corporeal, intellectual, and ethereal, who have defined the relations of each part to the others, who have weighed the capacities of each—have they accomplished anything beyond that already accomplished by the Egyptians ?

The fact seems to me to be this : they have reached the same conclusions in a different way.

Certainly we are better equipped to-day, in some respects, for exploration, than were the ancients. Could we but establish links between the exact sciences —or the sciences thus far rendered exact—and those at present termed occult, great progress would shortly be recorded.

No visible advance (I exclude the hermetic and theosophical *arcana*) has been made in these matters for many generations. Until very recent times, substantial men of science ignored the subject ; but quite an illuminating work could be compiled of the fragments of occult wisdom strewn through the writings of the poets—outcomes, not of inquiry, but of inspiration. Omar Khayyám, for all his hedonism, is richly streaked with gold, and Sir Edwin Arnold's *Light of Asia* I would place in the hands of every would-be inquirer as a textbook.

But now there is a promise of a new era; and one looks for great things when sorcery and science go hand in hand. In this way, and in this way alone, can we hope to progress; it is almost vain to look for an Apollonius of London, of Paris, or of New York.

" God still communicates with mankind," according to Sir William Ramsay, " using the voice with ' the sound of deep silence ' heard by the prophets of Israel and mentioned in the marginal notes in the Revised Version of the Bible; but, as a great French writer has said, to have miracles we must have saints; and there are few saints."

Forty years ago, he declared, scientists would have branded as a lunatic any man who said it was possible for a spirit to communicate with another spirit, lacking the interposition of the material. Yet to-day scientists admitted the possibility of such phenomena.

There is undoubtedly a tremendous future for psychical inquiry along photographic lines. The writer who conceals his identity under the *nom de plume* " A Member of the Society for Psychical Research," conducted a series of remarkable experiments of this kind some years ago. The experiments were conducted with the assistance of a distinctly mediumistic photographer.

The writer brought his " own marked plates, placed beforehand in the dark shutter," and watched the entire process of development in the dark room. Moreover, he used to visit the studio at odd times, and without giving the photographer notice of his intention.

He writes :

" The plates obtained under these conditions invariably disclosed a vague, cloud-like formation hovering near my own person, and sometimes showing distinct outlines of a form. In one or two instances features would become distinctly visible in this cloud-like emanation on the third or fourth plate—the very gradualness of the development of the form seeming to me to tell in favour of the genuineness of the pictures. I have thus obtained an infinite variety of pictures on plates prepared by myself, and remaining under my constant observation to the last. . . . Experienced photographers who have seen them maintain that they could be produced normally, although they also admit that this could not possibly be done under the conditions stated."

The labours of Lodge, Crookes, Ramsay, Barrett, Wallace, and others, must sooner or later bear fruit. It is quite absurd to suppose, in this age of discoveries, that we understand *all* Nature's laws. But the difficulty of demonstrating the existence of occult phenomena to the general public can only be likened to that of demonstrating the perfume of a rose to a person who has never possessed the sense of smell, the beauty of an autumn sunset to a blind man, or the distinction in flavour between Astrakhan and American *caviare* to one of defective palate.

Photography, to my mind, should prove to be the link joining the physical to the psychical. The experiments at séances, the experiments with the *planchette*, are all unsatisfactory. But think what might have been achieved by a photographer, provided with a flashlight apparatus, at one of Cagliostro's magical banquets !

Another avenue of research there is, which, however,

is all too rarely opened ; I refer to apparent cases of
" throw-back." Professor Richet mentions a French
lady, who wrote whole pages in Greek, although not
even knowing the Greek alphabet ; and in the *Gentleman's Magazine* for May 1760 is given an account, on
the testimony of Dr. Hooper, Capt. Fisher, and another,
of a boy at Reading who periodically was seized with
fits, during which he delivered lengthy theological discourses. As also bearing upon this phase of the subject,
I append a paragraph from F. L. Rawson's *Life Understood from a Religious and Scientific Point of View*.

" The head of one of the religious sects in England
once asked advice with reference to a man who had
been his stenographer . . . and who was then speaking
and writing Chinese fluently, having never known a
word of that language. He wanted to know whether
it was of God or of the devil, as this would make a considerable difference to his future policy. After answering a few questions he told me that the stenographer
at these times went into an ecstatic condition, and was
tongue-tied. By this he meant that he was unable
to answer questions whilst speaking or writing Chinese."

Proof is what a sceptical world awaits. According
to Mrs. Annie Besant a great Adept appears once in
every century whose task is to guide humanity a little
further onward to the hidden goal. The next of these
should bear in mind poor childish mankind's crying
need of something tangible—something to grasp.

INDEX